Abstract

Urban micro-businesses are often viewed as the economic engines for growth in both developed and developing nations. They are associated with concurrent changes in social values and provide fertile ground for studying change in global economics. This study examined the individual value priorities of two types of urban micro-business owner-managers in China: 108 ordinary store-front owners and 89 government-sponsored incubator entrepreneurs who receive subsidized rent for three years during their start-up. This revealed some of the subtle individual values related, in part, to Chinas emerging socialist market economy.

In 2004,197 micro-business owner-managers from Shenzhen, China, completed the Mandarin Chinese version of the Schwartz (2003) Values Survey. The values rated as most important were security, conformity, achievement, self-direction, followed by benevolence, and then, universalism, power, hedonism, tradition, and stimulation. These ratings differ from Chinese teacher and student individual value priorities and indicated that there are sectors of the Chinese society contesting individual value priorities.

Interviews of 6 of these micro-business owner-managers were also analyzed to discuss what these value priorities reflect about the complex social and economic orientations among micro-business owner-managers in China and what they may imply about attitudes and behavior in the nation›s emerging middle class.

Key Words: Chinese urban micro-businesses, Chinese individual and cultural values, ethical outlooks, and international development ethics in China.

ACKNOWLEDGMENTS

With grateful esteem for my committee members:

Marie Farrell, Ed.D.
Richard Appelbaum, Ph.D.
Robert Silverman, Ph.D.
Jan Taug, Ph.D.
Romie Littrell, Ph.D.

Special thanks to:

Dr. Shalom H. Schwartz, and Petr Kavalir, Ph.D.

With deep affection to my steadfast friends:

Connie Brennen, Joel Ficks, MaryBeth Stepanek,
Karen Bentley, Peter Fox-Penner, Ph.D.; Ann Davis, Ph.D.;
Larry Saunders, Ph.D.; Janet Steinwedel, Ph.D.;
and Kathy Geller, Ph.D.

With love and honor to my friends and colleagues in China:

Jie (Jenny) Jian, Cheng Feng, Doris Lian, Sue Wang,
Gan Hai Xing, Shirley (Bao Qin) and Mark Ye, Sun Wei Hong,
Wang You Ming, Liu Gen Ping, Liu Jin, Wang Hong Wei, Ye
(Mason) Qian, Zhu Haiqun and Zhou, Zhang Nasha, Nancy
Hong, Wu Hong Yan, Zhongming Zeng, Dragon Chen, Wang
Yang Hui, Winston Wu, Xing Feng, Ellen Pang, Wei Han Ping,
Xiou Zhang and family, Xiou Rong and family, Zak Lu, Jiang
Ping, Shenzhen Manager's Training College
and Shenzhen University.

Dedicated to my magnificent parents for sharing with me their love of knowledge and the world

Joan and Jack Wing

With love to my husband, children, in-laws, daughters-in-law, grandchildren, siblings and family:

Eugene Tsui,
Paolo Raino-Tsui, Sorell Raino-Tsui,
Chase Montgomery-Tsui, Bill and Florence Tsui, Kriselle Caparas, Tai and Caramia Caparas-Tsui, Gabriella Segal, Willy, Cindy, Paul and Jay Montgomery, Mary Ellen Wing and Jack and Emma Wing-Brice

In honor of:

My West Virginia great-grandmothers Mary Daisy Cook and Emma Wills Brennan and my Shanghai Chinese great-aunts Fong Wen Pei, and Fong Wen Yen

For inspiring me from the depths of their work and adventures:

Thor Heyerdahl, Illya Prigogine, Prince Kropotkin, Wang Zheng, Alexandra David-Neel, and Jane Addams

Table of Contents

LIST OF FIGURES

LIST OF TABLES

CHAPTER ONE

THE STUDY

Chinese Micro-Business Values, and Perspectives on International Development

Background of the Study

From 1999 to 2003, 1 had the opportunity to live in Shenzhen, China. For those four years, a time of accelerating social and economic reform in the country, I worked, travelled, played, and admired the phenomenon of change in the Chinese society. Chairman Mao's metaphor of "the iron rice bowl" had been replaced by what at first appeared to be thriving capitalism. As I observed the pros and cons of the nation's new market economy, I wanted to know the effects of the social and economic changes on the values of China's urban micro-business owner-managers.

Deng Xiaoping's policies, which set China on the current path to market socialism, launched the country on a new journey with a new metaphor, "crossing the river by feeling the stones." Following up on Deng's policies, China's Ministry of Science and Technology developed a plan for special high-tech incubators—that is, office building complexes that house and nurture technologically advanced micro-businesses.

The incubators are supervised by managers who provide the tenants with equipment and utilities and encourage cross-fertilization of ideas, products, and services among the tenants. Tenants can remain in the incubators for no longer than 3 years, after which they must survive outside on their own—or not.

At the same time, much less sophisticated micro-businesses, which I call "ordinary" micro-businesses, were springing up as millions of people, especially those who lacked the high level of education needed to fill modern high-tech jobs, migrated daily from the interior to the coast, particularly the nation's special economic zone in Guangdong province.

The high-tech incubator micro-businesses I observed in Shenzhen were operated by white-collar professionals and were assisted by government-funded management services and in-house training specialists. Nevertheless, like the ordinary micro-businesses, they were struggling for capital. At one extreme, was Mr. Xia, who was trying to market wire molds to the international community but knew little about how to develop customers or how to get his product to them. "Marketing," he told me, "is an underdeveloped field in China." This proved to be a recurring theme in the interviews on business attitudes and influences. On the other extreme was Ms. Miao, a former university professor of computer sciences. She used her technological research and know-how to launch her own software business in an incubator. This connection between education and incubator micro-business owner-managers proved to be another recurring theme in the study.

The ordinary micro-businesses I observed were usually housed in storefront spaces passed by multitudes of pedestrians who were their potential customers. The owner-managers typically operated without any standard business infrastructures, such as cash registers, by selling what they made or providing services. These ordinary micro-businesses often seemed quite futile and at times even defied the definition of a business. For example, I frequently saw bobbin-spoolers sitting out on the sidewalk, using archaic spinning machines to manually fill up bobbins with thread for local storefront tailors.

By 2001, the year in which China joined the World Trade Organization (WTO), I began to see the distinctions between Mr. Zhang, the shoe repair man who sat by the side of a foot bridge 3 days a week cobbling, gluing, and stitching shoes, and the Xiou family, with their bicycle repair shack, which also provided them with a home. The Xious were flourishing, had computers in the shop, used the internet, and were making plans to return to their inland hometown to retire.

What I experienced as a Western social researcher living in Shenzhen was a grand paradox. I was living in a burgeoning quasi-Third-World country with a market economy that was still governed by the parallel political philosophies of Mao Zedong's communism and Deng Xiaoping's market socialism. The Chinese government sanctioned the alignment of these conflicting values, and few individuals seemed to have any problems with this.

Many Westerners (e.g., Thurow, 2003; Sachs, 1997,2005) wrote about this Chinese acceptance of market economics as the inevitable supremacy of capitalism. However, I found other, deeper cultural forces operating as well, such as the Chinese tradition to seek harmony in all things and an ability to live with ambiguities—including conflicting economic and social philosophies. Thus, I was not surprised when, in June 2002, the new Premiere, Hu Jintao, announced to the Chinese people that capitalists and entrepreneurs could officially join the Communist Party.

When I completed my assignment in China in 2003,1 knew that the ordinary and the high-tech incubator micro-businesses were moving from the universities and countryside towns to urban centers to take up the cause of the new market economy. I sought to immerse myself in the lives of these Chinese urban owner-managers in order to focus on their business attitudes, influences, and ethical outlooks, with an interest in how international development ethics have influenced their values.

Fire in the lake, an image derived from a hexagram in the ancient Chinese *I Ching: Book of Changes,* symbolizes in this study, the differences between the incubator and ordinary micro-business owner-managers. The incubator micro-business owner-managers are the fire, working in the Center of the Torch, creating modern technology for the masses. The ordinary micro-business owner-managers are the lake, flooding the marketplace with products and services, reaching into every crevice of the nation. Together, they make the socioeconomic revolution that is modern-day China.

International development ethics.

As a social economic development researcher, I turned to international development ethics to examine the value structures of Chinese urban micro-businesses. International development ethics addresses the value structures of developing societies and cultures, also referred to as "periphery" or Third World nations, as opposed to developed nations, which are sometimes referred to as "core" or First World nations. Economists and sociologists perceive and examine structural links between national economic and social change, on the one hand, and local development practices, on the other (see, e.g., Bourdieu, 1977/2002; Olson, 2000; Peters, 2000; Sen, 1999; Stiglitz, 2002; Surin, 1998; Tu Wei-Ming, 1980). However, they tend to focus on broad issues, such as macro-economics, gross national indices, and structural power. They fail to address individual issues and influences, such as personal values. This study's purpose is to shed light on that oversight, in the case of China, by focusing on the values of men and women who own and operate micro-businesses in the free economic zone of Shenzhen.

China's prosperity was also largely influenced by foreign direct investment (FDI), which preceded privatization of China's State-Owned Enterprises (SOEs) and became an important strategy of the emerging Chinese market economy. The dynamic Chinese economy is based on policies of incremental economic reforms and the international economic principles, perceptions, and practices of foreign investments. Since 1999, China has even ceased borrowing foreign aid on concessional terms from the International Development Association (IDA) and now stands midway between being a semi-periphery and a core nation (International Development Association, 2002). At the same time, the increase in private sector development loans from the World Bank's International Finance corporation (IFC) has more than doubled (International FC, 2005).

Some of the reasons for China's economic growth are the gradual opening of the country's economic system through piecemeal market reforms from the late 1970s to the present. These policies have led to the rise of a Chinese middle-class (Bao, Chang, Sachs & Woo, 2002). Specifically, the government established Special Economic Zones (SEZs) to attract foreign investors. FDI flowing into China's southern coastal provinces of Guangdong and other coastal provinces provided the nation with the largest infusions of investment capital in the world, outside of the United States. At the same time, the FDI spurred competition for other provinces who demanded open policies for their regions, so they could compete fairly for investments with the coastal provinces.

According to Gallagher (2002), China's SEZs became laboratories of capitalism as foreign investor autonomy began to influence local business practices especially with the advent of foreign-Chinese joint ventures. For instance, there were important changes in the employment laws in these joint ventures, which prevailed over the socialist employment policies of the SOEs. The SEZs alleviated some of the problems of employment in the SOEs as they, the government, began to slowly dismantle the huge, costly, and inefficient state companies. Millions upon millions of unemployed workers flocked to the southern coast to work in the factories and fledgling high-tech companies of Guangdong. Nevertheless, many SOEs were (and remain) in crisis as the reforms are seemingly intractable.

However, private enterprise reforms in China have developed much more slowly despite the high levels of foreign direct investments (FDI). The barriers to traditional capitalism include time-consuming bureaucracy, lack of capital and financing, and inabilities to expand into regional and global economies. In particular, the political barriers for private enterprise (e.g., the role of public ownership in a market economy) are still debated within the nation. According to the Postrel (2000), the political argument for economic reforms using foreign capital investments is often couched as a nationalist economic argument that socialist labor policies must be scrapped so that Chinese companies can compete with foreigners.

Clearly, the more China engages in the international economy, the more her internal economic and social processes are stimulated. This stimulation, accompanied by the introduction of powerful market economic values, reinforces the concepts of freedom, self-direction, and personal autonomy.

Like the Chinese nation, micro-businesses that are astute enough to obtain financial loans, are transitioning from the peripheral, underground economy toward true market entrepreneurialism (Asian Development Bank, 2000). If this pattern continues, it should partly solve China's unemployment and underemployment problem. However, it remains unclear if the expected democratization of the nation will occur anytime soon.

Statement of the Problem

The present study measures the individual and cultural values of Chinese micro-business owner-managers in order to ascertain whether and to what extent international development ethics have an impact on their values. The study's focus is on two key themes: (a) business values in Chinese society, as represented through the survey of micro-business owner-managers; and (b) the perceived, self-reported effects of those values in two types of micro-businesses, those operating from ordinary storefronts and those private companies operating in government sponsored high-tech incubator buildings.

My goal as a researcher is to examine the role of micro-businesses in China. In turn, this examination may serve as the basis for future examinations of policies related to the creation of jobs in one, still largely underdeveloped nation.

Significance of the Study

China is unique among the world's many developing nations because of her new position as a world trade leader and the political alignment among most sectors of her society (Chu, Castellop, Churchill & Nourse, 2001). In a sense, China chooses to straddle the core and periphery processes of globalization, which makes understanding the values of its micro-businesses a critical contribution to economic, social, and philosophical inquiry (Baker, 1998). Nevertheless, in China today, approximately 260 million people, or 20% of the population, are either unemployed or underemployed (Zhang, 2001). Its labor force is divided into 50 % agriculture, 22%

industry, and 28% services. Additionally, the micro-business market remains filled with structural and cultural challenges in a country with millions of under-served owner-managers (Park & Zhang, 2005).

Creating opportunities for micro-businesses to develop constitutes a relatively important strategy for solving the problem; however, the structural challenges include financial, legal, and philosophical issues regarding the Chinese market. Every successful Chinese micro-business contributes to the society at large by creating jobs, earning profits, paying taxes, and developing investments; yet, financially targeting urban micro-businesses seems largely ignored by banks and policy discussions about the topic are just beginning in the Chinese Ministry of Finance (World Bank Group, 2001).

Part of the challenge relates to the legal and tax structures of these micro-business entities and the need for outreach measures to draw them into more traditional commercial banking relationships (Park & Kaja, 2001). Banks offering higher loan to value relationships, instalment loans, term loans, and various combinations of traditional continue to target the more financially well-off and well-connected, even among the micro-business sub-groups.

For ordinary businesses, the issues of loans need to be tied to the freedom to determine the way capital loans are used. Within a "top-down" banking environment, the owner-managers and their households may not respond as well to the government's initiatives. Both governmental and non-governmental loan systems to micro-businesses have performed well with loan repayment rates of 88% (Park & Kaja, 2001).

Philosophically, the government officials engaged in market reform in China are just beginning to experiment with ways to fill the gaps for micro-businesses to succeed.

These micro-businesses often take the form of what is called government sanctioned incubator projects.

People engaged with the government bureaucrats that manage the incubator projects report the lack of business training and ask whether loans should be tied to other social objectives and question the wisdom of approaching this issue in this way. Another problem arises as to the appropriateness of a company that appears to be thriving in the incubator staying in the incubator after an initial start up period of 3 years. Still another question relates to the ways in which high-tech micro-business will be measured.

The conflict between China's micro-business sector and traditional banking sectors lies in these structural challenges. In terms of overall strategy, the demands of the different groups of micro-businesses and how their needs can be met to create an urban financial loan system comprised of banks and cooperatives and flexible contract terms, especially regarding repayment structures.

The cultural challenges in a country with millions of under-served owner-managers present another set of issues that need careful attention because these micro-businesses are so clearly tied to household survival and reflect gender-related issues such as female heads of households (Baines & Wheelock, 1998). As noted, the coastal cities of China are exploding with migrating populations from the core of the country. Taxi drivers, restaurant owners, and young professionals with big dreams and hard work, take up the government slack to reinvest in their families and home-town communities (Ravallian & Chen, 2001). They fund schools, hospitals, and other programs back home, in the interior of the country. They send money home or return to their hometowns with entrepreneurial experience, new technologies, and new attitudes for the towns and villages of China's poorer provinces (Apter & Saich, 1994).

The present study is the first to assess two types of Chinese micro-business owner-managers and compare them using the Schwartz (2003) Values Survey (SVS). The results have policy implications for the future of micro-businesses and job creation in China.

Types of Chinese urban micro-businesses.

The Chinese government legally recognizes three basic kinds of private companies: solely-owned companies, partnerships, and limited liability companies. Politically, the government uses a variety of business models under the rubric of state-owned enterprises, township and village enterprises, and the private sector.

The private sector is further segmented into individual enterprises, joint ventures, and foreign enterprises. Within these categories, the private sector includes the subcategories of (a) individual business people or entrepreneurs *(getihu)*, (b) single industrial and commercial proprietors *(geti gongshang hu)*, (c) specialized households *(zhuangyehu)*, and (d) privately run enterprises *(siyingqiye)*. It is the first and fourth categories of micro-business, the *getihu* and *siyingqiye* that are the focus of this research.

The government has designated the *getihu* as the business sector that supplements the state and collective sectors. The entrepreneurs distribute consumer goods and services and provide employment. They are usually constituted, legally and politically as one owner-manager and up to eight employees. Many *getihu* petition the government to become *siyingqiye,* which allows them to employ up to 30 employees (International Trade of Canada, 2000). The *siyingqiye* have the background and the resources to develop in the high-tech sector of the Chinese economy. These companies, considered high risk ventures, are often funded with loans on the Principal's property.

Micro-businesses in Shenzhen, China.

In 2003, Global Entrepreneurship Monitor (GEM), an international consortium that annually monitors entrepreneurial activity, used a standardized model to compare the total entrepreneurial activity of Hong Kong and Shenzhen. These two cities, which border on each other, share the resources of the South China Sea. Over the past 10 years, they have experienced increasing integration to a point where, according to the GEM (Chua, Ho, & Le, 2003), the two cities can no longer be distinguished by the nature and extent of entrepreneurship.

In summary, the city's entrepreneurial strengths include its status as a "new immigrant" city, with more than 95% of its residents coming from other parts of China. The GEM Report rated Shenzhen's research and development commercial potential as fair, its private investment as adequate, its professional and commercial infrastructure as adequate, its government policies as relatively open, its market openness as good, its sociocultural environment for entrepreneurs as excellent, and its access to physical infrastructures as superior.

Shenzhen's weaknesses include huge gaps in venture capital; ineffective communication between the local government, entrepreneurs, and other local people; a huge gap in education and training in the primary and secondary educational systems (which overemphasize examinations); and the "flight" or mobility of technological talent, which originally flocked to Shenzhen but is now returning home or emigrating because of tightening policies and other factors such as missed opportunities.

The GEM report on entrepreneurial activity explained, in broad strokes, the ways in which the micro-business climate in

Shenzhen can be described as one of moderate opportunities and moderate necessities.

Chinese micro-business values.

Culturally, Chinese micro-business owner-managers have, over the centuries, cultivated local mercantile exchange practices in the many provinces of the country. Guangdong Province happens to be one of China's most enterprising cultures, and Shenzhen naturally reflects the government's strategy to harness entrepreneurship. One of the overlooked aspects of urban micro-businesses is the role of values and subsequent ethics among the owner-managers. Another important question in this study is whether the values of ordinary micro-business owner-managers are different from those of incubator micro-business owner-managers.

Conceptual Framework

This study adopts the position that international economic development values include democratizing influences, which have an impact on the traditions of developing societies. I assessed Chinese micro-business owner-managers' values, using Schwartz's Chinese version of the SVS (2003) for 10 individual values and seven cultural values (Appendix A).

Individual values.

Power: Social status and prestige, control or dominance over people and resources.

Achievement; Personal success through demonstrating competence according to social standards.

Hedonism: Pleasure and sensuous gratification for oneself.

Stimulation: Excitement, novelty, and challenge in life.

Self-Direction: Independent thought and action—choosing, creating, exploring.

Universalism: Understanding, appreciation, tolerance, and protection for the welfare of all people and nature.

Benevolence: Preservation and enhancement of the welfare of people with whom one is on frequent personal contact.

Tradition: Respect, commitment, and acceptance of the customs and ideas that traditional culture and religion provide the self.

Conformity: Restraint of actions, inclinations, and impulses likely to upset or harm others and violate social expectations or norms.

Security: Safety, harmony, and stability of society, of relationships, and of self. (pp. 468)

Schwartz's framework allows for individual values, priorities, experiences, and behavioral attitudes to emerge in order to further distinguish universal processes, which are tied to cultural influences. These elements reveal the complexity of value meanings among individuals and cultures.

In order to clarify differences, Schwartz (1994a) used factor analysis to categorize his values into four types of higher-order dimensions: (a) Openness to Change versus Conservation; and (b) Self-Enhancement versus Self-Transcendence. For example, Stimulation, which falls under Openness to Change, is in opposition to Conformity and Tradition, which fall under Conservation. The content of the 10 individual values changes with every situation, but the order of the values always remains the same.

The seven cultural values represent the interests of persons, groups, or nations and is defined by Schwartz (1994b) as, "A nation's institutional or organizational concepts of a value system become a guiding principle, or way of acting. The challenge is to understand and manage these values and to motivate individuals who establish sets of priorities among compatible and incompatible goals."

Cultural values.

Embeddedness: Commitment to maintaining the status quo; keeping to traditional order.

Hierarchy: Subservience to rules, roles, and obligations; unequal power distribution; unequal resource allocation.

Mastery: Self-assertion; orientation to change; exploitation of natural and social environments.

Affective Autonomy: Bounded individuality of a unique and autonomously acting self.

Intellectual Autonomy: Bounded individuality of a unique intellect and autonomous ideas.

Egalitarianism: Voluntary commitments, usually to moral equals.

Harmony: Acceptance of the world as it is; trying to understand and fit in and not to change or exploit it. (p.469)

Cultural domains, in which all basic human requirements are expressed, combine the anthropological, psychological, and organizational meaning of individual values. These domains represent the desirable influences that individuals choose to act upon and to evaluate their actions. Schwartz's original cultural analysis is based on both individual and cultural dimensions and assumes a seemingly objective position that states a new aim of values research towards human values as criteria as opposed to human values as qualities inherent in objects (Schwartz, 1996).

I examined the values of Chinese micro-business owner-managers by using Schwartz's (2003) standardized cross-cultural values survey (SVS) for China to rate their individual and cultural guiding principles. I surveyed 197 micro-businesses with the SVS and then conducted 10 face-to-face tape-recorded interviews with owner-managers, of whom I selected 6 for in-depth analysis, as these were most typical of the sample demographics.

Research Questions

The central inquiry in this study is: What ethical values are taking root among two types of Chinese urban micro-businesses in Shenzhen? To answer this question, I generated five research questions:

RQ1 : How do ordinary and incubator micro-businesses differ demographically?

RQ2: What are the self-reported individual values of micro-business owner-managers in Shenzhen, China?

RQ3 : What are the self-reported cultural values of micro-business owner managers in Shenzhen, China?

RQ4: In what ways do individual and cultural self-reported values of Chinese micro-business owner-managers in Shenzhen, China, differ by type of business (ordinary or incubator), by demographic categories, and by years of business ownership?

RQ5: In what ways do the self-reported values of Chinese micro-business owner-managers in Shenzhen, China, influence their business attitudes and ethics?

I explored the individual and cultural values of micro-business owner-managers through taped interviews and narrative analysis, and examined the ways in which the individual and cultural economic development values were taking root in China at the micro-business level.

Operational Definitions

The following definitions and the ways they were measured are as follows:

Micro-businesses are defined as businesses that are operated by one owner-manager with up to 8 full-time and 30 part-time employees.

Ordinary micro-businesses are businesses that primarily operate in locations accessible to foot traffic, such as storefronts and small service offices. In this study, many *getihu* fit the description of ordinary micro-businesses.

Incubator micro-businesses are government-supported office complexes designed to nurture private, high-tech businesses by providing a wide range of services, including management assistance, access to financing, business or technical support services, shared office equipment, flexible and affordable leases, and expandable space. In this study, many *siying qiye* fit the description of incubator micro-businesses.

Values, according to Schwartz and Bilsky (1987), are cognitive representations of three types of universal human requirements: biological needs, social needs, and institutional needs. These three universal requirements become conscious motivational goals or values, which are taught, shared, and communicated. Individual and cultural values were measured in this study through 58 values- related items and 10 demographic items on the Schwartz Values Survey Instrument ©.

Economic development is defined as factors that influence the growth or restructuring of an economy to enhance a community's economic well-being as measured by GDP and quality of life indices. Activities of economic development include planning to enhance the production, distribution, and consumption of goods and services, on a local, regional, national, or international scale.

Local economic development is an economic process that begins when a community acts to start-up, locate, expand, or retain enterprises that create jobs.

International development ethics is a value process that occurs when a local economy is vitalized by the useful distribution of capital (either financial or social) that arrives from foreign sources. International development ethics will be considered, in this study, as variables that relate to perceptions of self-direction and personal freedoms.

Assumptions and Limitations

Several assumptions were made. I assumed that micro-businesses are one of the main vehicles for economic growth in China and that, as a foreigner, I would be able to enter a culture in which I did not speak the language fluently but could still obtain the data needed to address the research questions.

Limitations due to the sample.

Despite measures to improve participant participation, it was difficult to attract ordinary micro-business owner-managers because they were often too busy to stop and take the time to fill a long and complex survey. Perceptions about the study and its length may have affected potential study participants' willingness to participate. This potential for selection bias is acknowledged.

All study participants who volunteered were interviewed and audiotaped. Those who elected to be interviewed may have had some bias in terms of education, since all but one was college educated.

CHAPTER TWO

REVIEW OF THE LITERATURE

Cross-Cultural Values, International Development, and Chinese Urban Micro-Business Structures

Overview and Context of the Chapter

This literature review is separated into three parts. The first section describes the theories of cross-cultural values, especially the theories of Shalom H. Schwartz (1992, 1993,1994a, 1994b, 1996,1999,2000,2001a, 2001b, 2003,2004; and Schwartz & Bilsky, 1987,1992, Schwartz & Sagiv 1995,2001a, and Schwartz & Bardi, 1997,2004). These theories evolved from anthropological, psychological, and organizational studies of individuals and groups in different cultures. The first section also assesses Schwartz's theories to measure the values of urban Chinese micro-businesses as the nation moves from a socialist to a market-based economy.

The second section of the literature review analyzes international development ethics, especially those emanating from recent economic reforms in China. This part includes the perspective, based on Sen's (1999) theory of consequentialism that Chinese micro-businesses are participating in a new development era. The discussion underscores the link between the values of individual micro-business owners and the ways in which participation in international development initiatives relate to these emerging values.

The third section of this chapter critiques socioeconomic theories of Chinese urban micro-businesses and focuses on the analysis of values between government-sponsored incubator micro-businesses and ordinary micro-businesses in Shenzhen.

The progression of the literature review is from cross-cultural values to economic development to the ways in which these apply to Chinese micro-businesses.

Theories of Cross-Cultural Values

The field of cross-cultural values gained scientific validity as anthropologists, psychologists, and organizational theorists developed an interdisciplinary discourse on cross-cultural issues pertaining to individuals and societies in transition. Anthropologists, studying everyday life in a variety of cultures, focused on societal values. Cognitive psychologists examined values from an individual rather than a societal perspective, focusing on the minutiae of behavior and motivation. Organizational theorists produced matrices of values based on extensive cross-cultural data.

Schwartz (1992,1993, 2000, and Schwartz & Bardi, 2004) addressed both individual and societal values from a cross-cultural perspective. Although based on certain assumptions of Western social science (e.g., that values can be quantified), Schwartz's theory of values is nevertheless a useful tool for examining the issues of shared values in China, as that nation makes the transition from a socialist to a market economy.

Anthropological antecedents to the study.

This study began with a desire to understand the transitional states of economic and social values in individuals in China. My first analysis came from observations and fieldwork in that society, exploring questions related to the economic and social structures of China's cultural economies. The emphasis on the study of the everyday lives behaviors. The assumption that urban Chinese micro-businesses are in this transitional state is based on the work of van Gennep.

Arnold van Gennep (1909/1960), a French ethnographer, produced the first cross-cultural theories of rites of passage, according to which individuals pass through more or less predictable stages during a life crisis. He called these stages "liminal states," referring to their transitory qualities. These stages, such as initiations, are chiefly the means by which to achieve social change or a change in social status without challenging the underlying structure of the community.

The ordinary and, to some extent, incubator micro-businesses in China exist in a liminal state because they are least likely to benefit from any state economic reforms. In fact, all Chinese private companies are still in their infancy in terms of access to finance, freedom from laws and restrictions, and access to global standard business practices. For now, there is a "lying low" approach concerning the ways in which they conduct their business activities. This may, in part, be because direct foreign investment has not produced many calls for social liberalizations (Stiglitz, 2002). Thus, despite their huge numbers and potential wealth, there remains a certain marginality or nonconformity about urban micro-business owner-managers as a Chinese socio-economic subgroup.

Victor Turner (1974/1995) used van Gennep's concepts to develop the idea of a "ritual man," who basically serves the same analytical purpose for cross-cultural studies that the

metaphorical "economic man" did for classical economics—
namely to clarify motives and behaviors. Economic man
was a model to inform the rationale for the ways certain
kinds of decisions are made. Ritual man clarifies motives
and behaviors in times of crisis and transition. In liminal
phases, Turner argued, social categories are sometimes
reversed or ignored, so people may experience new bonds
and relationships. Part of the ritual process may even involve
criticizing the existing social order.

Turner asserted that some members are allowed certain
freedoms because they are viewed as being on the margins of
society. Their criticisms are allowed because these individuals
provide some benefit to the nation or culture. This could be
true of the Chinese urban micro-business owner-managers,
since they create jobs but have questionable social and
political power. When they ever do assert their collective
power, or what Turner calls *communitas,* they could constitute
a real revolutionary force.

Bourdieu (1977/2002) advanced the notions of culture and
economics as symbolic power relations that are embedded in
our descriptions of everyday life. Thus, culture can be mapped
as an objective social structure that contains both a *habitus*
(the practical sense of the rules) and a *field* (the agent in a
context of possibilities) for individuals acting within the rules
of the space of that symbolic power. As Bourdieu (1977/2002)
stated:

It is significant that "culture" is sometimes described
as a map; it is the analogy which occurs to an outsider who
must find his way around in a foreign landscape and who
compensates for his lack of practical mastery, the prerogative
of the native, using a model of all possible routes, (p. 2)

Bourdieu (1997) mapped these fields of cultural and
economic production by drawing diagrams of what he called

observable power phenomena. He developed, from these field studies, the theory that there are modes of domination that structure all social, cultural, and economic capital. He stated:

Economic power lies not in wealth but in the relationship between wealth and a field of economic relations, the constitution of which is inseparable from the development of a body of specialized agents, with specific interest; it is in this relationship that wealth is constituted, in the form of capital, that is the instrument for appropriating the institutional equipment and the mechanisms indispensable for the functioning of the field, and thereby also appropriating the profits from it. (p. 184)

The initial analysis of Chinese urban micro-businesses, then, relates to structures that guide the economic and cultural spheres of observation and research (Polanyi, 1968). Using Bourdieu's (1997) theories, one could conduct a reflexive, simultaneous analysis of the observed historical relationships in micro-businesses. For example, in the international arena, even though China is now a member of the WTO, the nation is still viewed as a "non-market economy," or NME (Government Accounting Office, 2005), which places it as a periphery or semi-core nation in the international economic system.

The development of a private sector in China is far from complete in terms of legal structures and finance. Private companies remain less important than the massive state-owned enterprises (SOEs). The latter are undergoing wholesale restructuring of entire industries and regions of the country, and thus expending vast amounts of government resources and attention. At the bottom of the economic pyramid, the micro-businesses, although arguably more dynamic than the other two sectors, are dependent on local regulations and personal financing. The relationships between the SOEs (1), the large private sector (2), and the micro- businesses (3) can be mapped by using concepts from Bourdieu's (1997) field of cultural production (Figure 1).

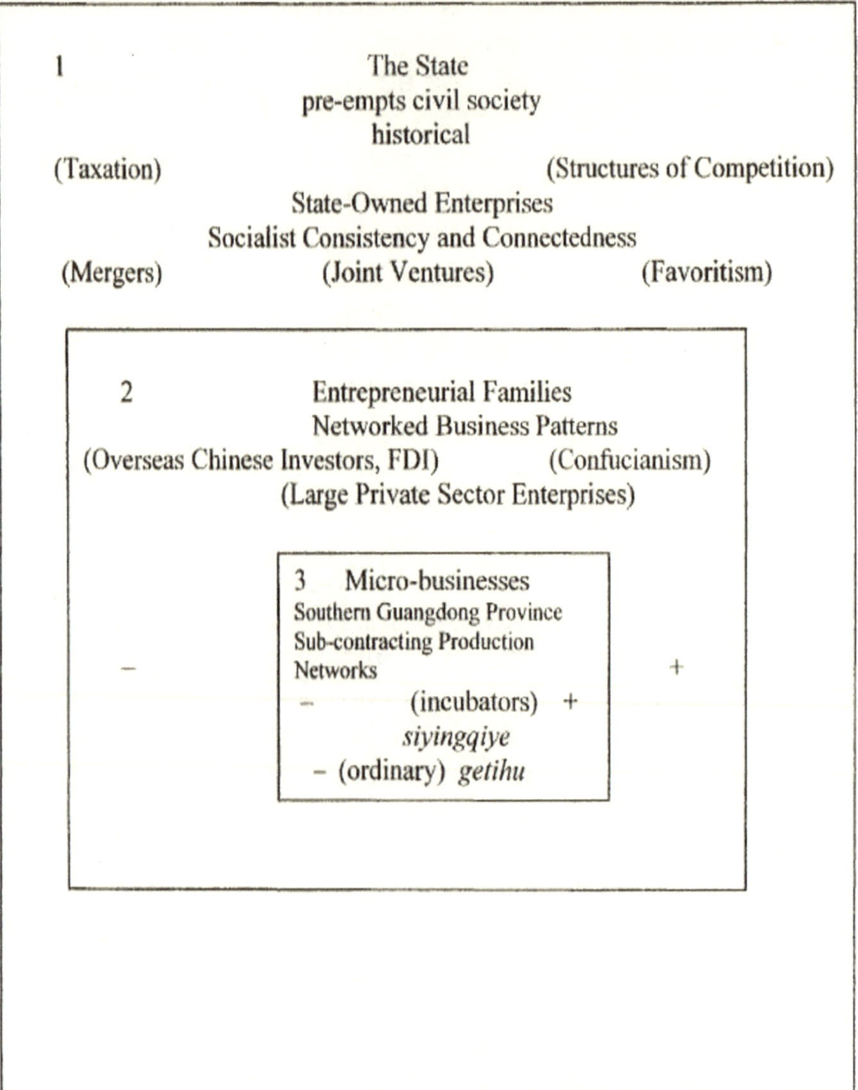

*Figure 1: Chinese urban micro-business
field of cultural production.*

The incubator micro-businesses resemble the SOEs, in that they, too, are government-sponsored and sector-based (in this case, almost exclusively serving the high-technology sector). The ordinary micro-businesses resemble the large private-sector businesses, in that they are largely family-funded. In terms of cultural production, the micro-businesses are permeable entities that generate more freedom and flexibility than the other two sectors of the economy.

The central idea that emerged from Bourdieu's (1997) later works which can be applied to socio-economic research is the intricate patterns of relationships exhibited in everyday life that add up to culturally- produced realities.

Clifford Geertz (1983, 1990) interpreted the daily life of individuals by concentrating on what he called their "frames of meaning." That is, he believed that the function of culture is to impose meaning on the world and make it understandable. Thus, returning to the theme that Chinese micro-businesses exist in a liminal state, one can suggest that culture provides answers for individuals in times of transition.

This concept of transition can be analyzed in terms of the historical and economic self-descriptions of micro-businesses. For example, most Chinese and their adult children remember the Cultural Revolution under Chairman Mao Zedong as a time of enormous personal and national upheaval (Egri, Ralston, Stewart, Terpstra, & Yu, 1999). Yet, most Chinese and their offspring feel that even though reforms under the direction of Premiere Deng Xiaoping called for "reform without losers," his near complete reversal of Mao's policies produced considerable controversy (Hinten, 1990).

In other words, the gradual economic path that Deng selected would have allowed for transition, not the drastic reversals of fortune seen in the collapse of other communist countries, particularly the former Soviet Union. Nevertheless, his policies required a social consensus about the new market socialist economy, which was to become the most important factor for personal and national prosperity.

However, this explanation needs further analysis—in part, due to the dizzying economic changes in China that have led to increased resistance to authoritarianism. George Marcus (1998) is the first anthropologist to claim that his field can study multiple cultures simultaneously, if it does so through the context of power structures. For example, Marcus studied issues concerning reproductive technologies (feminist anthropology), studies on pan-epidemics (medical anthropology), and biotechnology (e.g., Human Genome projects). Marcus analyzed the way individuals, "caught in the complexities of dominant regimes of power" (p. 19), view their own abilities and well-being. Marcus (1998) had earlier shown, with the Tongan culture, how people can take their economic power relationships with them even when they are geographically displaced around the world. He wrote:

Possibilities in the context of an internationally dispersed population are thus the crucial framework for assessing the life chances even for people who remain lifelong residents of Tonga. To be able to migrate is not essential for economically enhancing a family's position in Tonga. Rather, the capacity to call on international resources, continually or on important occasions, has become the crucial factor in influencing its local economic conditions, (p. 144)

Applying Marcus's concept to the complexities within dominant regimes of power helps to describe the Chinese micro-businesses in terms of their demands for change. These demands come from within *and* without the society. There is a Chinese adage that says: "Chinese have a long-term political view, but in business we look at our feet."

The micro-businesses may function within the nation as playing a part in the role of privatization, which is justified in nationalistic terms, and leaving the role of political reform to outsiders, and big investors. This is part of a valued personality type that opens the discussion to themes of agency and self-identity, cognition and culture, and even further to the goals, motivation, and behaviors of urban Chinese micro-businesses.

Psychological antecedents to the study.

Cognitive psychologists (e.g., Coombs, 1964; Cronbach, 1963; Rokeach, 1960; Tajfel, 1982; Turner, 1982, and Tajfel & Turner, 1986) took the discussions of valued personality types out of the realm of anthropology and rooted them in psychology, some through social identity theory and others by measuring values with psychosocial metric surveys. Social identity theory, championed by Tajfel (1982), described the ways in which the individual constructs an identity of the self, based on participation in relationships with other individuals or groups.

These early works in cognitive psychology are applicable to Chinese culture even though they are based in Western psychological traditions. These works anchor identification with a dominant group and authoritarianism as a trait of some individuals in a group. Social identity theorists argued that the individuals favored their own group because it enhanced their self-esteem. If individuals show less favor to those in another group and more to their own group, which would then give their group the most points, they thereby improve their overall self-esteem. Historically, most Chinese identify their ethnicity with the powerful Han group (206 B.C.-A.D. 220), which had the most uniting influence and the most wealth in the nation's long history. The Han were known for their administrative and diplomatic prowess, but most importantly, success in this group is based on individual merit.

China's history is also based on centuries-long imperial regimes and in the more recent histories of protracted and difficult occupations of the nation by foreign powers. Rokeach (1960) concentrated his research on reorienting the topic of authoritarianism and advanced the relationship of the individual to the group. He developed a more general term, "dogmatism," to describe a value of individuals acting as authoritarians whether on the left and right of political groups.

Rokeach (1973) distinguished four major categories of values, which the researcher would summarize as follows:

1. Personal values are those modes of conduct that are personally preferred.

2. Social values are those modes of conduct that are preferred for society.

3. Competence values are those modes of conduct that are associated with achievements and advancement in life.

4. Moral values are those modes of conduct that are associated with leading an ethical life.

Organizational antecedents to the study.

Rokeach (1979) was also first to note that specific and diffuse societies exist. Specific societies tend to compartmentalize relationships, whereas diffuse societies tend to extend relationships to all aspects of life. Specific societies allow and protect privacy, whereas diffuse societies regulate self-expression. Consequently, in diffuse societies, it takes much longer for people to get to know each other and make commitments to each other.

Hofstede (1997) built on these notions of diffuse and specific societal values when he concluded that there were "observable, measurable, and universal values" that could be defined in a matrix for all cultures. Hofstede's longitudinal work in cross-cultural organizational theory was based on surveys he conducted of IBM employees in countries all over the world, after which he created a classical model of value orientations. All cultural variations, he believed, can be categorized into five distinct social dimensions: (a) power/ distance; (b) individualism/collectivism; (c) masculinity/ femininity; (d) uncertainty/avoidance; and (e) long-term/short-term orientation. Hofstede's (2001) theory provided a model of values scales and a rationale for measuring cultural similarities and differences.

Power/distance defines the relative distance or closeness individuals in a society hold with the sources of power in that society. Individualism/ collectivism, the dimension he considered the most important, is based on the premise that, worldwide, there are two cultural frameworks within which individuals organize their identity. He asserted that most Western societies tended to have broad, individualistic tendencies, and most non-Western societies had broad collectivist tendencies. He also viewed these cultural frameworks in terms of their dominant (preferred) personality type, and he categorized them along masculine and feminine spectrums. In addition, Hofstede noted there are categories of culture that could be divided into how societies respond to threats, uncertainty, and challenges: some societies address uncertainty, while others avoid it.

Hofstede's (1983) values scales were criticized based on the methodology (Triandis, 1993; Trompenaars & Hampden-Turner, 1998) and on their interpretation and use, (Noorderhaven & Tidjani, 2001). Triandis (1993) criticized the values survey instrument used by Hofstede because the items were not independent variables and were somewhat incongruous. The face validity of some items was also called into question. For example, "Uncertainty/Avoidance" is composed of items such as "level of perceived stress," which seems to reflect a consequence rather than a self-construct. Furthermore, Hofstede's data were scrutinized because the sample was based on middle-class, white-collar workers in one corporation. More to the point, however,

Noorderhaven and Tidjani (2001) found the values scales showed support for only two of the four Hofstede scales. The "Masculine/Feminine" values dimensions did not hold in his survey, conducted in Africa, nor did the scale of "Uncertainty/ Avoidance." Nevertheless, Egri and Ralston (2004) found the Hofstede values scales to be robust, particularly because the sample had been more socially homogenous. Ultimately, Hofstede's work provided one of the first quantitative assisted comparisons of cross-cultural values on an international scale.

Later, Bond and Hofstede (1988) developed a work-related cultural dimension called "Confucian Dynamism" to address specific East Asian cultures. Confucian Dynamism includes a long-term orientation that is a dynamic, status-oriented ordering of relationships, a propensity to save, and a sense of shame related to "strategies for face-saving." Ting-Toomey (1999) integrated Hofstede's cross-cultural model of cultural dimensions with Confucian values from a communication perspective. She adjusted these terms to the way people from various cultures view themselves—which she called, following Kitayama and Markus (1991), "self-construals." These self-construals influence an individual's thinking, feelings, and motivations. Two types of self-construal exist for all people in every society: independent and interdependent. In China's case, Gao, Kim, Lin, & Ting-Toomey (1991) contend that the nation has deep-seated traditions of Confucian dynamism, which describe a set of personal values that combine traditional values and adaptations to changes in the economic environment. Chinese values often have the dual objectives of integrating the new and the traditional. Thus, Ting-Toomey (1999) explained:

For the Chinese, the self is both a center of relationships and a dynamic process of development within a network of relationships. In Chinese culture, to be aware of one's relations with others is an integral part of *zuo ren,* or "conducting oneself properly" in getting along with others. In sum, Chinese can never separate themselves from obligations to others, and a Chinese sense of self-worth is closely tied with kinship and social networks, (p. 78)

However, despite Hofstede's efforts to include a variety of cltures in his model and expand the basic theory, Trompenaars and Hampden-Turner (1998) made a concentrated analysis of organizational processes refuting Hofstede's (1997) seven-dimensional model which was based on inputs and outputs of cultural variables. They contended that Hofstede's model was too static to be of any use and some of the dimensions were not valid. For Trompenaars and Hampden-Turner (1998), the project of cross-cultural values research and analysis was to reconcile value differences in order to enhance organizational performance, a task of importance in the construction of international companies.

Schwartz's universal theory of values.

Schwartz's SVS (1992) first measured instrumental and terminal values as Rokeach defined them (1960). Instrumental values are desirable modes of behavior that lead to the achievement of terminal values—or in Rokeach's words, "desirable end-states of existence" (p. 21). Schwartz (1992) applied Rokeach's instrumental and terminal values to his research, although he redefined terminal values as "goals that are deemed desirable to attain during one's lifetime" (p. 26). Initially, Schwartz (1992, 1994a) mostly chose teachers at all academic levels to be the participants in his surveys because they were literate, were used to taking tests, were responsible for passing on their culture, and were behavioral role models. In addition, there were large numbers of them. Eventually, however, Schwartz recognized that profiling a nation through the eyes of only one group creates distortions. Subsequently, Schwartz (1996, 2000, 2001b) began to use the SVS on other cultural representatives, such as lawyers, corporate executives, and middle managers.

Schwartz based bis cultural findings on individual value traits that were prized within various cultures. Values, then, can be viewed as the top of a hierarchy of highly general and desirable motivational goals. Schwartz (1992) formally defined values as follows:

Values are an individual's concept of a transituational goal that expresses interests concerned with a motivational domain and evaluated on a range of importance as a guiding principle in his or her life. (p. 553)

The concept of a transituational goal departs from the Rokeach (1973) and Hofstede (1997) construct, in which one considers the individual's values only. Increasingly, this perspective of motivational goals became important among interdisciplinary fields that were merging into a cross-cultural paradigm. By motivational domains, Schwartz meant Rokeach's (1973) domains of "social motives, institutional demands, and functional requirements of groups."

The values that serve the individual and those values that serve collective interests create the central axis of Schwartz's values theory. The content of the 10 individual values, as plotted on the wheel (Figure 2), changes with every situation, but the order of the values always remains the same. The wheel, read clockwise, shows opposing and overlapping values. For instance, Power is opposite Universalism, and overlaps with Achievement and Security.

*Based on "Identifying culture-specifics in the content and structure of values, *Journal of Cross-cultural Psychology, 26(l):96.* Copyright 1995 by S. H. Schwartz & Sagiv, L. Used with permission of the authors.

Schwartz (2001b) provided a set of operational definitions that guided his cross-cultural values project, which can be summarized as follows:

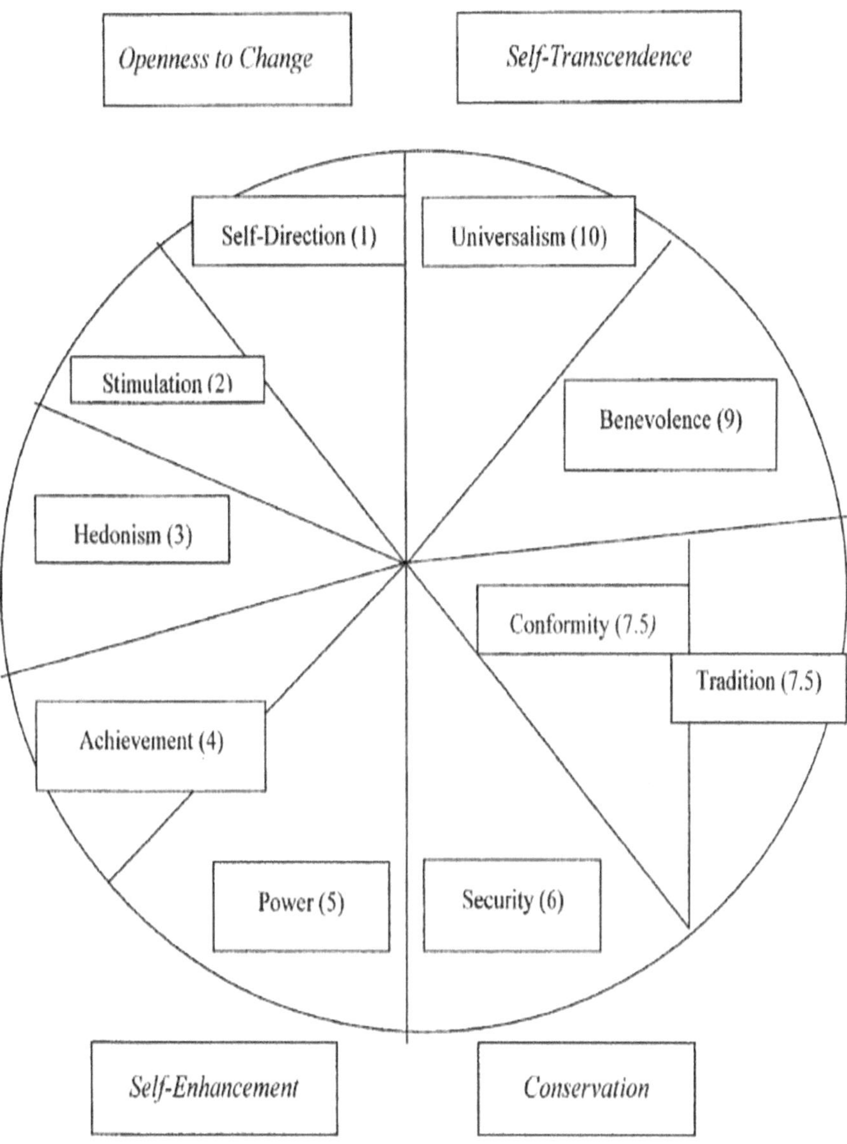

Figure 2. Theoretical model of 10 value constructs by higher order values and bipolar value dimensions. (Schwartz, 1995)

1. Most values have a range from unimportant to "near-universal" in their order and meaning, and as such can be defined as guiding principles or priorities.

2. The goal of the ideal individual in a culture must be moderately stable in order to serve as a meaningful guiding principle in life.

3. Motivational goals are the key to behavior and expressed interests.

A key here is that values are comprised of individual goals and interests, which represent the larger content of human motivations along the seven value dimensions of culture (Table 1).

Table 1

Development of Seven Cultural Values Dimensions
– Schwartz (1992-2000)

	Cultural Dimension	Cultural Dimension
Desired ways to guarantee responsible behavior that preserves the social fabric	Hierarchy Obeying rules, roles, and obligations, unequal power distribution, unequal resources allocation	Egalitarianism Behavior transcends self to promote the well-being of others Voluntary commitments, usually to moral equals
The relationship of humankind to the natural and social world	Mastery Self-assertion, change oriented, exploits natural and social environments	Harmony Accepting the world as is; tries to understand and fit in and not to change or exploit it
Desirable relationship between the individual and the group	Embeddedness Commits to maintaining status quo Keeps to traditional order	Autonomy (Two Types) *Affected Autonomy* - The individual is viewed as an autonomous, bounded entity steeped in his/her uniqueness; autonomous sub-groups include:

	Intellectual autonomy - Bounded individual of unique intellect and autonomous ideas.
Individual/Collectivism The relationship between the group an individual: preferences exist for loosely knit social relations in which individuals care for themselves and immediate families versus tight knit relationships and extended families; unquestioning loyalty.	

When viewed cross-culturally, values are individual goals, and as such they represent the interests of persons, groups, or nations. The challenge becomes managing life choice, or as Schwartz (2000) put it, "sets of priorities among compatible and incompatible goals" (p. 469).

Schwartz's studies on teachers ' cross-cultural values.

According to Schwartz (2000), teachers in 55 nations and students in 54 nations rated individual values in order of importance, from most to least, notably with benevolence as the top-rated value with self-direction and universalism in a close lead. Power was rated and ranked as the lowest value among the teachers and students.

Schwartz (2000) applied his values theory to socioeconomic concerns. Value consensus forms when members of a society acquire their values from informational institutions such as national media and a centralized educational system. The sense of what is important to a nation is likewise influenced by working conditions and divisions of labor in that nation. Thus, those in control of media, education, and labor markets may control the shared values of a nation. (Table 2).

Schwartz's ideas on values and work (1999) influenced recent notions put forth by Kohn (2001), which address job complexity that may enhance intellectual flexibility. Kohn suggested that, over time, the mental flexibility of the individual increases in jobs requiring higher levels of complexity. The value of self-direction needed to manage Chinese urban micro-businesses would then be higher than the benevolence values of the nation's teachers.

Cross-national cultural value types.

The highest rated cultural values in the Far East are hierarchy and embeddedness; the lowest are intellectual autonomy and egalitarianism (Licht, Goldsmith, & Schwartz, 2001). While both democratic and totalitarian regimes develop guidelines for how much freedom people must choose their values, individuals in an ideal democracy are encouraged to develop and express their own value priorities, lifestyles, opinions, and associations, whereas individuals in a totalitarian society are compelled to accept and comply with the values of the government. In other words, "social consensus decreases with democracy and increases with totalitarianism" (Schwartz, 2001a).

Littrell (2003) evaluated global business theory as it applies to China's interpretation of the rule- of-law and ethics. The values showed a greater relativity of goals, attitudes and influences, and opinions. As socialist societies, such as Maoist China, democratized, subgroups gained some freedom to reject dominant societal values. Schwartz (2001b) contended that such democratized subgroups in socialist societies may ultimately be responsible for dramatic social changes. For example, Deng Xiaoping's notions of "market socialism," which got him imprisoned for being a "capitalist roader," ultimately prevailed as China moved toward economic liberalization.

Non-Western approaches to cross-cultural values.

Although Schwartz studied people in 88 countries who spoke 144 different languages and dialects, some non-Western theorists, such as Kim (2002) and Kitayama (2004), have argued that his values theory still retains a degree of Western bias. To correct for this, they have emphasized the "cultural interdependencies" of individuals living in non-Western societies.

Kim (2002), a cross-cultural communication theorist, delineated two basic types of cultures: interdependent and individualistic. Interdependent cultures, such as those in East Asia, tend to view individuals' worth in terms their relationships and group memberships.

Individualistic cultures, such as those in Europe and North America, tend to view individuals' worth in terms of their ability to achieve. While these terms are relatively clear in terms of theory, Kim argued that all cultures are always and simultaneously interdependent and individualistic, depending on their situation and circumstance.

Kitayama (2004) argued that only indigenous researchers can fully understand and interpret an indigenous people's local knowledge. To approach this knowledge, non-indigenous researchers must focus on narrative methods, such as collecting stories, analects, and idiomatic expressions, and must allow for participatory interpretation of the data—that is, observed populations must be permitted to contribute to descriptions and analyses of themselves. This awareness of indigenous knowledge is obvious to those in the field of cross-cultural values research. While this is not to toss out the observations of potential researchers outside of a culture,

Kitayama suggested that they adhere to extremely rigorous guidelines of conduct and sensitivity and document their process thoroughly.

Somé (1999) brought an African perspective to the dialogue on cross-cultural values by noting that in non-Western societies, especially in Africa, ritual practices often perform the functions served by individual and organizational psychology in the West. One of the main purposes of ritual is to restore one's individual or organizational balance through letting go. Rituals may also assist individuals to navigate identity or community crises. For example, Somé (1999) described how the ash ritual is used for resolving issues that arise between members of families and small communities:

The people with issues walks into this circle and face each other, while everyone else sits outside, also facing one another. The person who called for the ash ritual speaks his or her truth about what is hurting. The emphasis is not on blame, but on how the actions of the other have resulted in hurt and bad feeling. The other person responds, emphasizing the motive of his or her action. The people present support them by guiding them away from accusatory language, such as "you did this, and I don't like your guts," and so forth. Usually a healthy imparting of one's feelings to the other results in cathartic understanding, and the whole session ends in embrace, (p. 190)

These rituals intensify relationships among all the community's members in ways that are almost impossible to replicate in modern Western societies or even to describe in Western terms because the sources of transformation and change may require a perception that comes "up from the ground," not from heavenly or divine authority. Clearly the non-Western research theorists call for reform in the major fields of anthropology, cognitive psychology, organizational theory and cross-cultural studies.

The Schwartz Values Survey supplies an analytical framework that transforms large cross-cultural data sets into "near-universal values." The resulting information creates a system of human cognitive activity and the motivating goals behind values. Applied by independent scholars to various studies, the research process increases the certainty of the existence of some basic cross-cultural goals, motivations, and behaviors. The SVS data can be supplemented with interviews to give the research a qualitative dimension.

International Development Ethics, China, and the Role of Micro-Businesses

Cross-cultural values are the building blocks of international development ethics, operating in tandem with economic equality among the world's nation-states (Ohmae, 1996). Ideally, these international development ethics that underlie the goal of current trends in global economic stability, promote practices that further that goal, and push for conditions that lead to social transformations, usually in the form of democracies. This section of the Literature Review identifies the nature of colonial and modernization theories and practices that led to current international development conditions. This discussion reviews the primary Western theories of international development and trade, and the ethical principles that have emanated from those development theories. The analysis includes several of the multicultural ethical challenges, in particular Sen (1987, 1992,1999, 2004), who contributed the economic theory of consequentialism, which in turn led to what he called "development as freedom." The section concludes with a discussion of China's re-emergence as a world power, the new social contract under market socialism, and the role of China's urban micro-businesses as agents of revolutionary change.

Peters (2000) observed:

Development is one of the most powerful intellectual
constructs and political slogans of the past half-century, giving
order and purpose to a world in which colonies disappeared,
in which virtually everyone acquired citizenship in a sovereign
state, but in which profound inequality remained, (p. 2)

Modernization.

Modernity launched the world on its historical path toward
development in the 16th century (Arrighi, 1994; Braudel,
1979; Frank, 1995a; Wallerstein, 1996) the details of which
occupied development theorists for decades. The origins of
international development ethics were a fertile part of this
history of modernity, which lasted over 5 centuries, until the
end of the 20th century. Braudel (1979) provided a long-term
historical account of events and contexts for understanding
international organizations. Subsequently, Arrighi, Hamashita,
& Seiden (1997) used the same method to describe the history
of Western cycles of flexibility, expansion, and fluctuation of
capitalist growth and capital formation over the long term, or
longue durée.

Frank (1995b) provided an in-depth macro-historical
account of simultaneous processes of the global economy
experience in civilizations such as China and India,
challenging the economic and ideological hegemony of
the European west. Wallerstein (2004) viewed the French
Revolution as the catalyst for the modern concepts and ideals
of worldwide legal citizenship.

Schumpeter (1911/1934), a conservative economist,
inaugurated a theory of economic development, according
to which entrepreneurs, by disturbing economic equilibrium,
are the cause of economic development. At the other end
of the political spectrum, Gramsci (1988) contended that

humanity is capable of continually improving its condition of existence without heroes. Gramsci cautioned that the rational Enlightenment notion of equality (and democratic rule) could lead to a reaction dedicated to its opposite—namely, fascism—the hegemony of the few over the many.

Weber (1922/1993) contributed to the understanding of economic ethics with an analysis of the western Puritan work ethic, but also differentiated the underlying social and cultural origins of international development ethics:

"Capitalism" existed among all these religions, even those religions of the type in occidental antiquity and the medieval period. But there was no development toward modern capitalism, nor even any stirrings in that direction, in these religions. Above all, there evolved no "capitalist spirit" in the sense that is distinctive of ascetic Protestantism. But to assume that the Hindu, Chinese, or Muslim merchant, trader, artisan, or coolie was animated by a weaker acquisitive drive than the Protestant is to fly in the face of facts. All these people import economic rationalism as the most important product of the Occident, and their capitalistic development is impeded only by the presence among them of rigid traditions, such as existed among us in the Middle Ages, not by lack of ability or will, (p. 269)

Throughout the 19th century, the United States and other colonial powers debated economic philosophy and policy, which contributed to a Western cultural inclination to discuss such issues as economic independence, minimal governmental intervention, and the widespread desire for profitable trade (Newell, 1999). By the end of the 19th century, colonialists, still motivated by the increasing plurality of cultures they had "discovered," believed that the raw materials and labor of these cultures was theirs by providence and force (Sahlins, 1995; Said, 1983/2002). Specialization of raw material economies included the classic model of a single export nation or "banana republic," organized along a Western thinking system of government.

The beginning of Western modernity expanded with efforts to modernize the underdeveloped world. Countries were considered underdeveloped or generally poor if they were "traditional societies" that resisted change. Peasants who resisted high-risk, capital-intensive technologies were regarded as "irrational." Local histories and cultures were dismissed as "barriers" to economic growth. The modern prescription for international economic development ethics created pro-capitalist and pro-urban growth (Todaro, 1997).

A linchpin of Western modern development theories were the ideas of Nurkse (1952,1959), who equated development with the growth of output. Contrarily, on the economic development side, Prebisch (1950/1962) and Singer (1950) took issue with disintegrating terms of trade between developed and developing nations and argued for the role of savings in developing countries and for improving "human capital" or social development as a prerequisite for growth. However, as these social policies became more difficult to implement, neo-liberalism took root, as Rostow (1964/1991) and other economic theorists suggested and called for large and capital-intensive industrialization strategies as a prescription for economic development of the Third World.

Development Theories

The current streams of international development ethics span the half-century since the Bretton Woods Conference in July 1944, where the United Nations (UN) and the International Monetary Fund (IMF) were established. These organizations provided structures, such as the World Bank, for the allocation of financial resources among developing countries. In addition, numerous academic studies were commissioned by these organizations to collect information from central international funding sources and enable more informed decision-making. The establishment of international organizations such as the IMF and World Bank also led to critiques of Western colonialism and modernization theories. The mid-20th century opened decades of discourse on what was called dependency development and its variations.

Dependency theory.

The story of development theories centers on the axis of capitalist processes and critiques of the goal to transform traditional societies even though the goal includes the intention to intervene on their economic behalf. In contrast to the modernization theories of the 1960s, those writings about the 1970s characterize this as a time of rapid growth of Western multinational corporations, particularly in Latin America. From Brazil and Chile, almost simultaneously, two theoretical schools of thought emerged on development: dependency theory and center-periphery, or world systems theory.

The concept of "dependency development" is reviewed here on two levels of conflicts: micro problems (such as local community-based development), and macro problems (such as the long-wave patterns of economic growth and globalization).

Cardoso and Faletto (1978) explained the ongoing condition of dependency as a result of unfair export trade practices. This was the situation viewed between the Southern "periphery" nations of Mexico, Central, and South America and the "core" United States and North America. Using a concept of "standardization," they explained dependency as a function of industrial capitalism. Therefore, the inequalities of trade were a direct result of standardization of industrialized companies, which emanated from the capitalist conditions of labor and labor divisions. The components of unfavorable trade relationships included corrupt and colluding governments, and risk-averting investors.

Singer (1950) and Prebisch (1956) are often viewed as the founders of dependency development theory. Singer (1975) revisited the notion of the terms of trade. He observed that the volume and terms of trade between countries that export commodities and those that manufacture goods, would deteriorate over time. In effect, developing countries would export primary goods that were then manufactured into secondary goods in developed countries and sold back to the poorer countries as commodities. These "value-added" manufactured goods would have a higher cost than the primary products from which they were created. Export nations would be less likely to import more goods over time and should therefore concentrate on building up their manufacturing capability. The solution would seem to be for developing countries to import resources for increasing their manufacturing base. However, this strategy led to debt structures that saddled many developing countries for decades at a time, thus reducing internal development. Prebisch noted another inconsistency under these internationalist capitalist processes: that developing nations reduced the amount of land and resources to feed their own people, which in turn required them to import goods from developed nations.

From his studies, Prebisch (1981) created a model for these inconsistencies, which he described as dependency development theory. The theory was based on the notion that wealthy nations increased their wealth at the expense of underdeveloped nations. Prebisch (1981) later concluded that most international, liberal capital markets were not necessarily economically progressive, making a distinction between economic growth and development. Over time, he argued, they did not provide the economic benefits they claimed. He observed that local communities of developing nations did not necessarily benefit from the structural changes in their traditional economic system. In fact, international economic development, while purporting to provide economic growth, increased strategies for financial aid, and created a system of dependency. This could be viewed as an extension of colonialism.

André Gunder Frank (1995a), a sociologist and economist, asserted the primacy of macro conditions on development—that is, economic development is affected by historical global forces that in turn affect local economies. Using the socialist concept of "capital accumulation," Frank (1995b) critiqued development in Mexico to show how cyclical changes within that nation affected local modes of production. Latin America, he argued, was economically structured to serve international capitalism. Frank (2002) extended this critique to the dynamic of the long-term role of markets and capitalism and the relationship of foreign debt in developing economies. For example, he found that merchandise imports from developing nations, were being purchased by developed nations as "payments for services." This practice contributed to the inaccurate representation of the so-called Third World debt service. He championed calls for relief from this burden of debt.

Frank's concept, that macro monetary policies created class oppression, strengthened dependency structures, and led to chronic underdevelopment. He argued that the IMF structural adjustment programs should be curtailed and that the socialist countries in economic demise should protect themselves from these and similar international development monetary policies, particularly rapid flows of capital in and out of a country.

World-Systems Theory.

International development ethics include a range of historical approaches, of which world-systems theory integrates the narratives of development. Originating in the 1970s, world-systems theory is an analysis based on the Polyani's (1944) structuralist perspective that global geographies are "multi-spatial and temporal zones" under a single political, economic, and social framework. The world-systems theorists assert that there has never been a world empire of a single political authority rather, there are only ongoing rivalries between geographical states. Therefore, this large geographic area, the world, only unites to create divisions of labor with significant internal exchange of basic or essential goods as well as flows of capital and labor. The priority of the world-system is capitalism, or the 'endless accumulation of wealth."

World-systems theories expanded the Prebisch-Singer thesis (1960) of "core," "semi-periphery," and "periphery," as inherent worldwide relationships. For example, Wallerstein (2000) analyzed that the divisions of labor flows between countries of the North and the South—or the First World "core" versus the Third World "periphery." Wallerstein, (2000) demonstrated the ways in which social oppression is built into the language and ideology of the powerful "Firsts," and how it begins to affect the less powerful nations. Economically, according to world-systems theory, capitalism can be bridged with the socialist economics and practices of the late 19th and 20th centuries (Arrighi, 1995; Wallerstein, 2000). In Wallerstein's (2005) world-system analysis, the "core" countries (European, North American) own the means of knowledge, production, and distribution, whereas the "periphery" of South America, Africa, and some countries in Asia, possess raw materials and human resources for production and services. The "Second World," such as several Asian capitalist countries and parts of mainland China, move in and out of periphery and core status, but are essentially tied to the world-wide enterprise of capitalism.

World-systems theories also expand on Frank's (1995b, 2002) thesis that geographic Latin America is part of a greater *world-system* in which capitalism differentiates the regional processes. He emphasizes that each nation state can be analyzed based on its mix of core-peripheral economic processes within it. The complex relationships of the world economy with its expansion and stagnation, creates spiralling trends of endless accumulation.

One key feature that world-systems theorists introduced is the socializing force of households in the world-system. Wallerstein (2004) used the unit analysis of "households" to describe capitalist cycles of accumulation, or what he calls "secular trends." Households, as opposed to tribes and clans, which are units of security, can be viewed as having some forms of the following trends: (a) subsistence work (such as uncompensated housework), (b) petty commodity production (a product made to sell outside the household), (c) rent, and (d) transfer payments. In other words, few households anywhere in the world operate without several types of income and these households (as opposed to individuals) are located within classes.

World systems theorists use their comprehensive analysis to recreate the emerging world-wide view of development and often view their notions as outside the paradigm of development, and perhaps more attuned to the forces of globalization.

Global development theory.

By the late 1970s, development in an international context began to refer to transnational economic strategies. Leavitt (1973) coined the term global development to describe standardized products and practices all over the world driven by low-priced, high-quality, and economically efficient production. By the 1990s, the impetus for globalization was corning mainly from the United States, the lone military super-power. Robertson (1992) described the paradox of the increasing interdependence of the world into "a single place" and at the same time, negotiates the distinct identities of nations within that single place. He said that the global situation entered a phase of uncertainty between the 1960s and the 1990s. Attempts to congeal a global identity met resistance. Given the premise of hegemony, the articulation of a global cultural identity (Feafherstone, 1990), exacerbated certain realignments of national societies and realigned at a rapid pace identities, terminology, and centers of power. For example, Stiglitz (2002) coined the term "Washington Consensus" to refer to conditions imposed by the United States that require any aid to developing countries for economic advancement to be market-driven.

Throughout the 1990s, the World Bank had continued to sponsor structural adjustment programs (SAPs) in underdeveloped countries in return for such adjustments as the privatization of water systems and the patenting of seeds. In effect, in exchange for a subsistence level of development, the poorer nations used the foreign aid money to pay for the services of Western transnational companies to build large scale engineering, mining, and agricultural programs. These policies came into sharp conflict with developing and traditional societies and, most importantly, with socialist societies. The former, such as India, produced compelling post-colonial dialogues on these issues. The latter, for example China, in 1972-73, opened the door, but only a strategic crack in order to control growth for direct foreign investment into the country.

Robinson (2004) described the rise of transnational corporations, as rooted in global neo-liberal market capitalism, clashing with the nationalistic aspirations, religious values, and perceptions of the developing world. Robinson proposed:

The emergence of global networks of accumulation requires stable rules for economic competition, which new capitalist and professional sectors are eager to construct, while excluding the rest of the population from meaningful participation in economic and political life. The "democratic consensus" in the new world order is a consensus among increasingly cohesive global elites on the type of political system that is most propitious to the reproduction of social order in the new global environment, (p. 83)

In the 1970s, many international relationships moved away from dependency toward other development models. There was an increased awareness of indigenous knowledge (IK), values, and practices, which led to participatory development movements in many third world countries. Standards changed for development institutions and it became unacceptable to dictate economic or political policies without including the members of those nations as stakeholders. Nevertheless, these ideas of inclusion were viewed as extensions of modern social democratic ideas from former colonizers to their former colonies (Olson, 2000; Stiglitz, 2002). Global development, an emergent paradigm in international economic development systems, is far from understood.

Subaltern theories.

Arguably, the strongest challenges to globalization are coming from intellectuals in post-colonial nations who call themselves "subalterns." The subaltern theories, while mainly focused on India's regions, provide relevant discussions for Asians (Rahnema & Bawtree, 2003). Founded in 1982, the Subaltern Studies Collective established a system of historical critiques of colonialist and nationalist perspectives. Amin (1995) provided general criteria for constructing alternative development within the capitalist world economy. Chattergee (1986), focusing on a rewrite of India's colonial history, examined the institutions of colonial society, peasant uprisings against the colonialists, international feminism and gender studies, and general problems of historical perspectives and interpretations. Spivak (1988), in her work on international feminism, chose a method called "strategic essentialism" to develop her thesis that even the Western term for woman sets up woman an individual, whereas in most subaltern countries, gender reflects the essence of a woman. For the purposes of solidarity and social action, these distinctions must be part of the broader international development ethics discourse. Obadina (2000), lamenting Africa's lost opportunity to integrate the best of its indigenous, alternative values in its economic institutions, nonetheless critiques the dogmatism of Marxism and the dependency theorists for establishing worldwide economic analysis based on "them-us." He argued, if everyone agrees colonial exploitation was wrong, it's time for Africans and other non-westerners to master and share in the benefits of a single civilization.

Current international development theories.

Escobar's (1995) anthropology of modernity, or developmentalism, explains more fundamentally the loss of the socialist dream of economic equality, or even the seemingly attainable capitalist ideal to eliminate worldwide poverty. Using a post-structuralist, political economy analysis, he views the eclipse of socialism by super-capitalism as a structure of international development. Escobar punctures the veil of the international development ethics paradigm by asking to what extent the development "experts" and institutions influence tangible development. His conclusion advances the "world systems" concept that the ethical discourse of development is responsible for widespread underdevelopment. Ivan Illich (1971/2003) had earlier described underdevelopment as a form of reification of consciousness, or "the hardening of perceptions of real needs into the demand for mass-manufactured products" (p. 97).

Since the domination of the United States as a superpower after World War II, Escobar (1995) contended that the "war on poverty" in the Third World has occupied a prominent place in the discourse of international development ethics beginning in the 1940s and 1950s when organizations such as the World Bank and the IMF were formed. He described an historical construct about the ways in which these institutions and the professionals who run them produce knowledge. He contended that when they use disparaging terms such as "aboriginal" or "undeveloped," they objectify the people into a problem. The underlying message is that these "savages" need to be transformed into *us.* Thus, when the institutions and professionals encounter the Third World, they enter with that bias. Escobar (1995) wrote:

Any model, however, whether local or universal, is a construction of the world and not an indisputable, objective truth about it. This is the insight guiding the analysis of economics as culture. The coming into and dominance of modern economics meant that many other existing conversations or models were appropriated, suppressed, or overlooked. There is, then, an orientalism in economics that must be unveiled-that is, a hegemonic effect achieved through representations that enshrine one view of the economy while suppressing others, (p. 62)

Escobar (1995) also asserted that when Western institutions and professionals try to modernize "Third World" peoples, the latter begin to think of themselves in alien terms—that is, as tools of production and consumption. "People and nature," he wrote, "are separated into parts, or recombined into market economies, or objects of exchange knowledge" (p. 61). Escobar contended that in the 1940s, the World Bank defined poverty on a worldwide scale as a gross national product (GNP) of less than $100 per year per capita. This provided people with a concrete yardstick to compare themselves to others—usually unfavorably. However, the economists, dependency theorists and world systems theorists had pointed out earlier that GDP is a "stylized fact" (Ros, 1994,2000) that can camouflage levels of output. GDP can measure output levels, but is also based on many differing internal scales of efficiencies such as the ratio of workers to the total population, knowledge, and natural resources. For example, in the 1990s, the share of manufacturing exports produced by developing countries grew by 150%, rising from 11% of the total world export of manufactured goods to 27% in 1998 (UNCTAD Trade and Development Report, 2002). However, during that same period, the developing world's share of manufacturing new value-added products grew 40% rising from 17% to 24%. The value and volume of manufactured exports by developing countries increased gigantically more than the actual income obtained by the producers (Ravallian & Anand, 1993).

Meanwhile, developed countries in the same time period decreased their exports of manufactured goods from over 80% in 1980 to about 70% in 1999, yet their share of the world's value-added manufacturing increased from 65% to 73%. Even though Third World exporters did get rich, these nations received less and less for what they produced for sale in the world market. This is also reflected in the terms of trade for manufactured goods.

Escobar pointed to the work of Gudeman and Rivera (1990) to demonstrate the value of indigenous ways of life and relationships and how these provide alternatives to Western economic development. For example, indigenous people live and work in the same place, so there are no issues around clogged transportation arteries, pollution, and all the stress that comes with these. They operate under the ethical principles of conservation, reuse, and low consumption. Traditional economies, these authors argued, are also more flexible and resilient than outsiders realize, so the latter, before imposing external changes, need to look more deeply into the cultures and economies they are trying to "fix." In other words, local innovations and gains can be preserved as part of the modernization process.

Escobar affirmed that development specialists can mediate between the economic practices they discover in the field and those that they are mandated to implement from outside by using the concept of "cultural difference." The key to understanding cultural differences is to recognize that there are legitimately different forms of knowledge.

Todaro (1997) asserted that development economics has no universally accepted doctrine or paradigm. Modernization theories but also other paradigms, including development theories, have lost a considerable amount of their validity, or have reached an impasse (Leys, 1996). This occurred, in part, because capitalism today, as unlimited accumulation and growth, depends on new knowledge systems and new investment sources, such as pension plans, real estate, mutual funds, and other portfolios (Surin, 1998). Most developing nations cannot structurally compete with these new capital markets, and only the modernist hybrid nations (such as China, India, and Indonesia) are evolving within those markets.

The dependency and world-systems theorists had rejected the tenets of the stages of modernization, which Gallagher (2002) claimed, in retrospect, may have occurred in many newly developed nations. In particular, she pointed to Rostow's (1964/1991) third and fourth stages of capitalist modernity, specifically the drive to maturity, and the stage of mass consumption. Certainly, both India and China provide examples of countries in these stages of economic development.

The world-systems theorists were perhaps too structuralist. In combining the structures of capitalism and socialism and linking individual and national futures, world-systems assumed an agency-less way to do things. Social values that direct the questioning back to a purpose, or a direct set of goals to guide actions, are antithetical to the world-system, therefore negating some cultural viewpoints. The world-systems theorists were also criticized because of their non-linear approach to modes of production, challenged on their premise that national and cultural structures are based on a single economic maxim, and dismissed by their hyper-hierarchical theory, which claims to be a grand narrative, but has no central actor.

However, the failures of Western international development ideologies can be said to match the failures of economic socialism, specifically regarding non-Western multiculturalism. These failures have produced severe challenges to the ideals of global capitalism. While development specialists gained some understanding of the importance of local land-based economic approaches, which incorporate dynamic multicultural concepts, the most important task of development remains to stabilize the economics of the households in the developing world.

Sen's Theory of Development as Freedom

Sen (1987) contended that the field of economics, after Adam Smith, evolved in such a way that human motivation became very narrowly defined as the pursuit of wealth. Smith himself, Sen argued, was a moral philosopher who viewed economics as much broader than this. Its ultimate purpose is to support the basic goals of life. As Sen noted, economics asks Socrates' classical ethical question, "How should one live?" The very etymology of the word economics tells us this, for it derives from the Greek oikos (οικοσ), "household," and nemein (νεμειν), "to manage."

For decades, Sen (1987) wrote, economists viewed human beings as strictly rational creatures who made consistent choices and maximized their self-interest. Thus, Léon Walras (1874/1954), among other so-called "Marginalists," developed the general equilibrium theory that came to dominate in the new (numerical) school of economics, or what Sen called the "engineering approach" to the field. This trend of marginal utility evolved into utilitarianism and Keynesianism. In addition, Pareto's (1906) criterion of optimality, a fundamental theorem of welfare economics which relates to market equilibrium, provided yet another extremely limited way to assess social achievement.

Sen did not want to lose these engineering approaches to economics but intended to bring them back to their original purpose, which was to enhance well-being by emphasizing such things as the intrinsic value of work, pride of ownership, and civic order. In other words, he wished to reconnect economics to ethics.

Consequentialism and ethics.

The way Sen (1987,1992, and 1999) did this was by first viewing human beings as agents or managers of their own well-being. The problem was, how does one measure this agency or management? Sen answered this question by focusing on a process from welfare economics called "consequential reasoning," which determines the intrinsic value of things and their instrumental roles by calculating the consequences on other things. Therefore, consequentialism calculates whether decisions based solely on self-interest generate greater efficiencies than decisions based on advantages to the society.

Sen's (1999) theory of economic consequentialism returns an ethical foundation to economics by replacing wealth with well-being as the primary objective. This provides a justification for financing micro-businesses in China as one way to merge socialistic ideals with capitalist market mechanisms to alleviate the economic inequalities in the millions of households in that country.

The ways in which Western international development ethics evolved applies to China today, whose development compressed into decades what took centuries in the West.

Social Economic Analysis of Chinese Urban Micro-businesses

Sen's (1999, 2004) conclusion, that decisions based solely on self-interest produce fewer efficiencies than decisions based on advantages to the society, can be applied to China as it transitions from socialism to market capitalism. That is, in order to understand China, one must understand that the people have no "self-outside of their roles and relationships (Fei, 1992).

Today, although many in rural China remain in poverty, the West has not imposed its will on China by overt force but by the attractiveness of its civilization and the belief in the desirability of material progress and prosperity. At present, China has solidified its desire to regain its status with the rest of the modern globalizing world. However, Fei (1992) suggested that even though China has grown out of its dependence on agriculture, the general social and cultural relevance of the nation is its ties to and from the soil.

China's re-emergence as a world power.

China has been a world economic power, if not a military one, for centuries (Frank, 2002; Sheff, 2002; Wang, 1998). For most of modern Western history, the prevailing fallacy has been that China has remained a feudalistic country with closed and protected borders (Said, 1983/2002). In fact, in the 14th century, the *Hakka kongzi* miners, from the southern regions of Guangdong Province, explored trade routes and established colonies throughout all regions of East Asia. When they reached new territories, they planned with the local populations to share the mining profits with them, and they also established small shops for trade. This was quite different from the plundering style of the colonizing Westerners. The Chinese instead chose a long-term economic ethic with which to exploit foreign resources by integrating into the foreign communities (Peng, 1995).

In the 16th century, the tailors of Zhezhiang, a province in the north of the country, especially those from the city of Wenzhou, created a family-based trade guild of unprecedented capitalist strength. The influence of these tailors reached all corners of Chinese society in terms of fashion and market share. Their textiles became one of the nation's principal exports (Zhang, 2001). The descendants of the *Hakka* Chinese became the economic elites of Hong Kong and many Asian countries and have been investing in China since the 1970s. Their contributions make up roughly 40% of the foreign direct investment in China (Fligstein, 2001). In addition, the tailors of Zhezhiang and those regional family-based enterprises that followed their model constitute one of the largest economic trade industries in the world, the Chinese apparel industry (Appelbaum, 2005).

According to Trescott (2002) the most prolific theorist on modern China is H. D. Fong (1902-1985), a Yale-educated economist whose work at the Institute of Pacific Relations (IPR) in the 1930s and 1940s provided extensive data on textile industries and the problems faced by China as the nation began to industrialize. He pointed out that the government, as an investor, perpetuates the institutions that make industry inefficient: the continuation of family-based systems, which most often led to lack of capital, poor accounting and personnel policies, and corruption. Fong also favored the population control advocates such as Margaret Sanger.

Modern China.

China's evolution from the end of the last dynasty in 1911 to half a century of communism and then into the new market socialism cannot be fully comprehended without feeling the magnitude of its population. Population is the conscious center of the discussions in China on all social and economic levels. For example, students discuss population as the most important environmental factor facing the nation. In their own words, "people are pollution."

China's population explosion is rooted, in part, in the agricultural consolidation that took place in the early Qing dynasty (1644-1911), when food was plentiful, but people continued to have large families (Huang, 2004). Now, with more than 1.3 billion people to feed, clothe, educate, and create jobs for, China's government exerts strict control over many aspects of civil society, including reproduction. However, in recent years, the government has loosened its control over many aspects of the economy, and this is gradually leading to social freedoms.

East Asian capitalism.

China's economy continues to organize, in part, on agrarian, pre-industrial institutions based on family relationships, social homogeneity, rapid industrial development, and weak legal structures. "An important function of the family," Whitley (1994) wrote, "has been the reproduction of particular authority relations in respect for established hierarchies" (p. 220). These authoritarian relationships permeate most organizations in the country. For example, managers tend to see themselves as fathers and treat their workers in paternalistic ways.

Within this authoritarian system, social homogeneity has contributed to the rapid industrialization of the nation because of the persistent consensus about the way things need to be done. The weak legal structures created some barriers to development because of the unimportance of formal contracts and agreements, which makes it difficult to interact efficiently with Western nations. China has skirted this, however, by doing business with other Asian nations, which operate under the same principles, and by becoming so big that the West must accommodate to it.

Explaining authority.

This notion of Chinese institutional markets is furthered by Biggart's (1997) perspective, rooted in Weberian sociology of non-Western societies, that the structures of Asian organizations are based on institutional authority and relationships. They contended that the rationality of these institutions and relationships are "socially produced and culturally maintained" (p. 20). In other words, the reasons for economic exchange and material pursuit can be different, depending on the country of origin. They mapped out the Asian institutional organizational model by addressing the norms of exchange, the networks of financial relationships and obligations, and strategies of accumulation, using four of Weber's (1922/1993) elements: (a) economic action as social action; (b) embeddedness of economic activity in institutional settings; (c) institutional logic; and (d) the multilevel nature of an institutional argument.

In contrast to the Western concept of economic man, the Asian cultures viewed economic action as a social one first. The relationships fostered in the economic action are of importance, and attention is given to the details of the transaction in terms of goals, motivations, intentions, behaviors, and responses. Whereas the Westerner may also look at the instrumental or intrinsic value of an economic transaction, the Asians view economic transactions as continuity based on socially embedded traditional practices and influences both past and present.

Relational logic and ritual.

To take this idea further, Biggart (1997) noted that the multiple logics of Asian organizations tended to be based on factors such as 'Values, networks, and relations, and socially constructed rules" (p. 28). In other words, the rules of the organization are reproduced by the relationships between actors within the system, and the patterns in the system rely on a great deal of specificity. The institutional analysis allows simultaneous study of both the micro and macro level of relationships.

Orrù, Biggart, and Hamilton (1997) also found that the networks of an individual's social relationships are the most important factors in Asia for getting businesses financed, supplied, and staffed. Chinese society is strictly ordered from top to bottom, so relationships become institutionalized in the logic of social networks. One example of this is seen in the concept of *ganxing,* the intuition and feeling one has for another person, which is often considered a necessary part of hiring in China (Yang, 1995).

Yang documented the nuances of Chinese urban social practices and its many layers of personal relationships and guidelines of interaction with the art *guanxixue* as the backbone of Chinese urban socio-economics. During the Cultural Revolution (19631973) guanxi relationships were exposed and prohibited. When these restrictions lifted, guanxi relationships persisted, yet took on an informal or underground quality that operated in communitas; that is people came together, associated for a purpose of guanxi, and then the relationship either evolved or dissolved away once fulfilled. This perception is supported by ongoing work in China on management and leadership that Littrell (2003) described and situated as the ongoing use of *guanxi* as the ethical source for business relationships in China.

Chinese Urban Reforms

In China's Reform Era (1976-presenf), vast economic networks were rebuilt on such structures of temporary mutual aid. For example, some relationships are not accorded the same treatment as *ganxing* (an emotional "heart" connection), and are best described as *renqing,* or observing the proper social norm in any given situation. *Renqing* allows for offering of small gifts, banquets, and other sociable forms of interaction. Yang (1995) suggested that the relationship between *guanxi,* which gets things done but holds obligation and indebtedness, and the observance of *renqing,* which holds lesser degrees of obligation and indebtedness as a relationship are the beginnings of how Chinese urbanites understand market relations.

The evolution of China's enduring civilization produced social and economic consequences particular to the nation's historical and aesthetic experiences. When asked, most cab drivers and tailors in China will explain that Chairman Mao was 67% correct in his thinking when he rallied a national defence against the Japanese invaders and radically transformed the country. Many have carried forth the spirit of new China that began in 1919 during the May Fourth Movement when students and workers united in the common cause of ridding China of foreigners and not conceding to their power.

Nevertheless, some assert that the Chairman's economic policies were only 33% correct. In the long view of China's history, the communist revolution lasted only half a century. According to the "man on the street," communism had largely failed economically (Easterly, 2001).

Chinese market socialism.

China prides herself on the practicality of her solutions (Fei, 1992; Yutang, 1935/1998, DeBary, 1962). According to Huang (2004), the first practical form of modern social economic development was initiated in the early part of the 20* century when the Chinese economist Ma Yin Chu (1902-1992) developed a theory of population in order to stem the tide of China's growing masses. Ma warned that the threats of overpopulation on the environment, the economy, and the political stability of the emerging nation were too dire to ignore.

In effect, Ma proposed the deeply controversial countercultural solution of one-family/one-child. Huang (2004) interpreted population control as the beginning of China's economic reform era.

The socialist economist Sun Yefang (1961/1984) promoted a Chinese interpretation of the Marxist "law of value," stipulating that the trading ratios of products are a real cost structure of production, and this cost structure ultimately reduces to the average units of human labor-time currently required to produce different goods and services.

Sun defined this "law of value" as a function of simple exchange in the course of the expansion of trade, markets, and the circulation of capital. In China, he argued, social priorities ensured that people got what they needed, which was good, but insofar as resources were wasted because of lack of sensible cost-economies, it was bad. His proof for the law of value was the lack of clear relationships between the exchange-value of goods traded and what it really cost to produce them (Sun, 1961/1984).

Later, Sun's version of the law of value coalesced with the policies of Gu Zhun (1957/2001), a Chinese revolutionary, according to whom the Chinese needed to build a socialist market economy based on the "actual circumstances" in China, not on theory. A specific and complex society such as China, Gu argued, must be deeply investigated to discover the role that the law of value plays in economic exchange.

Both the law of value and Gu's policy of "actual circumstances" used profit-making as the economic indicator for economic efficiency. These ideas were unpopular during the Maoist Cultural Revolution in China, and both Yefang and Gu were jailed for espousing them. Later, under Deng Xiaoping, these economists and others like them returned to favor (Deng, 1996). Fei (1992) mentioned that Deng's initial social and economic reforms, in the period between 1976 and 1984, were first adopted in the countryside and met with great success.

During the first urban reform years (1984-1989) of Deng Xiaoping prompted a revival of Hu Fuming's (1961/1978) pragmatic thesis " seeking truth from facts," a theory once espoused by Mao but for which Hu had been jailed. Hu stated that the truth of all theories must be tested in practice. After Mao's death, Hu's ideas were used to reassess the authoritarian methodology of Maoist socialism. According to Huang (2004), the combined concepts of Ma, Sun, and Hu formed the basis of the Third Plenary Session of the Eleventh Central Committee of the Chinese Communist Party (Deng,1978).

Metaphors of the new market socialism.

In March 1986, when Chairman Deng Xiaoping established reforms and called for a new market economic strategy, he used the metaphor "crossing the river by feeling the stones" (Hoong, 2001, p. 191). This gradual strategy was established, Deng said, because for China to survive, the country would have to become part of the world economy. When necessary, however, this process might become gradual and even include backtracking, such as continuing forms of subsidy to unprofitable state-owned enterprises. Although this unprecedented development and the need to open the country to the world were accepted by the government, the intelligentsia, and the working people, the impact on the nation's social structures proved considerable (Wang, 1998).

Deng's ensuing urban reforms set in motion the consequences of socialism and market efficiencies that signalled China's focus on questions of economic reform. China's advanced socialism supported the strong belief in a social contract, a theme relevant to both Western and

Chinese society (Cheek, 1994), but one which played out quite differently. Under Deng opening policies, the Ministry of Science of Technology became the central focus for government-sanctioned high-technology entrepreneurship. The government assisted these entrepreneurs with rent subsidies for the first 3 years of start-up. He metaphorically described these incubators of high-technology as "the center of the torch," which meant that China's bright future was based on the high-technology sector.

Tang and Parish (2000) viewed the consequences of the Chinese social contract as a system of "high over all equality," but also a system based on top down dependencies and close reliance on personal contacts, or one's need for personal connections and kin relationships. The generalized rules of these dependencies had a debilitating effect and led to the decline of idealistic socialism. The ways in which these socialist systems shaped the lives of ordinary Chinese people were intricate bureaucratic structures that proved to be economically inefficient (Olson, 2000). The personal connections aspect of the social system was fraught with corruption (Yang, 1995).

The role of ordinary Chinese urban micro-businesses.

Ordinary Chinese micro-businesses, which were inhibited by the Maoist Communist government on ideological grounds, sprang up almost immediately in the countryside after Deng Xiaoping took charge (Eastman, 1988; Fei, 1992). Once the agricultural communities shifted from planned programs to commercial enterprises, the urban sectors followed (Fei, 1992). Ordinary micro-businesses are now being encouraged by the Chinese government, which recognizes their economic efficiencies and their potential for jobs and wealth creation. The relative economic performance of different markets across societies and different organization of those markets have led scholars to consider the reasons multiple structures exist and how they can produce successful economic outputs for societies (Lincoln, Gerlach, & Takahashi, 1992).

The role of Chinese urban incubator micro-businesses.

The year 1986 marked a watershed year for high-technology in China. Deng's advisors in the Ministry of Science and Technology presented a long-range strategy for a high-technology revolution, which he called the "first productive force," and which he saw as the chief source of China's social and economic development.

At the same time, Deng wanted to advance China's commercial high technology industry sector, an important strategy to the coastal cities and in China's inland townships, making use of the flexible medium and small sized industries that had gained considerable economic strength. These industries were comprised of non-government enterprises and were quickest to grow, gather market information, source materials, provide incentives to workers based on company profits, and operated in modernizing environments.

These companies developed their own systems for pensions and social security of their workers and owners. For example, the *Zhongguancun* technology street in Beijing is the most successful location for start-up enterprises in China (Qi, 1999; Sheff, 2002), like Silicon Valley in the U.S.A. In order to reproduce this dynamic, nongovernment environment, the government set up incubator buildings to house the research and development of start-ups with a preference for micro-electronics, computer and information sciences, telecommunications, bio-technology, new materials, lasers, and highly efficient energy industries.

Qi (1999) described the goals of these non-governmental incubator companies as making decisions on their own accord, developing a market orientation, encouraging an internal flow of information, and distributing profits based on the proportion of the companies' success.

As a result of this technology-based economic vision, China has been able to take advantage of the many university-based scientific institutions and to encourage them to commercialize their activities and "enter the sea" *(xiahai)* by going into business. By the mid-1980s, there were approximately 1,000 research institutions with over 300,000 scientists and technical personnel (Qi, 1999). For example, Legend, the computer, is probably the most famous brand examples of a Chinese institute-incubated company (Sheff, 2002).

Micro-Business Owner-Manager Values in Shenzhen, China

Today, there are close to 400 high-tech incubators around the country, 14 of which are in Shenzhen. These local markets have complex and stable social structures that are based on the strong national and international multinational institutions *(The Globalist,* September 2005). Many have corporate headquarters and offices in Shenzhen including CNNOC, Haier, Lenovo, China Mobile, Carrefour, and more recently, Wal-Mart. Proximity to Hong Kong has allowed the Shenzhen residents to prosper through exchange and tourism. Repeated interactions of buyers and sellers based on reputation of participants in those markets are essential to this success (Prahalad, 2005, Tsai, 2002).

The incubators in Shenzhen operate in a climate of fierce competition. However, according to the supervisors of the incubator buildings with whom I spoke, roughly 80% of new incubator businesses succeed.

The system of market socialism introduced by the People's Republic of China is quite different from the original attempt of the Soviet-style economy (including the *perestroïka* reforms of Premier Mikhail Gorbachev) introduced into the countries of Czechoslovakia, the former Yugoslavia, and Viet Nam, whose market elements improved economic growth (Olson, 2000). Like most socialism in reform, Chinese market socialism attempts to retain some government control of economic infrastructures and heavy industry while giving local markets more freedom.

Unlike other reforming socialist states, under this system, private ownership and entrepreneurship can flourish as secondary markets, in particular the light manufacturing and service sectors.

Thousands of micro-businesses survive in the thriving streets of Chinese cities like Shenzhen. These owner-managers can set prices, sell in the open market, and retain profits as an incentive to improve and increase services and products. Many economists would argue that China, rather than having a system of market socialism, has evolved into modern Chinese capitalism. Accordingly, Castells (2000) remarked that the successful organizations are those that can create knowledge and efficiently process information in the new global economy.

In this sense, the network enterprise makes material the culture of the informational, global economy: it transforms signals into commodities by processing knowledge, (p. 189)

The present study extends the socioeconomic perception that Chinese people like groups in every society in the world must have some form of markets and traders that promote economic competition. As Fukuyama (1999) noted:

The desire for material progress is obviously a universal drive. I think that there's a fair amount of evidence that a desire to exchange on the market is also a universal human attribute. In those places where market exchange is not practiced, it is almost always because the state or other form of governmental authority prevents it. (p. 24)

In the context of ethical values, the question arises as to whether or not the proliferation of micro-businesses will ultimately produce greater ability in the Chinese people to choose their own goals, and if these goals will also lead to the distribution of benefits to the greater society. I used Schwartz's (2003) SVS to examine the current values that take root at the micro-business owner-manager level in China, and I interpreted business behaviors, influences, attitudes, and ethical outlooks from 6 taped interviews as an additional approach to examining these values.

CHAPTER THREE

METHODS

Cross-Cultural Values Surveys and Ethnographic Interviews

Setting

The study was conducted between July and August 2004 in Shenzhen, China, and three surrounding districts, which have a combined population of approximately 10 million. Shenzhen was the first area in the mainland of China to establish a special economic zone for opening Chinese markets. This study was conducted in individual micro-businesses during hours of operation in ordinary stores and incubator offices.

Research Design

This study included a one-time survey that I administered followed by face-to-face interviews. The 197 participants spent an average of 30 minutes completing (a) a 58-item questionnaire, the Chinese version of the Schwartz Values Survey, or SVS (Schwartz, 2003) (Appendix A); and (b) a 9-question, demographic, self-description survey modified from the SVS English version (Appendix B). Ten of the participants volunteered to participate in a post-survey interview that lasted between 30 and 60 minutes. Those interviews, facilitated by a bilingual translator, were audiotaped, transcribed, and back-translated for language validation (Pym, 2001).

Sample

The participants from whom the sample was drawn were micro-business Owner-managers in Shenzhen who were affiliated primarily with one of two local district business associations: the Shenzhen Small and Medium Enterprise Credit Guarantee Center (CGC) or the Science and Technology Bureau of Nanshan Shenzhen-International Business Incubator (IBI). The CGC has approximately 500 micro-business owner-manager members in Shenzhen and the IBI has over 500 micro-business in Nanshan, Shenzhen and over 500 in the district of Longgang. I distributed 250 questionnaires to both associations and their affiliates. Additionally, a few business participants asked me if they could copy and give surveys to friends and business acquaintances whom they thought might meet the inclusion and exclusion criteria.

Subsequently, I interviewed 10 volunteer participants and selected 6 of these participants based on the study's demographic typicality. These 6 included 1 male and 2 females from ordinary micro-businesses and 2 males and 1 female from incubators.

Inclusion criteria.

There were two criteria for micro-business owner-managers to participate in the study: (a) they could have no less than one and no more than eight full-time employees and no more than 30 part-time employees; and (b) they may have applied for or already received loans or non-monetary assistance from the CGC or the IBI.

Exclusion criteria.

Simple street merchants were excluded from the study, as were individuals who worked on farms, in rural areas, or in any other geographic location that was difficult for the researcher to access by local transportation.

Data Collection Instruments

The study used two types of data collection instruments: the Chinese version of the Schwartz Value Survey, or SVS (Schwartz, 2003), and one-on-one, self-developed interviews based on Interview Protocols (Appendix C).

Translations of materials.

I hired local university students to translate the written surveys and professional translators to serve as interpreters during the interviews. This was because some of the participants spoke Mandarin and others spoke Cantonese.

The Schwartz Value Survey (SVS)

The SVS (Schwartz, 2003) is a pan-cultural, data collection survey designed to empirically assess individual and cultural values among nations of the world and their subgroups. For this study, a Chinese version was translated from English into Mandarin Chinese and then back again into English to ensure language validation. It was then tested among a variety of Clmiese-speaking teachers and students in mainland China, Taiwan, Singapore, and other Chinese enclaves in Southeast Asia (Schwartz, 1994a).

Schwartz's (1992) original SVS model identified four types of higher-order values derived from factor analysis: (a) Openness to Change (self-direction and stimulation); (b) Conservation (conformity and security); (c) Self-Enhancement (power and achievement); and (d) Self-Transcendence (benevolence and universalism).

The SVS survey includes 58 questions related to values: 52 to capture core values, and 6 to capture spiritual values. The initial 30 questions concern terminal values (nouns such as *equality* and *wisdom),* and the latter 28 questions concern instrumental values (adjectives such as *capable* and *humble).* Participants rated each of 58 values on a 9-point Likert-type scale, from —1 ("opposed to my values") to +7 ("of supreme importance"), based on whether each participant considered the statement to be "a guiding principle in my life."

Validity of the SVS.

Validity, defined as the quality that examines whether an instrument measures what it seeks to measure (Kerlinger, 1979), was tested and confirmed for the SVS several times since 1987 (Licht, et al., 2001; Schwartz & Bilsky, 1990; Schwartz & Sagiv, 1995; Schwartz, 1992,1994, 2000, 2001b, 2004). Construct validity of the instrument first measured instrumental and terminal values (Schwartz, 1992; Schwartz & Bilsky, 1987), which were based on the work of Rokeach (1960). Schwartz and Bilsky (1987) used the 36 Rokeach variables in the first SVS surveys to collect empirical data on core values and to predict their own 7 universal values or guiding principles, which Schwartz (1994a) later expanded to 10 universal individual dimensions and 7 universal cultural dimensions.

Schwartz and Sagiv (1995) have woven divergent and convergent processes into the validation methods of the SVS. For example, at first, he used criteria to differentiate and develop variables of value differences (Egri, et al., 1999). Later, Schwartz used consensus criteria to validate his instrument (Schwartz, 2001a). This method of measuring agreement and disagreement concerning values has enabled

Schwartz to create an open platform for other researchers to develop and adapt his instrument.

Reliability of the SVS.

Reliability is the quality of a data collection instrument that indicates whether an instrument consistently yields repeatedly the same results so that it can be said to be accurate each time it is used (Kerlinger, 1979). Reliability was established for the SVS in a pilot study I conducted in China in 2004 (Appendix D). I used a test-retest method on micro-business owner-managers in three different provinces of China. These managers were similar in inclusion criteria and the other intended sample. Overall test-retest reliability was established at 0.85. The test-retest procedure confirmed that the top three core values in the Individual Values Dimension remained, in descending order, Universalism, Security, and Benevolence; and that the top three core values remained in the Cultural Values Dimension; Embeddedness, Egalitarianism, and Affective Autonomy.

I also computed Cronbach's alpha (Cronbach, 1963) to assess the internal reliability of the data collection instruments. These were the 10 individual dimensions of the SVS (conformity, tradition, benevolence, universalism, self-direction, stimulation, hedonism, achievement, power, and security) and 7 cultural dimensions (embeddedness, hierarchy, mastery, affective autonomy, intellectual autonomy, egalitarianism, and harmony.) Cronbach's alpha was established at .50 or higher for all but two values, conformity and hedonism (Kerlinger, 1986).

Scorability.

Values items were averaged for each of Schwartz' 17 scales to compare them with data collected in other studies Schwartz conducted. For example, the average score for benevolence was derived from the 197 scores for questions 33, 45,49, 52, and 54. Each individual item was averaged in each survey before it was scored in the dimension of benevolence.

Additionally, I created an average rating score across all values items for each participant. Schwartz confirmed that the Chinese population tended to give lower ratings than other cultures to surveys and produced slight adjustments for cross-cultural differences in scale. He directed me to add 4.0 for China to the total score for each Chinese participant (Personal Communication, 2004). For example, if a participant had a total score of 225 for the 58 questions, I adjusted that score to 229 before calculating the mean.

Coding,

The collected surveys were coded numerically as they were collected. Later, the codes and data from the survey answers and demographic pages were entered into an SPSS 12.0 statistical database program numbered 1-205. After program statistics were run, there were 197 valid surveys to use for further statistical calculations.

The 10 audiotaped conversations were first coded with alias names prior to transcribing. Then one tape transcript was coded into nine categories based on the conceptual framework of the study. This process created a codebook for the narrative aspects of the study. Samples of the codebook and transcript were then given to second parties to verify meaning. The codebook was corrected or clarified based on these findings. Finally, all narrative transcripts were coded using the corrected codebook (Appendix E).

Utility.

In general, the SVS proved easy to administer among the sample population. Overall, the surveys were completed accurately and filled in completely by the participants. Among those participants whose comments were highly favorable, the survey was an interesting activity to participate in and provided them with a greater awareness about values and how they are useful in daily life. Those participants who disliked the survey said that it was too long, took too much time to complete, and was too impractical to benefit their life.

Costs

The $2,600 in expenses for the study included: $900 for travel to and around China; $400 for tape transcription; $400 for back translations; $300 for interpreters; $280 for photocopies and supplies; $200 for living accommodations; and $120 for gratuities to the participants.

The Interviews

The second data collection instrument that I used was a self-developed, 3-4 item, 30-60-minute, interview protocol to examine the international economic development values that have an impact on these Chinese urban micro-business owner-managers. The protocol questions were derived from the questions that had undergone content analysis during the pilot study (Appendix F).

Trustworthiness and credibility.

I established the trustworthiness and credibility of the audiotaped interview questions by using experts in the micro-business field. These experts were selected from local universities, business associations, and private business sector to assist with the inter-rater reliability of the interview questions.

The 10 volunteer interviewees in this study from which 6 were selected (based on gender, type of business and their descriptive narratives) were asked the same three-four guideline questions. These questions related to their personal business practices and values, awareness of market economics, and other subjects that emerged in the semi-structured interviews about values surveys and responses to the SVS instrument.

The participants usually invited the researcher to their place of business and agreed to respond to questions in the face-to-face, interview. One sample question was:

In your opinion, what are the strengths and weaknesses of your micro-business?

Additionally, I asked the participants to respond to questions about job creation and market economic reforms in China. I also encouraged them to talk about relevant people or experiences that were important to them as micro-business owner-managers. When all 10 interviews were completed, one of the interpreters and I transcribed the English language questions and answers, leaving room for the Chinese-language questions and answers to be added later in back-translation (Scollon & Scollon, 1995/2001).

Procedures

Access to study participants.

I explained the purpose of this study in copies of a letter, written in English and Chinese that I distributed to hundreds of potential participants in storefront and incubator micro-businesses. The letter also explained where copies

of the survey could be obtained, how it should be filled
out, and where it could be dropped off. A contact number
was also provided for individuals who would be interested
in participating in a 1-hour audiotaped interview with the
researcher. Ten people called, and all were interviewed
(Appendix G).

Protection of Human Subjects.

The Fielding Graduate University Internal Review Board
approved this dissertation research on August 17, 2004,
prior to any contact with the participants in the final study
(Appendix H). Protection of human subjects was of the utmost
concern in this survey. Data collection procedures adhered to
the confidentiality clauses and commitments required by the
IRB committee and Fielding Graduate University, as well as
standard national academic research ethics for working with
subjects in foreign countries.

It was important for the researcher to establish
relationships with local business groups and organizations,
which facilitated the researcher's procedures, especially
obtaining anonymous participants. The questionnaires were
made available to members and affiliates of these associations
on a strictly volunteer basis. The questionnaires were then
deposited anonymously in a central pick-up location or
returned to me via an interpreter or my address by mail.
Either I or the interpreters collected completed surveys from
these anonymous pick-up locations at business centers and
incubators.

All data generated from this study were protected on my
personal computer and back-up CD-R floppies. In addition,
final copies of all data were stored on removable hard-drives
and will be retained for 5-7 years. Also, once transcribed,
I stored the taped interviews on my premises and I will not
use them for any other purpose than those disclosed to
participants in this study.

The Pilot Study

I conducted the pilot study in three provinces of China in April 2004 to examine the reliability of the data collection instrument and to refine my data collection procedures. Subsequently, I decided to study only one province, with better procedures for obtaining participants and protecting their identities.

The pilot study demonstrated that the SVS was appropriate for undertaking the larger dissertation research on micro-businesses. I also decided to expand the interview format to a full-fledged 1-hour taped interview session. The pilot study also included a semi-structured exit interview of about 15 minutes in length, which asked the participants three questions concerning how they felt about taking this kind of values survey and to ask if any items in the survey stood out for the participant. These exit interview questions were not validated but were used to determine the efficacy of conducting longer in-depth descriptive interviews in the future. Seventeen of the exit interviews had Chinese-English back-translations.

Data Management

I first entered the data into the SPSS 12.0 program using the variables from the SVS Scoring Sheet (Appendix I). The statistical program SPSS 12.0 accepted 197 of the 205 returned surveys as valid, rejecting the remaining 8 for various statistical reasons. I then recoded, cleaned and prepared the data for analysis. Recoding also occurred on variables in education and number of years in business for purposes of analysis.

Data Analysis

The study addressed five research questions:

RQ1 : How do ordinary and incubator micro-businesses differ demographically?

RQ2: What are the self-reported individual values of micro-business owner-managers in Shenzhen, China?

RQ3 : What are the self-reported cultural values of micro-business owner managers in Shenzhen, China?

RQ4: In what ways do individual and cultural self-reported values of Chinese micro-business owner-managers in Shenzhen, China, differ by type of business (ordinary or incubator), by demographic categories, and by years of business ownership?

RQ5: In what ways do the self-reported values of Chinese micro-business owner-managers in Shenzhen, China, influence their business attitudes and ethics?

Survey analysis and procedures.

For research question 1, demographic items for ordinary and incubator micro-businesses were compared using cross-tabulations with chi squares and analyses of variance.

For research questions 2 and 3, I developed frequencies, means, and standard deviations on the 10 universal individual values dimensions and 7 universal cultural values dimensions of Schwartz and Sagiv's (1995) theoretical model. Next, I listed these in decreasing order of reported frequency. Frequencies were also run for two survey items that seemed to reflect Western values but were not averaged into individual values: "Choosing one's own goals" and "Privacy."

For question 4, I entered each individual value, cultural value, and the two specific items above (Choosing One's Own Goals and Privacy) as a dependent variable into an analysis of covariance (ANCOVA). The between-subjects factor was ordinary business or incubator business. The analyses controlled for gender, recoded age (16-25,26-35,36-55), recoded education (0-9,10-11,12, >12, Have missing data), and recoded years in business (0-4, 5-16, Have missing data).

Preliminary analyses showed that marital status (no partner) correlated significantly with self-direction and achievement, and religiosity correlated significantly with universalism and power. Thus, I used these items as controls in analyses for those specific values. I also used the average value rating across all participants as a control in analyses for the 10 individual items, but not for the 7 culture items, as specified by Schwartz. For example, values placed on three individual survey items—security *(M=* 4.80, SD = .60), choosing one's goals *(M=* 5.12, SD = 1.47), and privacy (M= 4.58, *SD* = 1.55)—were also relatively high. Participants in ordinary micro-businesses also had higher scores on: choosing one's goals (M = 5.30, *SD* = 1.42) compared to participants in incubators *(M=* 4.89, SD = 1.51), *F* (1,195) = 4.10, ρ < .04, ns; and on privacy *(M-* 4.79, SD = 1.45) when compared to incubator micro-businesses (M = 4.31, SD = 1.64), F(I, 194) = *5.33, p* < .03.

I also conducted a preliminary analysis to see whether results would change significantly if participants with missing data for education and years in business were excluded from analyses (rather than being included because a separate code was devised for people with missing data). The results of the ANCOVAs did not change significantly but reduced the total N for the analyses. Thus, I retained in the analysis recodes for participants with missing data on education and business years.

Interviews and analysis procedures

I addressed research question five (In what ways do the self-reported values of Chinese micro-business owner-managers in Shenzhen, China, influence their business attitudes and ethics?) through ethnographic style interviews, an approach that is nearly antithetical to survey and quantitative analysis, in order to emphasize the spirit of individual owner-managers. In this part of the research, I extended the survey on values by discussing, with volunteers who had taken the survey, their specific business influences and attitudes, as well as their ethical outlooks. I used four primary sources in this qualitative process, including (a) ethnographic theories of Geertz (1983) and Marcus (1998); (b) techniques of Bourdieu and Waquant (1992) and van Manen (1997); (c) direct use of the "intermezzo" style based on Easterly's (2001) global development; and (d) the open-minded approach advocated by Chinese sociologist Yutang (1935/1998). A secondary source for my interview approach included Fontana and Frei's (2000) strategies to categorize emergent ideas in interviews.

In part, I was inspired by Geertz (1983), who offered cross-cultural researchers a concept for developing a meaningful account of the physical, emotional, and interactive relationships in any cultural study—a concept he called "thick description."

I was also inspired by Marcus (1998), who developed the concept of "rapport" in anthropological studies, which refers to building relationships between researchers and their subjects. Marcus advised researchers to be aware of the changing stakes involved in dealing with different languages, translations, and internal critiques:

Not, I think, to make ethnography the frame to write essays or "do" theory, but to expand and innovate the possibilities for making arguments through description, the delineating of processes, the orchestrating and representation (or evocation) of voice, (p. 13)

Bourdieu and Waquant (1992) suggested that any "space of interaction functions as a situation of linguistic market" (p. 257), and that the researcher must recognize that the preconstructed space of a conversation enables certain power structures. The researcher needs to be aware that he or she has created a form of domination over the space that the conversation takes place within. This symbolic power leads to decisions about objectivity and subjectivity. Researchers who follow what Bourdieu thinks of as the highest forms of sociology create a space in which the participants understand themselves as objects of interest. That is why, with one exception, I interviewed the participants in their workplaces, which gave a certain amount of power over me, which we then renegotiated.

Max van Manen (1997) developed specific procedures for interview analysis based on a technique of phenomenological bracketing of the "lived space," or the feeling of one's existence in body and time. In transcripted interviews, it is important to start with the understanding of an individual's "lifeworld," whose meanings are "multi-dimensional and multi-layered." Interviews then usually manifest in terms of themes. In Van Manen's pedagogy of thematic analysis, he included a holistic approach that looked at the interview text and then pulled out the phrases that capture the fundamental meaning or significance of the "lifeworld." This phrase-pulling is an interpretive act. Fontana and Frey (2000) explained a technique called "analytic bracketing" to address multi-levels of meaning in interviews:

The use of this analytic bracketing allows the authors to analyze interviewing in its coherence and diversity as an event collaboratively achieved, in which product and process are mutually constructed, (p. 665)

I ended up using several parts of these interview methods in order to categorize topics, group them, and look for themes. I even took the liberty of expanding the themes into metaphors when I needed to. For example, when I read the work of Easterly (2002), a global development specialist, I took his theme of a musical composition, in which the researcher uses various "instruments" to create leitmotifs. This image fits the overall emotional component of my interview process. The micro-business owner-managers in this study were part of a composition of perspectives.

In particular, the words of Yutang (1935/1998) resonated with my notion that I approached the interviews in China with a sense of openness. The result of this qualitative part of the study links the role of the individual and his or her differences in values, personality, attitudes, and behaviors to the contextual "dwelling-in" (Polanyi, 1968), the milieu of an international development hybrid: the Chinese urban micro-business. The particularization of values was important to Schwartz's (2000) "near-universality" of the values measurements.

Interview Bias.

Ethnographic researchers in China benefit from understanding the socioeconomic frameworks of the Chinese people. My overall research approach in the interviews stemmed from my personal view that cross-cultural researchers must be aware of and analyze interview bias. In other words, my being a female American scholar created a certain kind of power relationship with my interviewees. This was particularly true with respect to doing research in a developing country, and using a filter of translated conversations.

Interview Coding.

The tools I employed in this interview section of the study included research on local demographics, observations, collecting and analyzing "exit survey" feedback during the pilot study, written descriptions in my journals, and written scenarios. I also videotaped scenes of the micro-businesses, although for purposes of anonymity, none that participated in the study, nor did I use the videotape with my interviewees. These accumulated ethnographic works were simulated into the analysis of the interviews.

The Schwartz Values Survey provided the conceptual framework for the qualitative interviews. In effect, the database was created from the parsed statements (language) in the interpreted narratives. The conceptual framework was verified by inter-rated reliability to determine the interpreted language and meanings. Number each parsed statement from codebook categories and subgroup categories. Two people were selected as inter-raters for reliability and provided with the codebook at the same time. I explained the thinking behind the codebook terms and asked the inter-raters to parse the codebook. One inter-rater agreed closely with me while the second did not agree as much. A third rater provided the necessary difference in opinion. After more explanations, an agreement was reached between me and all the inter-raters. Changes were made to both sides.

The codebook was then developed based on demographics, business type and values. These concepts were numbered and divided into sub-groups based on individual values, cultural values, international development ethics, business attitudes and business types. The vital aspects of the narrative content were developed based on the code book criteria.

I then selected one of the 10 interview transcripts to use as the "coding transcript." The coding was based on ideas I explored in using the conceptual framework in my pilot study. These ideas included three "exit interview" questions that I asked regarding the participant's response to taking the values survey and six other questions that were validated in the study's pilot by a group of Chinese business men and women. These questions included (a) In your opinion, what are the strengths and weaknesses of your micro-business? (b) In your opinion, what influences and business attitudes are important in your micro-business (c) What are the micro-business owner-manager's individual values? (d) What are the micro-business owner manager's cultural values? (e) Overall, what ethical outlook do you hold as most important to operating your micro-business, and (f) In what ways, if at all, do you feel the effects of the international market economy in your micro-business.

I used concepts from these questions in the initial coding, which were then narrowed to five: For example, whenever the participant spoke about international values, I marked that statement in the text, coded it green, and logged it on the following spreadsheet in Table 3 in order to find patterns of discussion topics and issues.

Each of the parsed statements were grouped by the conceptual framework categories and numbered. These statements were reviewed for the patterns and trends in the data. In some cases, the data repeated itself in each interview showing the similar statements from each interviewee. These patterns were then presented by research question 5, *In what ways do the self-reported values of Chinese micro-business owner-managers in Shenzhen, China, influence their business attitudes and ethics?* Examples from the respondents were used to illustrate the answer to the research question in terms of major categories and subcategories from which frequent themes or similarities emerged. Differences were then accounted for in terms of contrasting themes.

Table 3
Codebook Construction

From Z-Taped Transcript	Codebook				
Codes	**Blue**	**Red**	**Green**	**Pink**	**Brown**
	Chinese Micro-business Owner-Manager Individual values	Chinese Micro-business Owner-Manager Cultural values	Interna-tional de-velopment values	Owner-manager attitudes in his/her micro-business	Years in micro-business and individual values
1	1/ economic necessity	1/the idea is to survive as a society	1/small business mirrors a society	1/ everyone wants personal success	1/history of per-sonal achieve-ment
2	2/gain prosperity	2/histori-cally, peo-ple want success	2/-create a product	2/teacher turned business-man	2/former IT college professor
3	3/personal achieve-ment	3/division between intellectual and practical pursuits	3/client wants and theory are not the same	3/IT profession	3/ company based on IT
4	4/create own business	4/ focussed on market demands	4/focus on market demands	4/started small	4/growing from a small to a large business changed the company values
5	5/it was my idea	5/compa-nies must change their val-ues	5/the company's growth changes its values	5/ openness is good	5/pattern is to be open to in-ternational values

Two outside readers then reviewed the Schwartz values model and conceptual framework and took the exact same transcripts to rate the statements of the selected interviewee. The outside readers had difficulty distinguishing between the owner-manager's individual values and the owner-manager's attitudes. After another round of coding with outside readers, I retained three of the major concepts for coding the final six selected interviews.

Final narrative categories based on codebook ratings.

The final categories for narrative analysis included (a) Chinese micro-business owner-manager individual values; (b) Chinese micro-business owner-manager cultural values; (c) and international development values. I then analyzed all 6 selected tapes for relevant groupings based on these three final codebook concepts. Next, I outlined and compiled patterns and differences among the interview transcripts, using quotes to build narrative outlines on each of the micro-business owner-manager participants.

Content analysis of all 6 interviews included ethnographic interpretation of interview situations, analytical bracketing of the interview text, and category development for comparing both micro-business types. These categories were then compared for similarities and differences and developed into themes.

The discussion synthesized both the 10 individual and the 7 cultural values that Schwartz defined with the attitudes, influences, and ethical outlooks from the interviews.

CHAPTER FOUR

FINDINGS WITH ANALYSIS, and INTERPRETATION

Chinese Urban Micro-Business Owner-Managers' Clarified Values and Voices

Survey and Interview Results

The purpose of this chapter is to report, analyze, and interpret the demographic and descriptive findings in relation to the research questions detailed in chapter 1. The chapter first presents quantitative data based on surveys. Qualitative data based on interviews follow with a description of everyday practices that characterize the values among Chinese urban micro-business owner-managers.

Intended and Final Sample

Intended sample.

The intended sample for this study was to be 500 micro-business owner-managers operating companies in Guangdong Province, Shenzhen City, China, who met the inclusion criteria of employing 8 or fewer full-time employees and up to 30 part-time employees at the time of data collection. In addition, the participants in the study were to be associated with a local loan guarantee center, business association, or incubator institution.

Final sample.

The final sample consisted of 109 ordinary and 88 incubator micro-business owner-managers. The ordinary owner-managers participated through micro-business groups and their affiliates. The incubator owner-managers were connected to a throughout China, including Shenzhen and surrounding districts. The survey collection process went as smoothly as could be expected, given the voluntary nature of the study, the hectic pace of most micro-businesses, and the owner-managers' language and cultural resistance to standardized tests.

Geographic origins of the final sample.

The participants came from a wide variety of Chinese provinces to seek opportunities in the coastal city of Shenzhen (Table 4).

Table 4

Final Sample of Participants' Original Home Provinces

Province (N = 197)	Number	(%)
Guangdong	105	(53.4)
Sichuan	10	(5.1)
Henan	9	(4.6)
Hunan	9	(4.6)
Hubei	9	(4.6)
Guangxi	8	(4.1)
Shiangxi	5	(2.5)
Heilongjiang	4	(2.0)
Chongqing	3	(1.5)
Hainan	3	(1.5)

Shandong	3	(1.5)
Anhui	3	(1.5)
Yunnan	2	(1.0)
Fujian	2	(1.0)
Jilin	2	(1.0)
Shanxi	2	(1.0)
Inner Mongolia	1	(0.5)
Zhejiang	1	(0.5)
Gansu	1	(0.5)
Liaoning	1	(0.5)
Missing Data	14	(7.1)

Gender, age, marital status, education, parents ' education.

The basic demographic information on the 197 participants revealed some differences by gender, age, education, and marital status (Table 5). In this sample, there were slightly more females than males. A plurality of the participants was between the ages of 26 and 35, followed by participants between the ages of 16 and 25. Slightly more than half of the participants were married. In the education category, almost half of the participants had less than a high school education, but a little over 10% had 13 or more years in school. Their fathers, on average, had

slightly more than a high school education, whereas their mothers, on average, had only completed 7th grade.

Participants with missing data.

Ordinarily, respondents with missing data are excluded from data analyses, reducing the size of the sample and introducing unknown patterns of bias into the results. I decided instead to include two of the larger groups of these respondents with missing data in the analyses in order to increase the sample size for the analysis of values, because the values components of their surveys were complete. I created a category "Missing Data" for education and number of years in business and included respondents with missing data on these items in the analyses.

Table 5

Gender, Age, Marital Status, Education,
and Parents' Education of the Final Sample

Demographic Item	N	(%)	M (SD)
Gender	197		
Female	103	(52)	
Male	92	(47)	
Missing Date	2	(1)	
Age (M, SD)	197	–	30.00 (8.02)
16-25	68	(35)	
26-35	79	(40)	
36-55	48	(24)	
Missing Data	2	(1)	
Marital Status	197	–	
Married	98	(50)	
Single	79	(40)	
Living together	12	(6)	
Divorced	1	(1)	
Missing Data	7	(40)	
Education (M, SD)	197	–	8.47 (3.80)
0-9 years	93	(47)	
10-11 years	36	(18)	
12 years	35	(18)	
13+ years	21	(11)	
Missing Data	12	(6)	
Father's Education	191	–	12.42 (3.15)
Missing Data	6	(3)	
Mother's Education	170	–	7.09 (3.63)
Missing Data	27	(14)	

Ethnicity, Size of Birthplace, Religiosity, Years in Business, and Occupation

In order to understand the participants' background, demographic data were collected into three categories (Table

6). Most of the participants were Han Chinese. The largest category grew up in small cities (less than 500,000) residents. To nearly all the participants, religion was of little importance. The participants had been in business just under 5 years. The two most common occupation types were manager/ entrepreneurs (29%) and self -employed salespersons (23%).

Table 6

Ethnicity, Birthplace, Religiosity, Years
In Micro-business, and Type of Occupation

Demographic Item	N	(%)	M (SD)
Ethnicity	197		
Han Chinese ethnicity	182	(92)	
Non-Han Chinese	11	(5)	
Missing Date	4	(2)	
Birthplace	197		
Big city	47	(24)	
Small city	68	(35)	
Suburb	47	(24)	
Farm	24	(12)	
Missing Data	11	(5)	
Religiosity	197	–	.92 (1.55)
Years in Micro-business	197	–	4.74 (2.87)
0-4 years	95	(48)	
5-16 years	87	(44)	
Missing Data	15	(8)	
Type of Occupation	197		
Manager/entrepreneur	57	(29)	
Self-employed/Salesperson	45	(23)	
Other	32	(16)	
Other professional	24	(12)	
Technical	17	(9)	
Blue collar	12	(6)	
Student	2	(1)	
Home service	2	(1)	
Farm owner or worker	1	(1)	
Missing Data	5	(2)	

Findings Related to the Research Questions

The study asked five questions, the responses to which are presented in the order asked. The participant characteristics were considered and examined as they related to the research questions on the two types of micro-business: ordinary and incubator.

RQ1. How do ordinary and incubator micro-businesses differ demographically?

Women were somewhat more likely than men to be in the ordinary micro-businesses, and, conversely, men were somewhat more likely than women to be in the incubator micro-businesses (Table 7). The participants in the ordinary micro-businesses were somewhat more likely to have finished high school than those in the incubators, and they were also somewhat more likely to have missing data about their education. The participants in the incubator micro-businesses were significantly more likely to have been running their business for a longer number of years (5.65) than those in the ordinary micro-businesses (3.99). The incubators were also more likely to describe themselves as professionals outside the designated categories, and were less likely to describe themselves as self-employed/salespersons.

I used Chi-square analyses to examine these data for differences. There were no significant differences between incubator owner-managers and ordinary owner-managers on ethnicity $[\chi^2(2) = 3.30, ns]$, birthplace $[\chi^2(3) - 1.27, ns]$, age $[F(l, 193) = .55, ns]$, recoded age $[\chi^2(2) = .04, ns]$, education $[F(l, 182) = .02, ns]$, father's education $[F(l, 189) - .82, ns]$, mother's education $[F(\backslash, 168) = .00, ns]$, marital status $[\chi^2(3) = .91, ns]$, or religiosity $[F(l, 195) = .59, ns]$.

Table 7
Number, Percent, Chi-square, and F-Rations for Gender, Education, Years in Business and Occupation by Type of Micro-business

Demographic Item	Ordinary		Incubator		
	N	(%)	N	(%)	x^2 or F
Gender					2.50+
Female	62	(58)	41	(47)	
Male	45	(42)	47	(53)	
Education (M, SD)					9.39*
0-9 years	50	(46)	43	(49)	
10-11 years	14	(13)	22	(25)	
12 years	23	(21)	12	(14)	
13+ years	12	(11)	9	(10)	
Missing Data	10	(9)	2	(2)	
Years in Business (M, SD)	99	3.99 (2.34)	83	5.65 (3.19)	16.34****
Years in Business	109		88		16.66****
Less than 5 years	65	(60%)	30	(34%)	
5 or more years	34	(31%)	53	(60%)	
Missing Data	10	(9%)	5	(6%)	
	109		88		
Type of Occupation	109		88		33.12****
Manager/entrepreneur	27	(25%)	30	(34%)	
Self-employed/Salesperson	35	(32%)	10	(11%)	
Other	20	(18%)	12	(14%)	
Technical	11	(10%)	6	(7%)	
Blue collar	6	(6%)	6	(7%)	
Other Professional	4	(4%)	20	(23%)	
Student	2	(2%)	0	(0%)	
Farm owner or worker	0	(0%)	1	(1%)	
Home service	0	(0%)	2	(2%)	
Missing Data	4	(4%)	1	(1%)	

Note: Cross-tabulations, using chis-square, showed a significantly higher percentage for the category within the business type marked [a]. + $p < .10$ * $p < 0.5$****

RQ2. What are the self-reported *individual* values of micro-business owner-managers in Shenzhen, China, and how do these differ by business type?

Individual values, as defined by Schwartz (1992), are desirable, transsituational goals, varying in importance, that serve as guiding principles in people's lives. The crucial component among values is the type of motivational goal they express. Schwartz (1992) derived 10 core values recognized in cultures around the world.

I used ANCOVAs to ask about the ways in which the ordinary and incubator micro-businesses in Shenzhen differed on the SVS individual values (Table 8).

Individuals in both types of micro-businesses scored relatively high in security values. They also scored relatively high on values of achievement, conformity, and self-direction.

The results from ANCOVAs also showed that the participants in ordinary micro-businesses had higher scores on security and marginally higher scores on self-direction than incubators did, whereas participants in incubator micro-businesses had marginally higher scores on stimulation. In contrast, both groups of participants placed relatively little value on the individual values of hedonism and tradition.

Table 8

Means, Standard Deviations, and F Statistics from ANCOV as: Individual Values by Total and by Business Types

Individual Value	Total N = 197		Ordinary N = 109		Incubator N = 88		F
	M	(SD)	M	(SD)	M	(SD)	ANCOVA
Security	4.80	(.63)	4.89	(.67)	4.70	(.56)	5.77*
Achievement	4.36	(.82)	4.32	(.91)	4.40	(.68)	.09
Conformity	4.33	(.64)	4.33	(.63)	4.32	(.66)	.04
Self-direction	4.18	(.70)	4.24	(.70)	4.11	(.70)	2.69+
Benevolence	4.11	(.75)	4.11	(.81)	4.10	(.68)	.42
Universalism	3.95	(.63)	3.96	(.64)	3.94	(.62)	.00
Power	3.38	(1.20)	3.28	(1.25)	3.50	(1.13	1.56
Hedonism	3.35	(1.20)	3.36	(1.28)	3.34	(1.11)	.02

| Tradition | 3.34 | (1.08) | 3.40 | (1.15) | 3.27 | (1.00) | .02 |
| Stimulation | 3.27 | (1.32) | 3.13 | (1.35) | 3.43 | (1.29) | 2.88+ |

+ p < .10   * p < .05

RQ3. What are the self-reported cultural values of micro-business owner managers in Shenzhen, China, and how do these differ by business type?

Cultural values, according to Schwartz (1994b), represent the interests of persons, groups, or nations. He defined them as, "A nation's institutional or organizational concepts of a value system become a guiding principle, or way of acting. The challenge is to understand and manage these values and to motivate individuals who establish sets of priorities among compatible and incompatible goals" (p. 469).

Table 9 also shows the perceived importance of the SVS cultural values scores among the participants. There were no significant differences in cultural values between ordinary businesses and incubators. These values are presented in descending order for the total group and for both types of business.

Mastery, which reflects an individual's attempts to gain skills and competencies, was the most important cultural value for all the micro-business owner-managers. Egalitarian scores, which may reflect individual moral values in the context of cooperating with others in society, also scored high. Participants gave mid-level scores to the importance of embeddedness, which reflects the status quo, and on intellectual autonomy, which reflects the unique intellect and ideas of a bounded individual. The micro-businesses also had mid-level scores on harmony, reflecting an aesthetic order, but low scores on affective autonomy and hierarchy, reflecting a bounded individual self and subservience to rules, roles, and obligations.

Table 9

Means, Standard Deviations and F Statistics from ANCOVAs'
Cultural Values by Total ad by Business Types

Individual Value	Total N = 197		Ordinary N = 109		Incubator N = 88		F
	M	(SD)	M	(SD)	M	(SD)	ANCOVA
Mastery	4.44	(.63)	4.38	(.67)	4.51	(.58)	.71
Egalitarian	4.15	(.57)	4.18	(.58)	4.12	(.55)	1.02
Embeddedness	4.05	(.37)	4.04	(.35)	4.07	(.39)	.96
Intellectual Autonomy	3.84	(.90)	3.86	(.90)	3.81	(.91)	.28
Harmony	3.63	(1.07)	3.63	(1.13)	3.64	(1.01)	.06
Affective Autonomy	3.46	(1.16)	3.35	(1.11)	3.60	(1.22)	1.66
Hierarchy	3.42	(1.00)	3.40	(1.02)	3.45	(.97)	.23

RQ4. In what ways do individual and cultural self-reported values of Chinese micro-business owner-managers in Shenzhen, China differ by demographic categories and by years of micro-business ownership? Correlation coefficients were used to determine significant or marginally significant correlations between values and demographic items for the total sample are shown in Table 10. The Beta coefficient shows the magnitudes of the correlations between a demographic item and a value.

Analysis of Demographics and Values Across All Items

Education.

Compared to the least educated participants, those with a high school education had higher scores on the individual value, power, and marginally higher scores on the cultural value of universalism. Participants with a high school education also had relatively lower scores on the values of hierarchy and marginally lower scores for achievement. Alternately, when compared to the least educated participants, college educated participants scored relatively high on the cultural value of intellectual autonomy and on the individual value of self-direction. They had relatively low scores on embeddedness, security, conformity, and harmony.

Age.

Compared to participants less than 36 years old, those more than 36 years old had marginally lower scores on Self-directedness, and lower scores on choosing one's own goals and privacy.

Gender.

Among the males compared to females in the sample, self-direction, intellectual autonomy, and hierarchy are rated more important, whereas stimulation is rated more highly and security somewhat more highly among women.

Marital status.

Participants without a partner or spouse had relatively high scores on self-directedness but relatively low scores on achievement.

Micro-Business years.

Those in business 5 or more years compared to those in business less than 5 years, scored marginally higher on the cultural value of affective autonomy.

Religiosity.

Religiosity correlated positively with universalism and negatively with power.

Missing Data

Missing data/education.

When compared to the least educated participants, those with missing data on education tended to place more importance on values of tradition and hierarchy, marginally less importance on mastery, and significantly less importance on security and benevolence

Missing data/micro-business years.

Participants who had missing data on micro-business years also had relatively high scores on stimulation, affective autonomy, and choosing one's own goals. They also had relatively low scores on benevolence.

Mean Ratings Across All Items

Participants who, on average, tended to rate all values as high, tended to have relatively high scores on privacy and choosing one's own goals, and relatively low scores on security.

Table 10
Significant or Marginally Significant Demographic Correlates of Individual and Cultural Values: Regression Coefficients from ANCOVAs

Demographic Items	β	$<p$
Education (High School Graduate compared to < 12 years education)		
Power	.64	.01
Universalism	.25	.07
Achievement	-.30	.08
Hierarchy	.56	.006
Education (College compared to <12 years education)		
Intellectual autonomy	.79	.0001
Self-direction	.54	.001
Embeddedness	-.24	.008
Security	-.31	.04

Demographic Items	β	$<p$
Conformity	-.48	.002
Harmony	-.52	.05
Age (36 or older compared to <36 years of age)		
Self-directed	-.33	.06
Privacy	-.66	.05
Choose own goals	-1.25	.0001
Gender (Male compared to Female		
Self-direction	.40	.0001
Intellectual Autonomy	.33	.01
Hierarchy	.30	.04
Security	-.16	.07
Stimulation	-.38	.05
*No Partner/spouse (compared to Married)		
Self-Direction	.27	.03
Achievement	-.30	.04
Micro-business Years (5 or more compared to <5 years)		
Affective Autonomy	.35	.09
*Religiosity		
Universalism	.06	.04
Power	-.12	.04
Missing Data/Education (compared to question responders)		
Tradition	.80	.03
Hierarchy	.64	.05
Mastery	-.39	.06
Security	-.45	.03
Benevolence	-.71	.004
Missing Data/Micro-business Years (compared to question responders)		
Stimulation	.97	.02
Affective Autonomy	.79	.02
Choose Own Goals	.52	.04
Benevolence	-.50	.03
Mean Rating across Survey Items		
Privacy	.78	.0001
Choose Own Goals	.59	.0001
Security	-.14	.04

Interpretations of the Survey Findings

Demographic and values data.

Participants' self-reported values associated with their demographic characteristics for significance creates statistical profiles from the sample. For example, the profile of micro-business managers aged 36 or older showed relatively high values placed on the cultural values of intellectual autonomy, and hierarchy. These high scores show a priority in the cultural value dimensions with less emphasis on their individual or personal values. These male owner-managers aged 36 or older also showed low scores on values of self-direction, and the lower values of privacy, and choosing one's own goals. Their low scores on self-direction, privacy, and choosing one's own goals may represent a conscious choice or socialization to be group-oriented.

Egri and Ralston (2004) indicated that the 36 and older age group grew up during the period of what they called a "Communist Consolidation (1954-1961)" and in the early part of the period of "Cultural Revolution (1961-1971)," (p. 211). These individuals may also have viewed privacy as a luxury because they grew up in times of extreme poverty. By contrast, women in this age group showed higher values for security and stimulation.

Gender related differences.

Male micro-business owners showed relatively high values placed on hierarchy, self-direction, and intellectual autonomy (freedom, broadmindedness, curiosity, and creativity), possibly reflecting a wish to fulfil a culturally traditionally male role as self-sufficient economic provider but also feeling free to express oneself in that role. The owner-manager role may also have given men a sense of intellectual autonomy and self-direction insofar as the role involved strategizing, quick decision-making, and responding to crises.

In contrast, female micro-business owners placed higher priorities on the value security (including family security). Women micro-business owner-managers may have tended to value security, in part, because it represented the importance of control in the family domain and also represented social stability and harmonious social relations associated with a female gender role. Wang (1999) suggested that women in China's history and during times of great social change tend to be both "constructs and agents of that change." For example, during the cultural revolutions, women's status had been linked directly to the future of China. The women in this study may also have valued stimulation as a part of the social transformation that many women undergo when they are able to make a living for themselves and for their families, and, at the same time, participate in a wider variety of roles.

Marital status.

Many of the women in the study are young and unmarried. People without a partner or spouse had relatively low scores on achievement. Low achievement among those who are not partnered may in part indicate ambivalence towards investing in and serving the needs of others or serving the group. People without partners also tended to be more self-directed. Self-direction is a quality that includes setting goals, organizing, and being more open to change, and these individuals may have had less sense of responsibility without partners in the household.

Micro-Business years in operation.

Those participants in micro-business 5 years or more also had relatively high scores on affective autonomy and choosing one's own goals. Perhaps micro-business owners who had remained in the micro-business longer felt more successful in meeting their chosen goals and felt that they could now enjoy themselves and the fruits of their labors. Some participants defined themselves as manager/ entrepreneurs and may have started several micro-businesses, prior to taking the survey. They may not have known how to answer the question about their number of years in micro-business if they had had more than one micro-business. Those participants could also have placed high value on stimulation. Perhaps people with a low threshold for boredom also skipped some questions.

Religiosity.

Interestingly, religiosity also correlated positively with universalism and correlated negatively with power. Universalism (e.g., social justice, equality, and broad-mindedness) focuses on positive social relationships, which can include people outside the dominant group, such as minority groups. People with a religious orientation might tend to emphasize the spiritual ways that people are similar and should be treated alike, rather than the ways in which people might be controlled or dominated.

High response scores.

Some participants tended to rate all items on the survey as relatively high, which I corrected using a cultural mean. This is typical of the Chinese population according to similar studies using the SVS instrument. However, the participants tended to have relatively high scores on the variables "privacy" and "choosing one's goals" and at the same time had low scores on security. People who were more private may not have wished to reveal their true feelings on a survey, and may have chosen to give responses they thought were socially desirable. Those with low scores on security (which includes an item about valuing social order) may also have been more individualistic (consistent with having high scores on privacy and choosing one's own goals) and may have been eager to claim a variety of individualistic values as their own.

Demographics by business type.

Compared to participants in ordinary micro-businesses, those in incubators had slightly lower education levels different than expected. Originally, I thought this group would have an overall higher level of education as they are more influenced by high-technology, and subject to incubator guidelines that might show a bias toward more educated owner-managers.

Compared to participants in ordinary micro-businesses, those in incubators had been in business longer, and were more likely to consider themselves professionals as opposed to considering themselves self-employed or salespeople. Participants in incubator micro-businesses may, at some point, have had strong connections to government officials and information that enabled them to join the incubator program. The participants who had been in micro-business longer, or professionals with specific expertise, may have had more of an opportunity to make such connections and become incubator owners. This group was also expected to have high scores in self-directed values more common to their affiliates in other business communities. I found that the high value scores in stimulation among incubators also stands in contrast to their reported conformity values. These findings suggest that further analysis is needed to better understand what the meaning of this is in this segment of the sample

Combined demographics and values.

The study also asked how participants in ordinary micro-businesses and incubators differed on demographics and values. Participants in ordinary micro-businesses scored relatively high on the value items of security, privacy, choosing one's own goals, and self-direction. They may have perceived that they had more restrictions and fewer advantages than incubators and may have realized that their survival would be based almost exclusively on setting their own goals for achievement. People who tended to value privacy may also have preferred their own independent micro-businesses, and because they tended to be older, may not have been familiar with a more recent incubator structure.

Inter-Group values.

The hierarchical mean rankings in the table below indicate only slight variations in values, none of which are statistically significant (Table 11). While there were no statistically significant differences among the values of both business types, participants in incubator micro-businesses types scored slightly higher means on achievement, relatively lower on security and relatively higher on stimulation (defined as values placed on a varied life, an exciting life, and daring). In contrast, the ordinary micro-business types placed a slightly higher value on security and tradition and little importance on stimulation.

Table 11

Individual Value Priorities of Ordinary and Incubator
Micro-Business Owner-Managers*

Ordinary N = 109	Mean Rank		Incubator N = 88	Mean Rank	
Individual Value	M	#	Individual Value	M	#
Security	4.89	1	Security	4.70	1
Conformity	4.33	2	Achievement	4.40	2
Achievement	4.32	3	Coformity	4.32	3
Benevolence	4.11	5	Benevolence	4.10	5
Universalism	3.96	6	Universalism	3.94	6
Tradition	3.40	7	Power	3.50	7
Hedonism	3.36	8	Stimulation	3.43	8
Power	3.28	9	Hedonism	3.34	9
Stimulation	3.13	10	Tradition	3.27	10

*In descending order, numbered by importance, based on data in Table 7.

Individual Values of Chinese Urban Micro-Business Owners

The value hierarchy of Chinese urban micro-business owner-managers, when viewed in isolation, suggests a socioeconomic group where the average owner-managers place supreme importance on maintaining a safe social and physical environment (security ,1st) and avoiding interpersonal conflicts (conformity *2nd,3rd*) through the important characteristic of seeking success according to their social standards (achievement, 2nd and 3rd) as guiding principles in their lives. On average, they place a high importance on their autonomy in thinking and acting (self-direction, 4th), while these actions are guided by the somewhat less important motivational goals of cooperation and supportive social relations (benevolence, 5th). On average, they deem it only somewhat important to extend their concerns for supportive relationships to others outside of the members of their immediate group (universalism (6th).

While the ordinary owner-managers show some interest in maintaining tradition (tradition, 7th), the incubator owner-managers instead slightly prefer the idea of pursuing selfish interests at the expense of others (power, 7th). Gratification of sensual desires (hedonism, 8th) is slightly more important to ordinary women owner-managers, whereas incubator owner-managers pursue their goals with slightly more sense of novelty and excitement (stimulation, 8th). The ordinary owner-managers place very little importance on selfish pursuits and the exploitation of others (power, 9th) nor on novelty and excitement (stimulation 10th), whereas the incubator owner-managers place very little importance on sensual gratification (hedonism, 9th) nor upon upholding tradition (tradition, 10th).

Intermezzo: Interviews with Chinese Micro-Business Owner-Managers

The SVS survey and quantitative results for near-universal individual and cultural values is not the end of the story in this study. The following qualitative section is of equal importance, bringing into focus the lives of six micro-business owner-managers, all of whom took the SVS survey and volunteered to be interviewed by me. The purpose of this section is to give the reader an understanding of the context of these men and women working in their businesses (Scollon & Scollon, 1981).

The two business types emerged in the research process during the pilot study. When asking permission from local business local officials to conduct a survey I discovered that there were hundreds of private micro-businesses, nearly all in the high-tech sector, in large government owned building complexes. It seemed natural to survey these start-ups in addition to the storefront owner-managers by way of comparison. Through their variety and complexity, the people within the Chinese urban micro-business culture reveal their minute and subtle differences in personality, experiences, attitudes, and behaviors.

The 6 interviewees were selected for their demographic typicality in their business category. All but one of the interviews took place at the micro-business sites at various times during the workday. The exception took place in the evening in a restaurant at the request of the female participant.

The procedures I used to interpret these interviews included semi-structured, questions that had protocol and coded transcripts using the study's values framework. Each of the 6 interviews is followed by topics and issues that were categorized from the texts. At the end of each group of 3 interviews, I compared and contrasted the themes that emerged for that micro-business type using a technique called analytical bracketing in which I make a reflexive interpretation. I then interpreted the patterns that emerged between the two types following the same process but then tied to relevant literature.

My role as a researcher was to reflect on the conversations, look for themes in them, and interpret the themes for the reader. The 6 interviews were written in conversational formats, using direct quotes with line coding from the transcripts. In order to recreate the interview environment, situation, attitudes, influences, and outlooks of the interviewees, I used my journal notes written soon after the interview. These interviews add human portrayals to the quantitative data.

Interviews with Analysis and Interpretation

This section of the results chapter analyzes six narrative taped transcripts from interviews with ordinary and incubator micro-business owner-managers, who answered the following research question:

RQ5. In what ways do the self-reported values of Chinese micro-business owner-managers in Shenzhen, China, influence their business attitudes and ethics?

This section separates the six interviews and interpretations into three ordinary and three incubator micro-business owner-managers who completed the SVS (Schwartz, 2003) in August, 2004 and volunteered to be interviewed shortly after taking the survey. These interviewees included three women, one housed in an incubator building and two operating out of street-level storefronts, and three men, two housed in incubator buildings and one operating out of a street-level storefront. The average age of the 6 interviewees was 32 years-old, just slightly older than the average for the total survey sample which had an average age of 30 (ordinary age mean = 30.03, incubator age mean = 30.99, ns). All these owner-manager interviewees varied in terms of the size, scale, and scope of their businesses.

Two of the interviewees provided products and services; three provided products; and one only provided services only. Two of the micro-business owner-managers were from Guangdong Province, and the other four came from the northern provinces of Hubei, Hebei, and Hunnan, and one from eastern Xiangxi province (Table 11).

Table 12							
Personal and Business Characteristics of the Interviewees							
Interviewee	Business Type	Sex	Age	Location	Business	Number of Owners to FTEs*	Native Province
Bebe	Ordinary	F	32	Storefront	Cosmetic Services	1:1	Guang-dong
Evanna	Ordinary	F	43	Storefront	Hair and Fashion Design and Services & Manufactur-ing	1:8	Guandong
Marty	Ordinary	M	21	Storefront	Noodle Restaurant	2:1	Hubei
Alistair	Incubator	M	32	Incubator	High-Tech Cable Man-ufacturing & Services	4:10**	Hunnan
Zorro	Incubator	M	42	Incubator	High-Tech Cartridges Manufac-turing & Services	2:5	Xiangxi
Cara	Incubator	F	24	Incubator	Simultane-ous Foreign Language Translation Services	2:2	Hebei

* FTEs = full-time employess
** Alistair had added 10 new employees the week of our interview.

Interview Setting and Context

It was August 2004; monsoon season in southern China, the northern edge of the Tropic of Cancer, where summer temperatures exceed 100 degrees Fahrenheit and humidity hangs at 90%. When the rains ceased, and the sun exploded through the mist, the light was so brilliant and heat so intense that it was like walking through a hot sauna cloud. The summer Olympics held in Athens, Greece blared on TVs and radios all day and well into the night. Each day, as China swept up gold, silver, and bronze medals, the country swelled and heaved in collective outbursts of applause and pride.

As I left my apartment each day, golden dragonflies sizzled in the air, pale geckos scampered under stairways, and napping green-and-black striped snakes on the sidewalk slithered away as they sensed my approaching footsteps. Like everyone else, I walked slowly, carrying a parasol to shield myself from the sun. I looked forward to the balmy winds that would blow in from the South China Sea in the evening.

I was staying in a guest apartment in the West Moving Sea Building (Chou Xi Lou) at the Shenzhen University campus where I had previously lived for 4 years. Every day, I went out to conduct one or more interviews. It was a four-block walk to Bing Hai Road, where I would catch a cab. By the time I climbed into one, I was always drenched in my own perspiration. On most occasions, I would meet my interpreter somewhere and go on together to the site of the interview.

Each of the 6 interviewees had taken the SVS survey prior to our meeting and each had agreed to the prearranged interview that was to be conducted with an interpreter. The participants did not know the interpreters and did not appear to be influenced by them in any way. All but one of the interviews took place at the micro-business sites at various times during the workday. The exception took place in the evening in a restaurant at the request of the female participant.

In each interview, I told the participant that I was a sociology doctoral student at Fielding Graduate University, in Santa Barbara, California. After the participant, the interpreter, and I had signed the consent form and a confidentiality agreement, I told the participant that my main purpose for the study was to discover what values Chinese urban micro-business owner-managers use in conducting their business. I explained that my interest in this topic stemmed from my having lived for 4 years in Shenzhen and having worked in community development in the United States for 25 years.

I gave the participants fictitious names but otherwise the context and comments of both ordinary and incubator micro-business owner-managers remained the same as in the original interviews.

Contextual Descriptions of the Ordinary Micro-Business Owner-Managers.

Bebe

Mr. Gan, my male interpreter, and I met for lunch at McDonald's, just across a footbridge from Shenzhen University in Nantou, a major district of Shenzhen, with a population of three million. Bebe's beauty shop was located on a busy street corner a block away. Bebe greeted us in the doorway of her 14' $\times$ 20' storefront. As she ushered us into her attractive shop smelling of jasmine, she told us that she has been at this location for the past 6 years. The shelves were packed with bottles of nail polish and cosmetics. The walls were covered with mirrors, which makes the shop look twice as big as it is. In the far left corner, there was a chair for facials and manicures, and right next to it, separated by a room divider, there was a small space where Bebe's mother, father, and 5-year old son were sitting on stools. The mother was preparing tea for me and Mr. Gan.

Bebe gently crowded us in behind the cash register at a makeshift table for our interview. She was petite at 4'-9" with a pale face, luminous against her tinted red hair. She wore hardly any makeup and no fingernail polish.

After we were seated, her mother served us tiny hot cups of *Gungfu* tea as Bebe folded her delicate hands on the table to talk. She told us that she is 32 years old and was born in Guangdong, Province. Her heritage was *Hakka,* a group of Han Chinese responsible for exploring and cultivating this tropical region. She was married and had one son. Her husband, a graduate in electro-mechanical engineering from Birmingham University in England, worked as the general manager for a British information technology (IT) corporation. Bebe explained that because her husband had a good job, she did not need to work for financial support. Instead, she was in business just to make herself feel good, keep active, and be able to take care of her family.

Bebe graduated from Jingan University as a scholar of Chinese literature and indicated that the reason Bebe started her own business selling cosmetics was, in her words, "dramatic." (11. B8) She had worked for the same corporation as her husband, but her newborn son became ill, which often forced her to stay home to take care of him, and so she finally quit.

Strengths and weaknesses.

When I ask Bebe to describe her business strengths and weaknesses, she begins by telling me that her "skin was not good" (B35) after she had her baby, so after trying various doctors and their remedies, she decided to take matters into her own hands by going into the cosmetics business. Her education, especially her major in Chinese literature, and some accounting and management courses that she took in college, helped her, she said, with her mission to make herself and other women look beautiful. She also worked in order to teach her son that his mother is an active person who can pursue her own dreams.

We stopped the interview for about 15 minutes while Bebe attended to questions from three female university students who walked into the shop. Two of them were Bebe's customers and had brought the third to introduce her to Bebe. This interruption allowed me to see first-hand the depth of the relationships that Bebe had with her customers. First, she carefully examined the new customer's skin with a handheld magnifying glass and then applied several products to the girl's face. As the girl sat there, Bebe gave her a handout about hygiene and diet. Then Bebe touched up the eyebrows of the other two customers without charge. In effect, Bebe appeared to have created a trusting family environment in the tiny cramped room. I also got to see the girls protesting that Bebe was selling Japanese products, especially since there had been recent demonstrations in the streets of every major city in China, protesting the Japanese government's refusal to rewrite its history books about the Nanjing Massacre.

After the girls left, I asked Bebe what weaknesses she had in business. She said: "Chinese people are opposed now to buying Japanese goods. And many of our products come from Japan and South Korea. So some customers come to us and ask which country the product belongs to, and I tell them it is Japan. Their reaction may not be great: "Oh, I won't buy Japanese goods! This is one effect from international politics" (11. B266-B270).

After the encounter with her customers, Bebe discussed another business challenge she had—namely, that she must visit factories where her Chinese products are made in order to confirm that they were not contraband. This was interesting because it focused on a common problem in her line of work. The Chinese government has few ways to control product development, so in effect the onus for verifying the authenticity of products lies with the buyer.

Influences and business attitudes.

To my question about influences on her business attitudes, Bebe said: "I feel it is much better for me to do my own business instead of working for a boss, because there is pressure at work between superiors and subordinates. To me, I totally have not got the pressure" (11. B148-B150).

She also brought up the value of work and the modern Chinese view of housework: "I think work is the biggest need of people. Work can fulfil us and help us to avoid being disjoined from the society. Taking care of kids doesn't mean useless work. There is a point of view in China that the woman who brings up kids is a useless housewife" (11. B197-B200).

Being self-employed gives Bebe the kind of freedom she says she needs: "The reason why I think I have got the freedom is very simple. For example, there is an emergency happening in my home and I need to be there. Back then I had to come to my superior and ask for leave. If he told me not to leave now and told me I should stick to my post, and I insisted on going home, I would be fired. However, now I can manage everything by myself. I can choose to make business temporarily suspended. Maybe I will need to bear loss of money, but I don't worry to lose my job" (11. B232-B239).

Bebe wanted to be creatively engaged in her work, not just to make money. "I will take it as my career throughout my life," she says. "I don't want to just earn one or five million [*yuan*] in the coming years. I do hope my interest could be a main part in my life and work. I can arrange my time, and I can have my own thoughts" (11. B76-B79).

Ethical outlook and values.

Underlying Bebe's ethical outlook were traditional Chinese family values: "As a Chinese woman," she said, "I think one of my most important values is to have a happy family. But I have a much more important ideal. Doing the business is not my only target. Another one is the education of my kid. I don't need to work completely. But I think my work can give him some experience of life" (11. B193-B197).

Analytical Bracketing of Bebe's Interview

I had originally anticipated that ordinary Chinese micro-business owner-managers would have little education and culture. Bebe clearly does not fit this stereotype. Her profile underscores the growing sense of personal control among China's middle class. She does not have to work to support herself, since she has a husband to provide for her and her son, so her job allows her to pursue her values of family, self-direction, and intellectual flexibility and freedom.

Family cohesion.

I was initially surprised that Bebe had had a college education, given that her work did not require that kind of background. However, then I realized that she had gone to school during the early reform era (1976-1980), when millions of young Chinese flocked back to universities that had been virtually closed for years (Waley-Cohen). It was clear from statements she made throughout our interview that Bebe's early life had been hard. She referred to the fact that her parents had been far away from her during some of her childhood, which she felt was a terrible thing to happen to a child. "I have seen a lot of joys and sorrows," she said. "The environment of the last generation was not good, so they worked very hard to earn money. In this process, bringing up and educating a kid seems to be a kind of restriction of activities, in fact, for those people who also wanted to make their families happy. They just didn't put the point of balance in its right place. And I hope this kind of sad story will never happen to me. Maybe if you earn a lot of money and give it to your kids, but if you neglect his or her mental needs, the consequence will be very serious" (11. B350-B356).

Bebe believed that her 5-year old son would learn modern Chinese entrepreneurial values from watching her run her micro-business. When she mentioned she only wanted to gross between one million and five million *yuan* ($125,000-$625,000 U.S.) over the coming years, she may have been influenced by Deng Xiaoping's remarks in 1986 (quoted in Huang, 2004) that Chinese business society would prosper if everyone aspired to earn middle-class wages, which would in turn lift the entire society out of poverty.

Self-Direction.

At first glance, Bebe's beauty parlor was like hundreds of other shops dotted along any given street in Shenzhen. One could assume that the people (usually women) who were running these small businesses were earning just enough to keep their families afloat. I saw them every day, opening very early in the morning and working very late into the night. Although Bebe faced fierce competition, she maintained very high standards for her products, a strategy that has always worked well for the merchant classes because they had the status of specialized brokers of goods (Fei, 1992; Huang, 2004; Tang & Parish, 2000).

However, in reform-era China, job shift patterns for the period from 1992 to 1996 indicated that individuals with higher education were entering the private sector as China's legal system advanced (Zheng, 2003). Bebe commented: "Although now the legal system is being perfected. Many people want to do business, since they want to be outstanding or improve the financial condition of their family. So, they have the pressure to start a business. However, I feel it is much better for me to do my own business instead of working for a boss" (11. B147-B150).

Zheng (2003) hypothesized about a "hazard rate" of individuals transferring to the private sector is higher for those with better education, administrators are much more likely to transfer to the private sector than professionals in the period from 1985 to 1991, and this increased in the period between 1992 and 1996, when Bebe was getting ready to open her business.

Bebe perceived her work as a vehicle for self-expression and a way to be her own boss. This contrasts with her grounding in traditional family values. Her attitude is in line with Kohn's (2001) theory that intellectual freedom is a key factor in self-identity and motivation for work.

Intellectual flexibility and freedom.

The sense of flexibility and freedom that Bebe expressed broke her out of the mold of the dominant state-owned and government administrative jobs that await many educated young women in China (Zhang, 2001). Bebe viewed her education as instrumental to her work goals. This attitude parallels what the philosopher John Dewey felt about Chinese women when he lived in Guangzhou for 3 years during the exciting reform years at the beginning of the Chinese modern republic. Dewey (1921/1973) compared the women's reform movements to the defining phases of great social change because women upheld the demands of family and freedom to develop their own lives.

She said, "I find the advantage of having learned Chinese literature is that it can raise a person's personality and improve their ability of thinking" (II. B171-B173). Bebe used her "cultural capital" (Bourdieu, 1977/2002), that is, the dominant cultural values of her society, based on knowledge, skills, and educational systems, by switching her profession and becoming an entrepreneur, and by focusing on things that remained culturally important to her, namely, family and society. In China, the dominant culture favors the educated (Yutang, 1935/1998) and the socialist (Fei, 1992). Bebe forged for herself f an aesthetic work that fit a part of her classical educational background, but at the same time she pursued a profession that went against some of the dominant socialist culture in which she was raised. However, she described her work to keep in touch with society: "Work can fulfil! us and help us to avoid being disjoined from the society" she said (11. BI 98-B199).

In the original framework of this study, I viewed this type of ordinary micro-business owner-manager not only as a sole supporter of an immediate family but also as an employer of extended family members or networks of family. The rather surprising results of the interview with Bebe suggested that the economics of the typical Chinese *getihu* (small family business) are changing as more and more well-educated people renter the merchant classes to seek their fortunes or to live more manful life.

Evanna

Ankle-deep rain greeted us as Mr. Cui, my interpreter, and I got out of the taxi in front of Evanna's store, where she sells women's hair products, clothing accessories, and jewellery. We were in the Futien district of Shenzhen, an upscale downtown area that is only 3 years old. The smell of coffee wafted out of a nearby Western-style café called Coffee Language, where a cup of regular Colombian costs as much as a typical meal in China.

Evanna's store, which was approximately 50 feet wide, was on street level. The hair accessories and other products in the display windows were made with the most elegant material and uniquely beautiful.

Two of Evanna's female assistants, waiting outside for us with umbrellas and towels, led us around the side of the building to the entrance to Evanna's office. When we stepped inside the door, they took our umbrellas, and we dried ourselves off with the towels and removed our shoes. They gave us clean slippers just as Evanna came out of her office to greet us.

At 5'-10", this lanky, kind-eyed, 33-year-old owner-manager exuded a quiet command and was clearly respected by her employees. On the short walk from the reception desk to her office, she dispatched two other female assistants on errands, signed for a FEDEX package, and hand-signalled to a woman, to join us in 15 minutes. This woman, I later learned, was her younger sister. Over her shoulder, she said in heavily accented English, "We're a learning organization," obviously referring to Peter Senge's work, especially *The Art and Practice of the Learning Organization* (1990).

Evanna directed us to a low couch 10 feet from her desk inside her office, which was separated from the rest of the business by a glass partition, through which could keep an eye on her staff. As I sat down, I knew that intimacy in business situations in Asia takes time to develop, but I did not feel comfortable conducting an interview from so far away, and asked Evanna in my basic Mandarin if we could sit closer. She immediately signalled to an assistant, who rolled in two comfortable armchairs, placing them directly in front of Evanna's huge desk.

I looked around as Evanna finished up on another phone call and I noticed that the office was brightly lit, modern, softly metallic, and uncluttered. Throughout the interview, Evanna would be consistently interrupted with calls, signing documents, and introducing us to key staff, including her sister.

As we settled into our seats, Evanna's assistant offered us packets of coffee or tea from a small tray she was carrying. Mr. Cui passed, but I helped myself to a Nescafé.

I interpreted Evanna's cultural cue of originally sitting me on the couch, in the most comfortable area of her office, as a sign of respect toward a guest. I quickly realized, seeing how busy she was, that I had to be highly efficient with her time. The fact that I spoke some conversational Chinese eased the situation somewhat, especially my use of apologetic words and phrases.

For the first 20 minutes, Evanna spent more time on taking phone calls and attending to other business than she did conversing with me. When I mentioned that my husband was an American-born Chinese and that our daughter had attended a Chinese public school, Evanna started to phase out her business work and focus exclusively on the interview. She understood quite a bit of English.

Evanna began the formal part of the interview by telling us that she had started her business 9 years before. Like both of her parents, who were college professors, she had graduated from a university as a trained K-12 teacher, but soon found that she disliked teaching. She then became an office manager in a bank and discovered that she had a talent for managing people. Nevertheless, she was not satisfied with her work and was looking around for something more interesting to do, especially if she could be self-employed. Realizing that she had an eye for fashion, she opened her business in 1995. It began on a small scale, but quickly grew, with Evanna doing all the legwork to make business sales connections throughout the country and beyond, especially in South Korea.

Strengths and weaknesses.

When I asked her to describe her business strengths and weaknesses, she immediately noted reliability as her strength. "When I say I am going to do something, I come through," she said (11. E45-E45). She also indicated that she hired very trustworthy people. "My biggest strength is that the company has very faithful people that are very dedicated to the company". "They don't steal ideas. They don't go out and try to copy things and make their own company" (11. E163-E165). Unlike many Chinese employers, Evanna said she did not like to socialize with her employees. She partly borrowed this attitude, she admitted, from Western management styles.

Evanna said, "Most of my time, about 80% or more of my time, is dealing with the products. I'm really concerned about the products" (11· E86-E87). Her biggest challenge at work, she said, was competitors who were ready to steal her ideas. For example, she recently had a contract with the Chinese branch of Wal-Mart to sell her line of hair products and accessories. Then an Italian company copied her products and underbid her with Wal-Mart. Fortunately, Evanna was able to prove to Wal-Mart that she had designed the products, and so the multinational chain broke relations with the Italians and signed on with Evanna.

Influences and business attitudes.

When I asked Evanna about the influences on her business attitudes, she said, "I don't feel that innovation is the key to my success. It's mainly keeping up with the trends. For example, I go to the conventions and see exhibitions so I know what's going on in the business and I have the foresight to keep ahead. At least, others think my products are fresh" (11. E194-E195 and E208). That is, she did not try to invent new products, but instead worked to improve her existing products by putting her own personal stamp on them.

Evanna had at least 20 people with whom she had contracts for designs. "We're always discussing new ideas and new possibilities," she said. "Then we make experiments. We have a new product, we look at it, we experiment, and test it" (11. E222-E223). In effect, Evanna's business entailed a business model called "continual improvement process," or, as she said, "We always have to be improving, or else we just get copied" (11. E233).

Evanna noted that she wanted to move slowly although she had been talking to business associates about expanding her business to Singapore and other countries,. "I think the WTO [World Trade Organization] helps the trade and fashion industry," she said (11. E253). "It's the first to gain recognition as a world trading block, and the Chinese fashion market is more and more a part of the global fashion market" (11. E253-E256).

Over the years, Evanna had built up a network of outlets to distribute her products. "I have over 100 store distributors in China," she said (11.E127). "And because of that, I am able to distribute products through the many stores. These stores are also reliable. They, too, carry through with what they say they are going to do" (11. E127-E130). "But," she also stated, "we are not yet good at managing or at marketing in this company, or in this country" (11. E97-E98).

Ethical outlook and values.

To my question about her business ethics, Evanna replied, "We're not trying to make a huge profit or anything. We're just trying to maintain steady growth" (11. E133-E134). Her reputation, she concluded, was based on honesty rather than competition. She was not interested in rapid expansion, going public, or expanding her exports beyond the Asian market, but instead just wanted to grow in China within an atmosphere of honesty and integrity. This outlook is heralded by many cross-cultural managers in the field of human potential (Merchant, 1998).

Analytical Bracketing of Evanna's Interview

Themes that emerged from Evanna's interview included her Confucian work ethics and her concepts of markets and competitive practices. She appeared to be straddling the strategies of Western managerial concepts and Eastern entrepreneurial models, and coping with increased foreign challenges to markets within her own country (Fu, 2002).

Confucian ethics.

Evanna's ethics were more those of a Chinese teacher than a Chinese businessperson, in that she related her business success to her own personal virtue. She truly combined Confucian rationality and spirituality (Yu, 2002) by structuring her business along the lines of family loyalty (*li*) and extending these familial relationships to her business dealings. Evanna has taken advantage of the privatization trends that began in China in the mid-1990s (Tang & Parish, 2000) while the form of her company resembles a traditional Chinese family business, with a benevolent authority figure at the top. For example, shortly before I interviewed her, she had hired newly trained MBA students as consultants to make financial forecasts and create marketing plans. As part of the new non-state economy, her business repackages innovative products and positions them in the national and international marketplaces. Evanna's almost zealous reliability paid off with many rewards, including increasing profits, the loyalty of employees and business associates, and the strength of her contracts with multinational corporations.

Evanna confidently used her reputation to compete with European and other countries for what she said was, "China's market share of the hair accessory industry" (11. EI 76).

Markets and competition.

Evanna frequented South Korea for her production and supply needs. This told me how extensive her family business networks must be. It is difficult and expensive for most Chinese to leave the country without special industry visas and passports (Hoong, 2001; Solinger, 1999). The institutional supports for Chinese clothing businesses and fashion trades are based on regional associations—usually from outside the mainland— that interact with local family businesses. These regional associations are pre-modern, neo-Confucian structures that have been in place for many centuries (Hamilton, 1997). Taiwan, Hong Kong, and South Korea provide the same general configurations for production and supply networks to Chinese family merchants today as they did in the past. When Evanna discussed her business decisions, she said, "What I do is try to find people who are experienced in the business and in similar businesses and get their advice on how to proceed" (11. E105-E106). The key here is that these networks exist among kin and extended family.

East-West entrepreneurial management fusion.

Evanna skilfully balanced two different management styles within the new Chinese capitalist marketplace and culture. In a very Eastern tradition, she said, "My vision is more of long-term growth. I am not so concerned with how much profit I am making today or tomorrow, rather I'm looking at growth in the long term" (11. E174-E176). For example, even though she had contracts with Carrefour and Wal-Mart, and those associations were doing well, she remained very cautious, noting that "we also are prepared that the products, while they are good for now, people may get tired of them and so we have to be ready for when things get less" (sic) (11. E186-E187). As Whitley (1994) noted, Chinese businesses focus on growth through "opportunistic diversification and volume expansion," as opposed to specialization. In other words, to stay afloat, they maximize their flexibility.

In contrast, Evanna's Western thinking of her company as a learning organization (Senge, 1990) allowed her subcontractors and employees to experiment with products, materials, and management techniques, liberating the multi-dimensional contributions of the individuals in her company. She described the management form of her company as "lateral"—that is, nonhierarchical. "I often meet," she said, "with different sections of employees, contractors, and clients. I'm very much a part of the overall daily activities of the business" (11. E153-E155). Her notion that she was not an innovator was an interesting modesty given the vibrant originality I saw in her shop. Her concept of being a master at reproducing, rather than inventing beautiful objects, may be derived from Ming dynasty approaches to art and mass production (Cleary, 1991).

Foreign challenges to Chinese markets.

Trust does not come easily in the Chinese business community because the small size of most companies means that the businesspeople do not work with many individuals outside their own family networks (Whitley, 1994). Evanna recounted how she faced fierce competition from an Italian company for a contract with Wal-Mart. "Although the Italian products were also very good, of a high quality" she said, "they were not honest, and their reliability in business was low. And so I was able to convince Wal-Mart that I was much more dependable and would come through. My reputation is based on honesty rather that competition. And so I think for this reason Wal-Mart went with me" (11. E120-E123). In effect, Evanna had adapted her Confucian spiritual values to modern international concepts of fairness and intellectual property rights.

Marty

My female interpreter, Nikki, and I took a cab past elegant estates and consulates over a hill into a deep jungle of factories. We entered Xili, a crowded, low-income factory district on the outskirts of Shenzhen. As we stepped out of the cab, we waded through the warm torrential southern China rain, the kind that shreds the leaves of banana plants. We jumped over deep puddles, wiping the water from our eyes that splashed up from the sidewalk.

Across a wide, muddy plaza, we could see Marty, a 21-year-old owner-manager, who waited for us in front of his noodle shop. He stood with his arms folded proudly across his chest, his legs spread wide, with a big grin on his face, looking like a happy king of the mountain.

With relief, we took shelter under his awning, where there were two boiling vats of scalding water filled with large churning noodles. Marty led us to a front table, one of 10 in his restaurant, which is approximately 15' by 30'. All the other tables were filled with customers. After a brief greeting, Marty offered to demonstrate his northern Chinese style of making noodles as they do it in his native province of Hubei. He and a male partner began this craft by kneading a long roll of dough on a table, expertly twisting and punching it until they had an arm's length slab a foot wide. Marty then lifted the slab into the air, which he deftly cut it into slices 1V2" wide, which one by one drop into the boiling vat below. Marty stirred the noodles with a huge ladle and then scooped some out into two large bowls, which he placed in front of us.

A boy assistant immediately brought us a tray of spicy condiments and fresh herbs, which we used to season our noodles before devouring them with delight. The tastes and smells in the restaurant were almost hypnotic.

Strengths and weaknesses.

When I asked Marty about his business strengths and weaknesses, he immediately mentioned that he is very easy-going with his employees, unlike his bosses when he worked for others. He added that there are many workers from the north living in the neighborhood and working in nearby factories, so he has a steady flow of customers. His products are excellent, he said, but inexpensive. He remarked, "I think I have an advantage now that I know what I want to do." (11. M305).

Marty knew that he is a first-rate noodle-maker and liked being his own boss, but he was not entirely confident about his marketing skills. He told me his weaknesses were, "The skills I need in the management. Making the noodles require more skills than I have now" (11. M517). Nevertheless, I noticed that he knows how to cater to his customers. For example, he has figured out how to attract many southerners, who tended to prefer rice to noodles, and who spiced their food differently from northerners.

Marty learned his trade in Shanghai, he said, where he worked at a locally famous noodle restaurant. He was lured to Shenzhen because the city was touted as "the new modem city of China." (11. M710-M711). However, he had concluded that the market opportunities in Shenzhen are just so-so, and that he might do better if he were to return to Shanghai. This fact, that Shenzhen was losing some its appeal to migrant workers, was supported in studies I had read about the business climate in the Special Economic Zones of China. These cities had undergone huge changes throughout the 1990s when large numbers of workers flocked to the coastal cities (Bao et al., 2002). There were so many people in transition and trying to make a living, that competition was fierce.

Influences and business attitudes.

When I asked him about the influences on his business attitudes, he replied that his main influence came from working in a famous Shanghai noodle restaurant. "I worked," he said, "and got the experience I needed by watching the skill of another." (11. M552). Marty's concern was to provide top-quality service and healthy food to his customers. "I want to be the best noodle-maker in Shenzhen," he declared. (11. MI032-M1034). His long-term plan was to move his business downtown and build up his reputation there. He said, "I want to open another restaurant. I want to be a manager at one place and have my friend at another." (11. M849).

Ethical outlook and values.

To my question about his business ethics, Marty replied that the key to his success was his health. He wanted to provide healthy, wholesome food for his customers and to maintain a healthy outlook about life. He said, "I want to provide the best service to my customers and *shenti,* health." (11. M900). When I asked him how he stays healthy, he says that, even though he has virtually no social life, he likes to dance to disco music in the back of his shop after hours, and he also hula-hoops for 7 minutes every morning while the vats are heating up.

Analytical Bracketing of Marty's Interview

Marty typified what I had expected when I first conceptualized this study. He represented the small, mostly unsophisticated restaurateur in a culture with an outstanding reputation for quality food. However, my interview with him highlighted how successful one can be at the bottom of the Chinese pyramid of business and society (Prahalad, 2005). Marty represented the trades that need to buy goods and supplies. Prahalad (2005) estimated that these tiny urban businesses and their low-income customers comprise 35-40% of the consumers in Asia.

Themes that emerged in Marty's interview included the tenacity of the migrating young Chinese workers and their quest for fortune, as well as the changing bonds of blood ties.

Workers on the move.

Hinton (1966) wrote an ethnographic account of the Communist Revolution from the perspective that the struggle for socialism, while extremely confusing and brutal had led to a new society based on brotherhood. After interviewing Marty, I realized that the image of Chinese urban micro-businesses as family-based *getihu* is perhaps fading as the post-reform generation in China comes of age. Marty's self-reliance has propelled him by sheer energy, talent, and willpower toward the fulfilment of his dream. His attitude is infectiously optimistic, for he sees the road ahead as bright, perhaps even brilliant. He is a perfect embodiment of the Western image of someone who pulls himself up by his own bootstraps. However, Marty retains some of the socialist spirit. When he arrived in Shenzhen from one of China's poorer inland regions to test himself in the emerging market economy, there were many inequalities in the system. Not least among these was the difficulty in getting residency status in an enormously competitive city of 12 million souls. But Marty was unafraid of the obstacles, and was even lured on by the challenges and opportunities.

The quest for wealth.

Hinten (1972), again writing about the abrupt changes in the Chinese society under Deng's rule, lamented the point in China's history where the people turned away from socialism to the various forms of capitalist wealth, growth and ownership. Although Marty had made it through most of his vocational high school, in many ways he represented an economically marginal group, for there were hundreds of thousands of competitors just behind him. There were few resources for restaurateurs like Marty to borrow money to grow their business. He recalled, "The idea of starting a business occurred to me during the Spring Festival (of2004), but the opportunities were not so good. Then I had worked for a boss and so I had to conserve my strength and store up money and energy. I saved the money which I earned from work." (11. M357-M358). Marty had to pay rent, adapt his products to customer tastes, and handle all other costs associated with the noodle shop. Prahalad (2005) suggested that the operating cost of an urban micro-business places an extraordinary emphasis on the price of their products which included innovation, distribution, manufacturing and general "costs of organization."

On the other hand, there were also hundreds of thousands—if not millions—of northern workers, with northern dialects, customs, and habits, who were eager to help someone from their hometown or region.

Changing blood ties.

On a small scale, Marty's story is precisely what Fei (1947/1992) noted when he described China's transformation from a rural society to one of regional mega-metropolises. This involved elaborate networks of people from various regions and subcultures reassembling in their adopted cities, still yearning for the dialects, customs, and foods of their native provinces. Cultural encounters among China's provincial sons and daughters are traditions not easily broken (Harrell, 1996). And this native cultural network is what appears to have created a loyal customer base for a young noodle-maker from the north.

When I returned to Shenzhen 6 months after this interview, the noodle shop was being run by someone else, a migrant Chinese Muslim (the *Hui* minority), who told me that Marty had moved his business downtown. So, he had taken at least one step forward toward fulfilling his dream.

Similarities Among the Ordinary Micro-Business Owner-Managers

There is a surprisingly sophisticated perspective among these individuals. They were all customer-centered businesspeople and informed wholesale buyers. Bebe, Evanna, and Marty considered granting me an interview an unusual request, but not a very important aspect of their extremely full and hectic workdays. They all continued working as they talked to me, which gave me a good idea of what their daily work was like. Bebe, Evanna, and Marty all had storefront locations, as do most ordinary Chinese urban micro-business owner-managers (Sheff, 2002; Zhang, 2001), which allowed me to see not only the products they sold but also the products they had to use in providing their services.

There were also many similarities among them in respect to business strengths and weaknesses, influences on their business attitudes, and ethical positions. For example, regarding strengths and weaknesses, all three felt liberated by their economic independence, such as Bebe's flexible schedule, Evanna's ability to engage in export markets, and Marty's mobility, but they were all also constrained by macroeconomic forces, such as boycotts of Japanese goods, unfair business practices, and a vast number of competitors. All three also felt that their marketing skills were weak. They understood their customers wanted information, trends, and choices, but all were unsure about the ways in which to market the capacity for their customers to consume. For instance, Bebe and Marty both catered to customers who could afford to spend within a certain price-range. They needed to come up with smaller, cheaper products and services, but were not sure exactly how to do that. Evanna seemed to be most in touch with market forecasting and unit pricing, but even she felt this was difficult to understand and implement. They were all very hands-on owner-managers.

As for influences on their business attitudes, all three cited networks of family and friends as their primary inspiration. Regarding their ethical positions, they all believed in continual self-improvement.

Several themes emerged from the interviews, clustering around the subjects of the Chinese owner-managers' sense of freedom, business motives, conflict with macroeconomic forces, and international development ethics.

Chinese micro-business owner freedom and flexibility.

The ordinary micro-business owner-managers expressed their freedom to pursue their interests and dreams through traditional Chinese network-based and associative business structures (Hamilton, 1997). Bebe built her business around the premise that her son and parents could be present as she worked with clients, which would create a harmonious environment for her and her family network. Evanna's ability to go in and out of the country, which is extremely difficult for Chinese citizens, demonstrates her powerful networks and associations within her industry. Marty's principal associations were regional—that is, he was economically and culturally linked to his fellow northerners. All three of these owner-managers launched their companies on their own by using the cohesion of their social relationships and affiliations to advance their businesses.

Bebe, Evanna, and Marty all felt confident of their customer bases, which were reflected in their references to the vastness of China's internal markets (Zhang & Yao, 2001).

This confidence is what appears to underlie their sense of freedom. They all spoke about the flexibility that their work allowed them.

Bebe liked being able to pick her products, work hours, and the way she related to each customer. Evanna liked to think of her business as a learning organization, which may suggest a flexibility of ideas, directions for growth, and employee and distributor relationships. Marty's flexibility can be seen in the many pages of his menu. His variety of ingredient combinations was a creative adaptation to his customers' tastes.

The only limitation on this freedom and flexibility was the obligation not to lose face by doing something immoral (Eastman, 1988).

Personalized business motives.

Bebe, Evanna, and Marty all had highly personalized motives for being in their line of work. Bebe used her products on her own skin in order to make herself beautiful and extended this skill with pleasure to her customers. Evanna's focus was on designing beautiful products for an international clientele. And Marty had not attended college, but wanted to be in a trade in which he could be self-employed. Starting out working in a restaurant at the age of 18, he was attracted to noodle-making and was able to open his own shop by the age of 20.

Macroeconomic forces.

Bebe, Evanna, and Marty all understood the subtle ways in which they interacted with market-based forces. Bebe knew that the Japanese cosmetics she sold were superior to the Chinese brands, but she adjusted easily to her clients' demand to boycott Japanese goods, figuring that they would use them again when the political situation quieted down (Ozkirimli, 2000).

Evanna is a small part of a powerful worldwide retail trade industry, and so she must attend a lot of conferences and trade shows in order to get the best deals in this rapidly changing environment.

Marty could see people in the street buying and eating cheap packaged instant noodles made by giant Chinese corporations, but he knew they could not afford anything better. His noodle shop offered an alternative for people who looked forward to a hot meal as the only luxury in their week.

Differences among the Ordinary Micro-Businesses

International development ethics.

The differences among the three ordinary owner-managers included Evanna's exclusive experience entering a contract with the multinational Wal-Mart. Her profile provided a unique angle on the theme of macroeconomic forces and international ethics. In the Western media, copyright infringement abuses are discussed as if these are standard Chinese business practices (Appelbaum & Robinson, 2005). Even though China's legal structure is under construction in terms of property and trading rights, Evanna, like so many other Chinese private businesses had to use the international governing laws and principles adhered to by multinationals such as Wal-Mart to redress her copyright issues (Sheff, 2002).

Migrant labor experiences.

Marty's story was the only one in this interview sample to represent the migrant labor experience, a kind of rite of passage, for millions of young men and women in China

(Zheng, 2003). As the Chinese government continually wrestles with the problem of migrant workers in the era of post-reform, Marty and others like him may represent a revolutionary element in Chinese urban micro-business society.

In a positive sense, Marty left home for the coastal centers of commerce to seek his fortune. Fei (1947/1992) described his people as tied to the soil and so the importance of *xueyuan* (blood ties) to migrating workers throughout the country. Since they must leave their native provinces to find work, their successes away from home ratified their ability to head a household. Turner (1974/1995) explained these impermanent affiliations as communitas. For instance, Marty's communitas was his cadre of northern workers.

Turner (1974/1995) theorized that if the informal communitas should organize, they have the potential to transform a society in revolutionary ways. While Marty's business was currently supported by his local factory-worker customers from the north, these informal affiliations were for the most part contractual and related to the rules of market competition. Marty experienced these informal ties as merely helpful to his overall business goals. However, the fate of his business was tied to the changes in the local factory hiring practices, which were largely due to wage competition from neighboring countries in the international marketplace. The global quest for cheaper labor confronts the Chinese society with what Tang and Parish (2000) observed:

China is now evolving from a caste to a class system of social organization. Chinese leaders may not have intended this, but over the years, desired or not, their policies produced a caste of privileged urban elites against a rural caste of have-nots. Those boundaries are beginning to soften, and society is adjusting slowly to this new reality, (p. 17)

As large numbers of migrant laborers arrive by the thousands from other poorer regions of the country, such as Inner Mongolia and the Qinghai Tibetan plateaus, they displace those workers from the north whose wages have increased, though ever so slightly. These labor conditions create unrest among all members of the informal worker groups in China's urban centers (Zhang & Yao, 2001). All the northern migrants, including Marty, face pressures to move on to other locations or perhaps to return to their hometowns. If the workers should take a stand and struggle for power in their adopted urban communities, they may create an unofficial, but organized labor movement.

Contextual Descriptions of the Incubator Micro-Business Owner-Managers

Alistair

I took a short cab ride down Shenanda Boulevard to the Nanshan district, which is surrounded by newly built freeways that fill the air with the fumes of exhaust pipes. Nestled in between off-ramps is a patch of office buildings that include the Center of the Torch, which is the name for all high-tech incubator complexes in the country. To get to my destination, we had to drive the wrong way down a narrow one-way street that had once been a bicycle path. I recalled hearing on the English language news hour that Shenzhen is adding 700 cars per month to its already congested streets.

Ms. Jiang, my interpreter, was waiting at the front entrance for me. We left the hot, muggy air of the street behind us as we entered the air-conditioned building and took an elevator to the fourth floor. Alistair sat waiting for us in a well-lit meeting room at one end of a long wooden table that can accommodate 20 people in large cushioned chairs. Potted schefleras decorated a large cutaway section in the middle of the table. Jiang told me that the room is used daily for all types of business meetings and must be booked. Alistair had reserved it for an hour.

Our host, a boyish-looking, casually- dressed, 30-year-old rose to greet me with a firm Western-style handshake, which is becoming more usual in China. Because he spoke excellent English (with an Australian accent), this was the only interview I conducted in English, and therefore Ms. Jiang simply listened to the conversation without interrupting.

Alistair dressed like a typical Chinese businessman: white shirt, black pants, black belt, and black shoes. Only the quality of the fabrics indicated his social status, along with his Rolex watch.

He invited me to sit in a chair next to his, offered me a small bottle of water, and said, "Have a rest."

"I'm an American," I reply. "We don't rest."

He laughs gleefully. "Yes, and time is money!"

Strengths and weaknesses.

When I asked Alistair about bis business strengths and weaknesses, he said that he is one of four young partners in this 1-year-old company, an electronic components manufacturer and distributor. His official position in the company, he said, was chief financial officer, but he "wears many hats," (11. 33) including production manager and personnel director, a position that he indicated put him in charge of hiring and firing. I soon learned that, just that week, he had hired 10 new employees.

Alistair indicated that he spent a considerable amount of time at the company these days. "All the top people in production and marketing," he said, "like to talk things over with me. I visited Beijing last week, helping the marketing guys to develop a potential big customer"(ll. A33-A35).

When I ask him to describe his customers, Alistair said, "We do both international and domestic trading. But they are not just small shops. They are Chinese, large, Chinese, private, multinational companies." (11. A456-A460). The reference to these large Chinese institutions such as *Hua Wei,* a private, multi-national electronic engineering firm located nearby, provided the context for the scale of his company.

As a supplier to these larger established Chinese firms, Alistair's entrepreneurial opportunities and risks were extremely high. "Because there are many things that happen in a small business," he said, "the company can do more business than it has, but we are not too regulated because we are small. Smaller companies tend to be more, much more flexible." (11. A74-A76). To my question about his business background, he replied that prior to starting this business, he had worked for 4 years as an engineer in a state-owned steel company in Heiliongjiang Province. Then he went to Beijing for 2 years to earn an MBA and later worked for almost 3 years in Shanghai as an investment manager in a venture capital firm.

When I noted that he had quite a wide range of experience, he said that he did not have much decision-making power when he was a quality-control engineer in the huge state-owned enterprise, and that he had few avenues to express his opinions. Furthermore, when he was an investment manager in the venture capital firm, the president made almost all the decisions, even though Alistair and his colleagues felt that they had much more integrity and technical expertise than the president did.

Despite Alistair's education and previous work experience, he felt that he has matured enormously, in a business sense, after only 1 year as an entrepreneur. Especially in his role as personnel director, he had to mediate conflicts among the managers and employees, which he characterized as very complicated but rewarding.

Alistair discussed how his company had made a profit in its first year, with gross revenues of five million *yuan* ($625,000). He mentioned that was very challenging because he and his partners were not able to get business loans from any banks and had to finance the company with personal loans. "It is very difficult, sometimes impossible," he said, "for small enterprises like ours to borrow money from banks" (11. A220-A221).

Another of Alistair's business strengths, he said, is that "all company decisions are made by group consensus." (11. Al 17-A118). The company's general manager, a man with considerable experience with start-ups, calls all the partners together to debate all important decisions. Alistair characterizes this style of management as traditionally Chinese. "When we are facing big questions, big problems," he said, "we always decide by group consensus." (11. Al 18). Or, he noted, "The general manager of this company, the most experienced with the business start-up, calls all of us to join him. He always puts the serious decisions on the table and we sit down, and discuss it. This is sort of a traditional Chinese family way, that is, it is the organizational way of how we solve such problems, by the group talking together. Even though I am not a marketing type," he continued, "we discuss marketing, and I give my opinions." (11. Al 19-A122).

A third strength of his company that Alistair mentions is its 10-year plan. This is mostly thanks again to the general manager, who has had a lot of experience in growing small businesses and making plans for them. Alistair described, "First, a team of small business people must have a good business model. We must know how to make enough money so that, we can feed ourselves, and to feed our employees.

To make the company at least profitable is the first challenge." (11. A97-A100).

A fourth strength of Alistair's company is that it pays somewhat higher salaries than industry average to its staff, as well as providing quality training, both of which attract talented applicants. Alistair used typical Western business language to describe the human resource approach of his company. "We also create value for our employees," he said, "because we provide a position, a place for all of us to make enough money to live in a respectable situation. And we have training program for each of us during certain times of the year, that is, no what matter the employee. For these reasons, we'll all working, and we'll continue to work in this company for several years." (11. A280-A284).

A weakness of the company is that its only way to grow has been to pay huge interest rates to venture capital investors. But Alistair felt this atmosphere of tight capital was changing. "I think it's changing. Last month, the president of this company chatted about this banking situation in Shenzhen. In the future, if we realize our plans in 5 years, in the coming 5 years, maybe the guaranteed loan company, or even a bank will give us a first choice. Right now, they are still funding the SOE (state owned enterprises) companies." (11. A259-A263). Alistair also felt lucky to have this loan option, since many other micro-businesses in the incubator building want this opportunity but have not been able to find backers.

Influences and business attitudes.

When I asked him about influences on his business attitudes, Alistair said that the general manager and the long-term plan were strong motivations for him to join the company. He believed that eventually his firm will be the "king of signal cable" in Asia. The reasons for the company's success, he believed, are that it provides quality cable products at lower costs, cheaper prices to the customers, and with faster delivery times than its competitors. The emphasis in dealing with customers, said Alistair, is less on *guanxi* and taking people out to banquets than on maintaining the highest possible quality for the company's products. Thus, market economics play a huge role in influencing Alistair's business attitudes (Yu, 2002).

As for the company's relations with its employees, Alistair says that he was still very much influenced by the notions of business practices that he was exposed to in the course of his MBA program, as well as by the consensus style of management at his company. Specifically, he mentioned,

We create value for the shareholders because all the partners, we put all of what we have into the company. We don't have a house, we don't have a car, we only have this company. So, this company, it must become more profitable. It should return to the shareholder, either in financial or in other methods. We create a value for shareholders. And, at last, we are creating value for our customers and our employees and the shareholders. (11. A297-A302).

Alistair emphasized that every employee is paid well enough to live comfortably and received customized training in his or her specialty at various times in the year. Therefore, according to Alistair, the employees are highly loyal to the company.

Ethical outlook and values.

To my question about his business ethics, Alistair replied that in past times businessmen had the lowest possible social status in China, but that now they have a much higher status, especially the big companies.

For such companies," he said, "the market works as it says, not the power of the relationship. Of course, we must do something to build up a relationship, but it's minor. We have our major focus onto this quality of products, in the supplying of products. That's what we are focusing on, instead of so-called relationships (11. A463-A467).

Yet, talking about money is still considered to be in poor taste. "Gentlemen," Alistair said, "never talk about money. Our potential customers are attracted to us because we are honest and well educated, which makes people feel comfortable"(ll. A565-A567). Alistair is somewhat conflicted over feeling ambitious, since traditional Chinese culture frowns on ambition, but he believes in being "comfortable."

Alistair has a clear notion of social responsibility. In creating value for its customers, employees, and shareholders, the company, he said, is "creating value for the whole society." (11. A304). Furthermore, Alistair noted that he is in the process of looking for a charity for his company to invest in that will promote the education of poor children. "For the Chinese traditional system, helping those who need help is natural to Chinese people," he explained. (11. A332-A333).

Finally, Alistair expressed a profound respect for nature. Even the ancient emperors of China, he said, who owned everything, still showed respect to nature. In recent times, however, leaders like Mao have not shown this respect, and that attitude, he feels, needs to be corrected. "Chin Tan," said Alistair,

is the place that the emperor would come to pray and worship the gods, the heavens. Well, I was thinking, the emperor in China, he owns everything, but even the emperor has some conscience, he has to worship the gods. What is the god he worships? The god is nature. He must pray for the nature, he must show the respect to the nature: to the great nature. But, in the past several decades Chairman Mao or any other Chairman of this nation and sometimes the president of other countries, they don't have any conscience. They don't respect nature. This is not correct. (11. A405-A412)

Analytical Bracketing of Alistair's Interview

Alistair is exemplary of the ways in which selected owner-managers in China appear to be searching to find their salvation in science and technology. The themes that emerged in this interview included perspectives from micro-business technology sector, *guanxixue* versus market force reliability of products and services, and social ecology.

Perspectives from the technology sector.

By allowing flexible business structures, the government is spawning companies that can adapt to the contingencies of a high-tech environment. The decision-making power of these companies rests with their own managers. Therefore, these torch enterprises sink or swim mostly by how they manage their own resources (Yu, 2002).

Alistair described the ways in which his company links its high-technology products to commercial, industrial, and international markets. Usually, the strengths of micro-business owner-managers reside in the technical or engineering degrees that they have acquired in universities or university research centers and the network of relationships they had formed there. Their work experience, especially in disassembling state-owned enterprises, also had contributed to the dynamic of China's economic transformation. Study or work abroad was an added benefit. This theme, of scientific solutions, has long been part of the socialist discourse (Wan, *People's Daily,* 1986) and remains current news.

Guanxixue versus market reliability.

Alistair had these experiences and was aware of what he called "the many ghosts within China's new market socialism." (11. A304-A305). In this regard, he wanted to replace Chinese *guanxi* business practices with reliable and friendly services. Such service is different from the shared feelings that one has in *guanxi* relationships, which are based on complex network ties that define the social position of the individuals (Huang, 2004; Zheng & Yao, 2001).

Yang (1995) summarized how the "rhizomatic networks" of China's business culture are interwoven:

What keeps the art of *guanxi* apart from market or commodity relation ~ is in fact that ironically its instrumentalism can only work through non-market *guanxi* ethics and non-objectified human relations, (p. 310)

Social ecology.

It appeared that Alistair had not completely abandoned the valuable aspects of *guanxi* relationships; rather, he seemed to have taken on an attitude of social philanthropy like that of China's former gentlemen-merchants (Eastman, 1988).

In addition, Alistair's awareness of China's lack of leadership on environmental sustainability reflected his connection to broader international discussions. Even though Alistair has immersed himself in the role of a young global entrepreneur, he shared his ideas on spirituality. Just as Chodorkoff (2003) argued that the rise of dominant liberal economic markets and the consequences of a globalizing cultures, is similar to the loss of the natural world's biodiversity, Alistair talked about reclaiming nature and religion, which for him is one, and it is rooted in an authentic Chinese of ethics, that gave him that spark of conscience toward an environmental practice.

Zorro

The elevator to the 10th floor of the business incubator building was dimly lit and extremely slow, packed with men going up. My interpreter, Ms. Jiang, shouted into her cell phone, *"Gang gang dao* ("We're here!").

As a female assistant greeted us at the elevator, Zorro's husky voice could be heard from his office at the end of the hallway. We entered a cluttered room with wide windows, through which I could see the smoky air hovering over downtown Nantou. To the left, the South China Sea was dotted with ferries and oil rigs, the blue-green images of the New Territories of Hong Kong shimmered on the water.

Zorro's office was decorated with heavy, carved dark woods with traditional Chinese calligraphy scrolls on the walls. Cigarette smoke clung to the ceiling. In a little side office, Zorro was talking on a cell phone and smoking a cigarette. At 6', he was taller than most Chinese men in the south. He had dark skin, bushy eyebrows, and was dressed in an ill-fitting suit, but he moved elegantly.

Still talking on the phone, he joined us in the main office, walking behind his huge, dark-stained rosewood desk. With an extended hand, he motioned us to sit down on a couch directly in front of him. The assistant entered with hot cups of delicious Hua Mu tea and placed them in our hands. Zorro hung up the phone and handed me his Schwartz Values Survey, which he told me he has just completed. He apologized for only having a short time to talk because some emergency has come up in his business. Therefore, I decided to go straight to the question about bis business's strengths and weaknesses.

Strengths and weaknesses.

Zorro explained that there was another digital technology company that he recently wanted to merge with, but the manager of that company was afraid that his business would be absorbed by Zorro's and his job would be phased out, so the merger could not take place. Zorro commented that the other manager's attitude was very common in China—that people are afraid that "big fish will always eat small fish." "In this example," Zorro said, "I had to cooperate with another manager of the company and talk about such ideas, and the other manager said 'yes, yes,' but I could not keep that merger together. That manager thinks that maybe my company will have more advantages. Maybe this company will win more contracts and be selected over the other. So, to combine, to make a corporate alignment, is important to do. But in order to do it, you must have the same values. That's important." (11. Z106-Z113).

But, Zorro added, he "is not afraid of being small and being swallowed by bigger fish. What is important is not one's size, but one's spirit." Having said that, he pointed to a scroll on his wall that read, "The mountain is not famous for its height; its name will spread far and wide if there is a fairy on it. The water is not famous for its depth, but only if it has a dragon in it." (11. Z205-Z206).

The issues of security, achievement and self-direction emerge in Zorro's discussion in terms of the interpersonal relationships that comprise everyday life among small businesses in the incubator. He expressed uncertainty about the newly allowed private mergers, its systems and safeguards, which are not always in place. People are nervous and rumors about several instances of merger fraud, the reason why. At the same time, Zorro relies on the roots of his traditionalism, a kind of non-conformity within the traditional culture, to describe the sources of his own inspiration. He describes his navigation within this system as the development of his own character, a kind of self-direction, a business focus that is practical, yet steeped in the parables of a more ancient China.

Influences and business attitudes.

When I asked him about the influences on his business attitudes, Zorro said that China must be open to how other countries do things.

There must be many ways," he said, "to do things from different countries. The world has many values, and maybe you can search for them in traditional cultures. I think people can learn from China, to learn the good and to try to get rid of the bad, beginning in herself or himself. That's the important things we should learn about cultural values - cultural values should serve the people. We can never be perfect - so these cultural values are just our results. (11. Z66-Z76)

Zorro spoke concretely about security and the survival of the nation. China's Confucian, agricultural, scientific, and socialist heritage merged in him more than in the other interviewees. He was very curious about the SVS survey, and wondered aloud about how many kinds of important values there are in the world. The survey became a bridge between this somewhat traditional Chinese intellectual businessman and me.

Ethical outlook and values.

To my question about his business ethics, Zorro replied that other countries can learn from China—especially about being peace-loving. "Up until now," said Zorro,

How could we have anything but a traditional culture, how could it be different within China? There must be the best value in every country but, you can never trade or change your way of being in your traditional culture. And if this kind of culture, China's culture, goes abroad - what is the best way to show who we are? We are peace loving. At least that we can try to show that to others. (11. Z16-Z21)

Analytical Bracketing of Zorro's Interview

Zorro presented a useful interview on the question of China's transition to a socialist market economy. His interview expressed the principles of China that stressed competition based on cooperation and the value of traditional relationships. When I asked him, "if there was an alignment among the values of the Chinese people, businesses, and the government?" he stated, "Maybe the government only had the end of the common good to make alignments at these different levels" (11. Z27-Z28). This perception of alignment from the state is in keeping with Chinese government economic policies (Brahm, 1998).

Competition based on cooperation.

In ancient times, there was a unity of values between buyers and sellers. The Chinese philosopher Mencius (372-289 B.C.E.), called these buyers and sellers "morally graceful merchants" (Harvey, 1999). Traditional Chinese ethics focused on interpersonal relations in a social hierarchy that governed all aspects of everyday life. In the exchange of commodities, the trading parties were considered equal in social status. But the sellers were supposed to be the most sincere. Their obligation extended the ethic of "righteousness" to the buyers.

Zorro expressed frustration about the many missed opportunities that he saw and experienced in the fierce market environment of his high-tech industry, which resulted in suspicion and corruption. He regretted that what he called the current climate of "big fish eats little fish" was so universal in

China. According to Yang (1995), these feelings are common. The *guanxi* gift giving practices among businesses once made it relatively easy to force others to become part of an exchange network. By accepting favors and gifts, the inherent obligation to give up some of their goods, connections, or power created a lot of fear, especially among people of lower rank who feel obliged in order to gain access.

Zorro's discussion affirmed Sheff s (2002) perspective that even though the Chinese state had given up direct control of business in favor of promoting broad economic policies, a position that is very popular in China, the new system does not operate effectively because of a basic lack of trust among China's newest entrepreneurs. Ohmae (1998) suggested that historically, China's opening up has seen the growth of a regional economic consolidation, in southern Guangdong Province and with the advent of Shenzhen SEZ status and proximity to Hong Kong. Zorro may reflect some of the frustration from missed opportunities that relate to this kind of regional growth.

The enduring spirit of a traditional society.

Zorro's outlook is a modern blend of Chinese commercialism, traditionalism, and socialism. Tu Wei-Ming (1980) called this view, the "moral universal" *(tang hsia-chi-shih),* which is a capacity to sense the presence of what "is" at every moment and giving up "everything that can be had (*I ch'ien fang hsia).*"

In this respect, the new market socialism that Zorro described might be just another link in China's long history, rather than something totally new. Zorro's commercial traditionalism and modern socialism was supported by the broader SVS data, which showed that benevolence *and* conformity ranked high among all the micro-business owner-managers.

Cara

I sat at a round table in a quiet private room in one of my favorite restaurants in Shenzhen, the *Yale Yuan.* A waiter took my order for a small banquet, including salt-baked shrimp on skewers, corn with pine nuts and onions, sweet and sour fish, greens with oyster sauce, red sauce tofu, and lotus root soup.

Five minutes later, Cara and the interpreter, Mr. Lu, walked in. Cara was dressed in pink from head to toe and looked extremely feminine. Mr. Lu wore sport coat and slacks and looked quite debonair.

I stood up and instinctively extended my hand to Cara, who placed her hand in mine, unsure how to shake hands. To demonstrate how to do it properly, Mr. Lu shook my hand vigorously. Then he introduced me to Cara in perfect English, although, as I learned later, he has never been out of China.

I sat back down, Cara sat to my left, and Mr. Lu sat to her left, facing me. Throughout the conversation, it was difficult to make full eye contact with Cara, because she mostly faced and addressed Mr. Lu as she answered my questions. Cara's preference to meet me outside her office reflected what I later came to see was her private nature.

Cara then told me her story that she and her younger brother, Xiou Biz, both in their late 20s, had just opened a new translation service office in a Shenzhen business incubator. They already had another such office in Guangzhou, where, she said, the market for such services is more competitive.

When I asked Cara how she started her business, she recalled that the idea came from Xiou Biz, who, from a very young age, was always looking for new things to learn and was especially influenced by ideas from the West. When he was in high school, he persuaded his parents to have an

American foreign exchange student live with the family for a few months. When he got the idea for the translation service, after graduating from the university, he wanted to prevent it from being a family business because he was afraid that inexperienced relatives would come to Mm, asking for a job. Therefore, he and Cara moved away from their hometown to open their business, and have not told anyone that they are brother and sister.

When I follow up about why Cara does not hire family members, she replied that family bonds in China are so strong that if relatives do not perform well, one cannot fire them. Nevertheless, in some respects, Cara's translation service is a typical Chinese family business. "There can be contradiction between us," Cara said about herself and Xiou Biz, "we will stand together when facing the problems from outside" (11. CI378-C1379). Cam's core values seem to be reconciled in this statement. The personal freedoms that she and her brother allowed for themselves in running their company— eccentric behaviors and new business techniques—did not dissolve the bonds of their consanguinity (Fei, 2002; Huang, 2004).

Strengths and weaknesses.

When I asked Cara about her business strengths and weaknesses, she replied that her business's number one resource (strength) was the qualifications of the teachers— Xiou Biz and two others—who were all university graduates of English departments, and who all had a very dynamic style for training their students. Xiou Biz based his methods on Richard Koch's (1998) 80/20 rule for time management (itself based on Pareto's (1906/1897) 80/20 economic principle): that is, that approximately 20% of one's efforts produce 80% of one's results. All the employees had to follow this principle, Cara said, because "if people just keep the traditional concepts, maybe it won't work nowadays because things are changing. People must keep open-minded so they can grasp opportunities" (11. C1025-C1026). In this connection, Cara mentioned that her parents were more positive and were more open than many other Chinese people of their generation.

Cara was clearly influenced by Western ideas and business techniques, but her intellectual autonomy was most inspired by the novelist Lu Xun, the author *K'uan jen ji chi* (Dairy of a Madman) and *Ah Q Cheng Chuan* (The True Story of Ah Q), who championed intellectual freedom and openly regarded traditional and communist social structures as metaphorically cannibalistic.

Another strength of the school, according to Cara, is that the atmosphere in the classroom is totally positive, with students only being supported, never criticized. Xiou Biz "just encourages students," Cara said, "and believes in them—that they are competent. He will tell them to stand on the shoulders of former generations" (11. C586-C587 and C597-C598). To foster this spirit of equality, the students and the teachers in the school called each other *"tongzhi,"* the socialist word for "comrade" (co-worker) in Chinese. This egalitarianism is not typical of the Chinese educational system at large, which is far more authoritarian.

A third strength of the company, according to Cara, is that the two employee teachers are very well paid, in part to discourage them from going out and starting their own translation services.

One weakness of the company, according to Cara, is that Xiou Biz is overworked and cannot help her with non-teaching aspects of the business, so she is also overworked. Another weakness is that they had not figured out the best ways to market or advertise their services. For example, they have their own web site, but they are not sure that it is the best way to attract new students and customers for translation services.

Another weakness of the company is that Xiou Biz, at age 25, is too young to be respected in China as a teacher, so they hide his age. "There is a traditional view in China," Cara says, "that teachers had better be a little bit old. So my brother often grows a long moustache and hair, and his moustache happens to be a little bit yellow," which makes him look older (11. C1205-C1207). Hiding his age, however, has cost the business publicity, because they have had to turn down requests from newspapers for interviews, since they were sure reporters would ask Xiou Biz's age. On the other hand, Cara has learned from her brother that no matter how young you are, you can become an expert so long as you focus on one field and stay optimistic.

Influences and business attitudes.

When I asked Cara about influences on her business attitudes, she said that her brother was the biggest influence. In addition, Guangzhou, she said, "was chosen for the business location because the most developed cities in China are Beijing, Shanghai, and Guangzhou. In Beijing and Shanghai, there are a lot of such kinds of language translation trainings. Only in Guangzhou, there was not too much translation training competition. The markets of Guangzhou and Shenzhen had not been developed" (11. C933-C936). I was surprised that Cara had few competitors, because the thousands of foreigners who pour into Shenzhen every week to attend business and technical conferences clearly need simultaneous translators.

Aside from her brother, Cara's main intellectual influences came from reading books. In addition to Lu Xun, she mentioned having read the biographies of famous Western women such as Mary Kay and Hilary Clinton.

Ethical outlook and values.

To my question about her business ethics, Cara repeats her point about specialization. "I think," she said, "we should focus on one small field and do well in it." (II.C1881).This theme is emphasized in their translation classes, in the office, and in many aspects of Cara's daily life, as well as in her brother's life. Their unofficial motto is "Be small, but be elite and have depth." (11. C546-C547). The elitism, however, is not, Cara added, expressed toward the students or the employees. Cara's perspective provides a glimpse into the ways of young Chinese women. Cara gave the sense the Chinese aesthetic tradition of an examined life (Jiang & Neville, 2002).

Analytical Bracketing of Cara 's Interview

Cara's interview covered themes about management roles for women and modernizing family-based businesses. She also provided a poignantly authentic description of the ways in which young people are trying to take in new ideas and change traditional business structures in China.

Management roles for women.

According to most analysts, socialism favored women, whether in China or elsewhere (Tang & Parish, 2000). Like many young female entrepreneurs, Cara chose to start a company with a family member, her brother. When I interviewed her, she was just setting up a new branch of her company in Shenzhen's unique high-technology incubator environment.

Her brother is the star of the classroom, while she takes responsibility for "everything else." At first, this traditional arrangement of male and female roles seemed familiar to me. Yet, I had no sense that Cara felt like a victim. "As a small business woman," she said, "I have to wear many hats and do a lot of work. It's just the problem of hands. If there is a shortage of hands, many things can't be dealt with in time. I can't be absent for any of these things." (11. C1466-C1468). Rather, I saw that Cara had full control over her aspects of the business, although she was deeply indebted to her brother for enabling her to use her managerial and organizational skills.

Chinese neo-family-based companies.

On the other hand, to be perceived as modern, Cara and her brother have hidden their true identities, which struck me as excessively cautious and vulnerable. When telling me about how she and her brother had to keep their identities secret, Cara said, "This kind of phenomena is very common, but it is not like the traditional Chinese way. From the beginning, we emphasized that we avoided making the company become like a traditional family business" (11. C1776-C1778).

Similarities Among the Incubator Micro-Business Owner-Managers

The incubator owner-managers had similar types of offices that housed their operations within one large office building. They expressed new and professional organizational styles, highly defined business goals, and they articulated many Chinese specifics of their market operations. Similar influences on their business attitudes included their personal academic skills and ensuing relationships from universities. They were each, in their own way, grappling with the complexities of the fast-paced, high-tech business environment.

In terms of weaknesses, all three of the incubator owner-managers felt that marketing was their major management obstacle. Freedoms to define their business goals, and show the Chinese face of the new socialism pervaded these discussions.

Experiments with organizational structures.

All incubator micro-business owner-managers spoke about their personal commitment to their organizations as extremely hard work but liberating in many ways. Alistair excitedly described a consensual, hands-on organization that allowed him considerable information that flowed freely among the four owners. For the first time in his career, he felt his input into the decision-making process to be of value. This equality among the partners existed despite the fact, he added, that he had a strong central figure as CEO. Alistair described a new organizational structure compared with the typical Asian business institution (Hamilton & Biggart, 1990; Sheff, 2002).

Zorro described the relaxation of regulations and rules and a general autonomy of entrepreneurs in China. Cara and her brother had set up rules of non-nepotism beyond the initial dyadic family structure (Zhang, 2001).

Each of these incubator owner-managers were experimenting with personal power, which exhibited some forms of liberation and other well-springs of internal conflicts. For example, during our conversation, Alistair spoke several times about his ambitious feelings which he tried to channel into more modest language and spoke of better customer services and charitable causes. Zorro forged his unique business personality in the cultural charm of China's genteel merchant class. He used Chinese metaphors to refer to the influence and persuasion power that is unseen in the force of a small Chinese company. Cara and her brother experimented with business roles in order to enhance their Western cache in order to attract their potential students.

Highly defined business goals.

All incubator micro-business owner-managers spoke about highly defined business goals. They all said they use business plans to run their businesses and reflect the kind of fiscal federalism that operates in China (Martinez-Vasquez & Bahl, 2004). Alistair combined the business plan with the 10-year, long-term planning associated with Confucian Dynamism (Bond, 1996). His business goals were defined in terms of quality and customer satisfaction: to be the best in all of China and Asia was a definite possibility. Zorro used the business plan to measure possible mergers and acquisitions. He defined business goals as finding the right companies and merging as key to succeed in the fast-changing technological environment. Lastly, Cara defined her business goals in terms of specific marketing plans to attract quality students and teachers: to be small but elite in providing their specific translation services.

The face of market socialism.

The incubator owner-managers discussed their businesses using the language of the new market socialism. They described their businesses in market terminologies even as they referred to policies that align with Chinese tradition. Cara, for example, went to elaborate means to keep the secret that hers is a family-owned business, yet readily states that when her brother needs her support, her alignment with him is unshakable.

The incubator micro-business structures reflected the embedded business values from China's past that re-emerge as a hybrid in their modern economy and society. For example, Alistair discussed the fact after he and his partners make a good deal of money that they will donate to charities. This is a practice he told us was derived from an old third century parable in Chinese literature.

The old beggar in the parable is really saving all his money to help the people of his village build a school. In Alistair's opinion this mythology carries considerable wisdom for Chinese society today.

Zorro described the familiar concept of capitalist small businesses clawing their way to the top and in the process pulling others down with them based on competitive fears within the society. While this idea is not entirely new, Zorro elevates the discussion about cooperation (Eastman, 1988; Huang, 2004) that once dominated Chinese thought. Cara on the other hand, still struggled to make her company grow by operating with an exciting and new family business model and expressed the need to stay on the pulse of what excites potential customers.

Differences Among the Incubator Micro-Business Owner-Managers

The notable differences within the incubator micro-businesses included professionalism and success and a strong degree of privacy.

Degrees of professionalism.

Alistair reflected the professionalism of a steadily increasing successful company in a stage of "takes off' (Sheff, 2002). From the beginning, Alistair aligned his business practices with those in standardized international markets, and profits had allowed him to hire at a higher official category of business operations. This professionalism was not as evident in Zorro's case, whose profitability in business still resided in his ties to local Chinese markets and sources of financial backing. Zorro shrewdly managed the company, but lacked the ability to grow with his current cadre. Cara's company was a fledgling at the extreme beginning of a start-up. There were no profits after 1 year and they hoped to expand into the Shenzhen area to gain other avenues. However, she noted that the overall professionalism of her company was being stretched too thin.

Degrees of privacy.

Cara's profile represents a sense of privacy among the incubator businesses that may stem from her specific business decisions and fears of competition. In a sense, Cara made her business more vulnerable to marketing problems by deciding not to be transparent about the qualifications of the principals. Hiding her brother's age for example, cuts the company off from free promotions and personality profiles in the newspapers. Hiding may also hamper their ability to associate within similar trade organizations. This sense of privacy seems to be driven by fear of competition. In the vast talent banks of China's universities, scores of possible competitors could be a real threat to them. However, this privacy practice, while it may serve some theoretical practical concept in the beginning, quickly loses its purpose as time goes on and leaves the organization with intractable, closed communication structures, difficult at best to navigate in the modern world.

Categories that Emerged from the Interview Analysis and Interpretation

The interviews produced several rounds of cross referencing of the conceptual framework to the transcripts and analysis of themes. These categories were also sorted for differences and similarities within the two types. These issue categories were also sorted for differences and similarities within the two types (Table 13).

Table 13

Issues Categorized from Interview Analysis

Business Type Owner	Categories of Issues from Interviews	Intra-Type Similarities	Intra-Type Differences
Ordinary Bebe Evanna Marty	Family Self-direction	Intellectual autonomy Personalized Business	Educated turn to merchant classes Migrant labor

	Intellectual freedom and flexibility	Motives	Manufacturing sector
	Confucian family ethics	Marketing challenges	Health as a value
	Markets and competition	Foreigners challenging their markets	Personal reputation
	East/west management styles	Confucian family business structures	Anchored in classical Chinese
	Foreign challenges to Chinese markets		
	Workers on the move		
	Quest for wealth		
	Changing blood ties		
Incubator Alistair Zorro Cara	Technology perspectives	Experimentation with new business structures	Multi-national Chinese corporation contracts
	Guanxi versus market forces	Market forces effect on guanxi	Critique of traditional business structures
	Social ecology	Non-conformist behaviors and attitudes	
	Competition as cooperation	Anchored in Chinese literature and views	Ecology tied to Chinese tradition
	Spirit of traditional society		Neo-nepotism
	New management roles/women		
	Chinese Neo-family-based company		

Source: Six Interviews with Chinese Micro-Business Owner-Managers

Intra-type Similarities and Differences Among the Ordinary Owner-Managers

When the three ordinary micro-business owner-managers discussed then-enterprises, they all cited highly personalized motives for what they were doing. One of the women had had a personal crisis. The other woman had been bored with teaching and stumbled into a professional opportunity. The young man was pursuing a dream he had had for several years to be, in effect, the Noodle King of Shenzhen.

All three discussed marketing as a skill in which they were weak, and they all felt, to varying degrees, that foreign products were challenging their markets. Also, each of them had Confucian family business structures, some with more and some with less extended business networks. Underneath it all, the three of them were unique intellectually autonomous individuals who felt free to experiment with their ideas about what they wanted from life.

Two of the ordinary owner-managers were local college-educated women, anchored in classical Chinese literature and values, both of whom had chosen to return to the entrepreneurial class to pursue the good life. However, one of these women highlighted her personal reputation as a professional designer and manufacturer, whereas the other one thought of herself principally as a merchant. The third owner-manager, a man, had migrated to Shenzhen with thousands of other laborers from a northern province, where he had only completed a high school education that had largely been inspired by socialist ideology. His main value priority was his health.

Intra-type Similarities and Differences of Incubator Owner-Managers

All three of these individuals were experimenting with new business structures in various ways, one with a democratic style of management, the second with joint ventures, and the third with a non-Confucian nuclear family business organization. Also, all three talked about how capitalist market forces are affecting guanxi relationships. The positive effects were that contracts were now being enforced by laws, that nepotism was being undermined, and that business deals were now being made more directly and efficiently. The negative effect was that it was difficult to overcome the forces and habits of guanxi relationships. All three were non-conformist individualists who advocated rebellious attitudes and positions. For example, one of them flatly refused to hire family members, which in traditional Chinese society is a radical notion. Finally, all three were inspired by ancient texts, Chinese parables, and modern writers who idealize the individual in China.

One owner-manager had highly favorable attitudes toward Chinese multi-national corporations, whose competition he found exciting. A second owner-manager, however, felt that these corporations fear change and taking risks with small entrepreneurs like himself. The third incubator owner-manager was not versed in international affairs and had no opinion on this subject.

Only one of these owner-managers was concerned about the ecological challenges facing China, feeling that the nation had to return to its ancient practices of agrarian resource management if it was going to prosper. One of the owner-managers devised a kind of neo-nepotism that placed extreme limits on family participation in her business, although her ways of handling business conflict were highly traditional.

Inter-Group Similarities, Differences, and Themes

There were many similarities and few differences between the two types of owner-managers that emerged from the interviews (Table 14). On the similarities side, all 6 interviewees were intent on expressing their intellectual freedom and flexibility, both in their business and personal lives. All 6 also provided services to customers, and 3 of them (1 ordinary and 2 incubator owner-managers) also manufactured products. Two interviewees in both categories mentioned wanting a "comfortable life" as part of their pursuit of wealth and happiness, and the same four interviewees discussed challenges to their businesses from foreign competitors and products. Two incubator and 2 ordinary owner-managers were concerned about their personal reputations impacting their businesses, using words like *honesty* and *reliability* to express how they wanted to be regarded. Four of the interviewees discussed what it was like to be an entrepreneur, but the 2 incubator owner-managers were wholly excited about this, while the 2 ordinary owner-managers were somewhat defensive because of traditional Chinese attitudes toward merchants.

On the differences side, the incubators were more technologically oriented in their discussions about everyday organizational issues. All three of them had a high-tech engineering-oriented vocabulary, whereas the three ordinary owner-managers spoke in more personal terms and never mentioned technology in any context. The incubators were focused on issues of mergers and acquisition of other companies, or their own company by others, which contrasted sharply to interviews with ordinary micro-businesses. The woman in the incubator was much younger than the other women.

Inter-Type Gender Issues

From the interviews, there were numerous ways in which the 2 types of micro-business owner-managers were different and similar by gender. Whether they were ordinary micro-business owners or incubators, the women tended to be more concerned with issues of security than were the men, a point Zhang (2001) noted. Bebe was the most secure of the three women, but was still haunted by the time in her life when employers had restricted her freedom. Evanna had clearly been violated by a foreign competitor who had stolen her designs, so she was, at the time of the interview, on "high alert" against patent threats. Cara feared that her teachers would leave and take her company's trade secrets with them, so she had a quasi-paranoid style, which was also reflected in her hiding the fact that her business partner was her brother. Of course, she was the only 1 of the 6 who was not directly creating the product or service of her company, for which she was totally dependent on her brother.

Table 14

Inter-Group Similarities, Differences and Themes

Inter-group Similarities	Inter-group Differences
Intelletual freedom and flexibility	Technology sector issues
Foreign challenges to Chinese markets	Megers and acquisitions
Reputation	Inter-type Gender differences
"Comfortable Life" business goals as part of quest for wealth	
Emerging status of the merchant classes	
Service sector	
Manufacturing sectors	

Discussion Themes from the Interviews

The final thematic analyses of the interview issues were integrated into the discussion chapter of the overall study which ties into key concepts from the cross-cultural, international development, and Chinese socio-economic foundational literature. The findings, analysis and interpreted topics and issues from interviews were examined for similarities and differences then synthesized into the following four integral themes: (a) Chinese intellectual and organizational freedom; (b) business motivations and goals; (c) macro-economic forces and Chinese market socialism; and (d) international development ethics complementing Confucian ethics.

The following chapter integrates Schwartz's (1999) conceptual values framework and work considering the results from both quantitative and qualitative sections of this study, and considering any lingering biases, produces a discussion of the overall results of the study.

CHAPTER FIVE

DISCUSSIONS

Chinese Urban Micro-Business Owner-Managers Values, Dynamics and Developmentalism

This chapter discusses Schwartz's (2000) cross-cultural values framework as it was applied to this study to micro-business owner-managers and the interpreted contextual themes based on 6 interviews with typical owner-managers. The statistical link from the survey data to the interview data will be discussed and then related to important foundational literature from cross-cultural communication theory (Kim, 2002; Ting-Toomey, 1999), the Chinese business theories of Tang and Parish (2000), the idea of "developmentalism" based on Castells' (2000) China analysis, and Sen's (1992) economic theory of consequentialism.

The importance of general values and specific contexts from interviews for comparisons in this study provided a range of discussions of Chinese socioeconomic development and processes. The integration of these methods, in my view, constitute a dynamic cross-cultural, East-West discussion of perspectives and contribute, in part, to the overall perception of western influences on international development practices. Upon closer observations of the ways in which owner-managers adapt to everyday customs, practices, scripts, and norms that they encounter, the cross-cultural values framework used in this study creates a montage of the socioeconomic life of modern China.

Discussion of Survey Rationale and Findings

From the SVS cross-cultural values survey the individual and cultural scores of the owner-managers measured their motivational goals based on the question: "What principles guide YOU in YOUR life?" (p. 1). In my own interviews, I turned this question into three: (a) "What are your business strengths and weaknesses?" (b) "What are your business attitudes and influences?" and (c) "What is your ethical outlook?"

Schwartz (2000) contended that the three requirements for individuals in societies to function are (a) cooperative relations among members of a group, (b) motivation of individuals to invest their cognitive functioning in ways that work to solve problems and to generate new ideas, and (c) self-gratification of an individual's desires. Schwartz (1996) placed these basic requirements into four orthogonal domains that were both oppositional and complementary.

The individual values of Chinese urban micro-business owner managers that emerged from the SVS survey data in this study can be structured along Schwartz and Sagiv's (1995) orthogonal domains of Conservation and Openness to Change, on the one hand, and Self-Enhancement and Self-Transcendence, on the other (Figure 3).

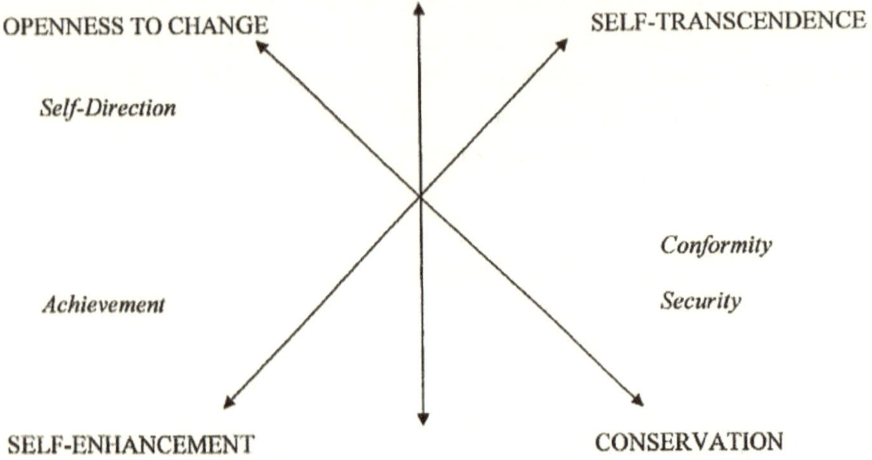

Figure 3. The structure of Chinese urban owner-manager values along orthogonal dimensions.

Value Domains

The top values of the owner-managers primarily fell into three of the four value domains: conservation, self-enhancement, and openness to change. The survey data showed that the ideal micro-business owner-managers had a consensus of their individual and cultural value priorities.

Individual values.

The Schwartz and Sagiv's framework (1995) had identified the 10 "near-universal" individual value dimensions that have oppositional and complementary structures, but are important because they are trans-situational and remain in the same basic configuration and overlapping motivational goals. For example, power overlaps the dimensions of security and achievement (Figure 4).

Of supreme importance is *Security* (safety, harmony, and stability of society, of relationships, and of self), followed by highly important *Achievement* (personal success through demonstrating competence according to social standards) and *Conformity* (restraint of actions, inclinations, and impulses likely to upset or harm others and violate social expectations or norms) values. They also placed importance on *Self-Direction* (independent thought and action—choosing, creating, exploring).

In the discussion that follows the values in the model describes the meaning of the four highest priority values of the owner-managers.

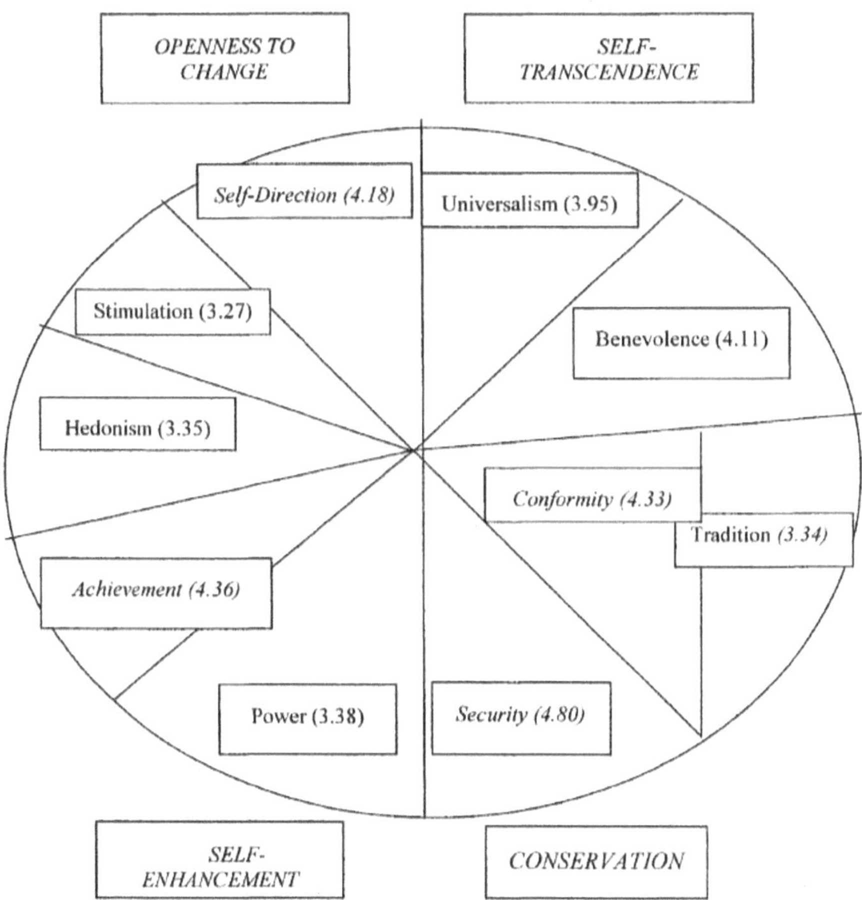

Figure 4. The structure of values among Chinese urban ordinary and incubator micro-business owners.

Based on "Identifying culture-specifics in the content and structure of values, *Journal of Cross-cultural Psychology*, 26(1):96. Copyright 1995 by S. H. Schwartz and L. Sagiv. Used with permission of the authors.

Security as family and social stability.

Security in the form of family and social stability is central to the identity of most Chinese urban micro-business owner-managers. Chinese businesses have been structured around family networks for centuries (Biggart, 1997). They may feel family (the equivalent in Chinese of "society") stability to be an important context for their business survival. For example, in general, it is difficult for micro-businesses to obtain loans. Thus, micro-business owner-managers must take out personal loans, which, as described in one of the interviews is often an onerous task, even if the company is generating substantial profits and potential. Most likely they will ask for family loans that may have other conditions or obligations attached.

In terms of social stability, these fledgling businesses often face a tenuous economic life. Running a micro-business is a considerable investment of time and effort, and yet owner-managers often must operate on the margins of their potential services and manufacturing sectors depending on their business networks and skills. Socially, micro-business owners may not feel assured that their property will not be unfairly appropriated by the government, they will not be too overburdened with taxes, and the exchange rates will not fluctuate much. Their security then rests with those connections of family that provide one sure safety net when all else fails.

Achievement as learned group behavior

Although some suggest the Chinese character eschews personal achievement for the good of the collective

(Hofstede, 1983), high scoring on individual values placed on achievement, for the sake of the collective, run strong in Chinese education and thinking. Achievement values for micro-business owners may also have been important in developing their business networks, developing skills to deal with crisis, and achieving success in a competitive environment. Bond and Hofstede (1988) referred to this phenomenon as "Confucian dynamism," which changed to "long-term and short-term thinking" (Kulich, 2004). In particular, the achievement value relates directly to values held by teachers and students in China.

Social transformations that manifest through the society place greater value on those who achieve higher returns for their levels of education and acquired experience. Increased education may also help people develop skills for task-oriented problem-solving (such as the common issue of how to hire and manage workers) and may facilitate technical innovation that leads to increased creativity and boosts social and economic productivity.

The achievement-motivated values may help explain the importance placed on mastery as the highest rated cultural value in this sample. High mastery values signal a society more readily able to compete and exploit advantages.

Conformity as a positive value.

Values placed on conformity in the West are likely to be interpreted as acquired responses to demands of maintaining the status quo (Schwartz, 2000). Conformity insinuates "sanctions" for self-control, risk avoidance, controlling forbidden impulses, and fulfilling needs oriented to the whole, and not the self. While these restrictions may seem to interfere with certain motivations, innovative ideas, and problem solving, participants in Chinese micro-businesses, a rather optimistic group, scored relatively high on conformity as opposed to tradition. This is noteworthy because it appears conformity can be interpreted in several ways: (a) conforming to the traditional rules of society; and (b) non-conformity within the traditional society, but conforming according to local norms (Schwartz, 2001a). Historically, micro-business owner-managers in storefronts and shop have been on the margins of Chinese may not perceive themselves as benefiting from traditional norms, although they may conform to local micro-business norms (Kulich, 2004; Triandis, 1993; Trompenaars & Hampden-Turner,1998).

Conformity is viewed in this sense to contribute positively to the society, like an expectation to help a stranger in the West (Bond & Yang, 1982)

Self-Direction as intellectual autonomy.

In the early part of the 20th century, Chinese social thought increasingly emphasized personal freedom and ideas balanced with social harmony. The legacy of the May 4th Movement (1919) and blossoming of Chinese republican democracy, was followed by war (1937), communism (1956), and the Cultural Revolution (1966).

Micro-business owner-managers in the current market reform era (1976-present), show high priorities of self-direction and a concern for personal freedoms that may have re-emerged in the form of economic motivations and goals. This flexibility to decide includes speaking, worshipping, and living as one chooses (Yang, 1995). The strong priority placed on self-direction values explains the importance this study sample placed on the individual survey items of "choosing one's own goals," while still placing a high value on overall security.

The more educated micro-business owners scored especially high on intellectual autonomy and self-direction, and were somewhat lower on conformity. Interestingly, as these owner-managers matured in age, they tended to show greater affective autonomy, or the pragmatic emphasis of one's ideas.

Gender and power issues.

The women in this study, like many in their country, talked about their power among the women as it relates to the greater society. Much of their power had to do with their education and the rising economic expectation levels of Chinese
women. By expressing their localized concerns as owner-managers, like those of other types of class struggles, the women related more to their internal reinvention of their role as women in business organizations. This reorganization of the traditional role of Chinese women in the economy took place during such key historical periods as the May fourth Movement and the Communist Revolution. Therefore, it is not, perhaps, an identification with other feminist struggles outside of China. Rather, in this study micro-business, women talked about their business values from their perspectives "as a Chinese woman," as an aesthetic right.

Alignment of Individual and Cultural Values

Schwartz (1996) used individual values of teachers and students as the cultural representatives of nations worldwide based on their literacy, the abundance of teachers and students in national populations, and their role as carriers of cultural values in their societies. For discussion purposes, I placed the hierarchy (rank) of individual values using the total sample of Chinese urban micro-business owner-managers' individual values compared with the hierarchy (rank) of mainland Chinese teacher and student values. These findings reveal individual values that connect to social-cultural information (Table 15).

The top three values of the total sample of Chinese micro-business owner-managers, on average, placed greatest priority on social stability (security, 1st). This was followed by a high importance placed on seeking success according to social standards (achievement, 2nd) and on avoiding disruption of social relationships for owner-managers (conformity, 3rd). The top three values of Chinese teachers and students, on average, placed greatest priority on seeking success according to social standards (achievement, 1st) followed by a high importance on autonomy in thinking and acting (self-direction, 2nd) emphasizing social stability and harmonious social relationships (security, 3rd).

Table 15
Chinese Micro-business Owner-Managers and Chinese Teachers and Students Values

N = 197 Chinese Micro-business Owner-Managers	M	Mean Rank	n = 1054 Mainland Chinese Teachers/Students (T = 589/S = 417)	M	Mean Rank
Security	(4.80)	1	Achievement	(4.50)	1
Achievement	(4.36)	2	Self-Direction	(4.48)	2
Conformity	(4.33)	3	Security	(4.42)	3
Self-Direction	(4.18)	4	Benevolence	(4.16)	4
Benevolence	(4.11)	5	Universalism	(4.06)	5
Universaligm	(3.95)	6	Conformity	(4.03)	6
Power	(3.38)	7	Hedonism	(3.15)	7
Hedonism	(3.35)	8	Power	(3.41)	8
Tradition	(3.34)	9	Stimulation	(2.92)	9
Stimulation	(3.27)	10	Tradition	(2.55)	10

Chinese urban micro-business owner-managers also placed importance on their autonomy in thinking and acting (self-direction, 4th) and their motivational goals for cooperation and supportive social relationships (benevolence, 5th) and extended these concerns to others outside of their group membership (universalism, 6th). Chinese teachers and students placed importance on their internalized motivational goals for cooperation and supportive social relations (benevolence, 4th) which they too extended to others outside of their group (universalism, 5th) in order to avoid disruption of social relationships (conformity, 6th). Both the Chinese micro-business owner-managers and Chinese teachers/students rated less important the values of power (7th and 8th), and hedonism (8th and 7th), tradition (9th and 10th), and stimulation (10th and 9th), and to varying degrees.

In this comparison, the hierarchy of values ranked in order from 1-4 satisfy Schwartz's basic requirements for cooperative relations among members of a group which motivate individuals to invest their intelligence and work toward solving problems and to generating new ideas. Values ranked in order from 5 and 6 reflect near-universal values among these two samples and throughout other nations (Schwartz, 2001b). The values ranked in order from 7-10 show there is a lesser importance on self- gratification between the teacher/student and micro-business owner-manager samples, although the teachers and students expect slightly more gratification than the owner-managers.

The Schwartz framework also identified seven cultural values that have oppositional and complementary structures relating to (a) the desired behaviors that preserve the social structure; (b) the relationship to the natural and social environment; (c) the relationship between the individual and the group; and (d) the individualist and collectivist perspectives and ways of communicating.

Based on their scores in the cultural dimension, these study's owner-managers can be described as basically assertive, change-oriented individuals willing to exploit natural and social environments (mastery). Owner-managers also assigned high importance behaviors that transcend self to promote the well-being of others (egalitarianism) and is opposite to hierarchical, unequal power distributions. The owner-managers place a high priority on their uniquely bounded individualism and autonomy as thinkers (intellectual autonomy). The owner-managers were basically individualistic but, overall, they prefer the close family relationships and extended families of their collectivist culture.

Discussion of the Interview Rationale and Findings

The interview data suggest that the study participants were also concerned with various levels of family business security, achievements based on moral goals, positive aspects of social conformity, and self-direction. As a whole, these owner-managers could be described as non-conformist individuals operating within a traditional society. The deeper meanings and differences on the placement of their value priorities tapped into related questions on their ethical outlooks.

I examined the 6 interviews for similarities and differences for the intra-group, inter-group, and collective perspectives. I then synthesized these perspectives into the following four themes: (a) Chinese intellectual and organizational freedom; (b) business motivations and goals; (c) macro-economic forces in Chinese market socialism; and (d) international development ethics complemented by Confucian business ethics. I looked at these themes through the lens of Schwartz's (1992) universal theory of values and relevant works by Kim (2002), Tang and Parish, (2000), Castells (2002), and Sen (1999).

Chinese intellectual and organizational freedom.

Chinese intellectual and organizational freedom, as represented in the values survey and the interviews of this study, revealed that "intellectual freedom" in China is based on a foundation of family security. This contrasts with the usual Western interpretation of intellectual freedom as the province of autonomous individuals.

All but 1 of the 6 interviewees discussed their intellectual freedom in terms of security, which ranged from personal to national to international spheres. Two of the three incubator owner-managers extended their discussions of security to the goals of society, such as issues of world peace, and protection of the environment. All 3 of the ordinary owner-managers spoke mainly in terms of the security of their families and businesses.

Chinese organizational freedom is also based on this secure extension out from a family structure or network of structures. China is commonly regarded in the West as a collectivist nation, an idea that goes back to cross-cultural attempts to categorize worldwide cultures. Hofstede (1983) developed the concept of an "individualist" West versus a "collectivist" East. Recently, Kim's (2002) cross-cultural work has added to the importance of distinguishing individualist and collectivist behaviors within each culture and its institutional organizations. Her cross-cultural descriptions provide concrete information about the nature of what is meant by Chinese intellectual and organizational freedom.

Kim (2002) used a non-Western approach called "self-construals," according to which individuals reflect their essential duality in the production of their identity and meaning. Interdependent Eastern cultures, such as China, promote a fundamental connectedness between the individual and his or her group. Identity is complete only after an individual joins the group and acquires "communication competence." Individuals in interdependent cultures often refer to goals in terms of "strategies of avoiding losses and fulfilling obligations" (p. 154), rather than achieving objectives. When predominantly interdependent individuals move to the self-construal of independence, they achieve self-enhancement through such "independent" strategies as entering contractual agreements and forging relationships based on contractual terms. Even so, they engage others through security-minded prevention strategies they learn from their culture.

In other words, the Chinese owner-managers' intellectual and organizational freedom is based primarily on their sense of security and the positive benefits of conformity. This is not surprising, since 4 out of the 6 interviewees came through periods of harsh political repression.

As interdependent individuals micro-business owner-managers may tend to use their intuition more than do independent individuals. For example, anticipating another's needs is a highly developed art form in most interdependent cultures (Kim, 2002). In addition, interdependent individuals use silence, rhythm, and timing to control what happens in negotiated situations, and they will most likely be judged accordingly by their peers. Chinese participants use parables and complex tales to drive home a point, the subtleties of which are often lost on predominantly independent individuals.

This kind of flux can be seen in the 6 interviews. For example, the interviewees were cautious and security-minded but had a deep sense of satisfaction about overseeing their own lives, especially regarding their professional achievements. One owner-manager, when asked how she develops plans, responded that she does this by cautiously "planning for times when business is not so good." Another manager catches himself in boasting about his financial success, which he realizes is maybe "not a bad thing to be ambitious," then he retracts that statement. Several owner-managers spoke of the sense of freedom they had "to wear many different hats" in the course of operating their businesses. While all 6 strove for excellence in their chosen work, their ambition was tempered by a traditional flux of Chinese notions of modesty and moderation. All 6 interviewees had a broad notion of organizational freedom, from the hours they kept to trying out popular Western management techniques. The 3 women, however, expressed a desire for greater privacy in their business affairs. The 3 men, on the other hand, desired greater excitement.

Lin Yutang (1935/1998), however, argued that the Chinese are not truly interdependent people, but rather independent. "The Chinese," he wrote, "are a nation of individualists. They are family-minded, not social-minded, and the family mind is only a form of magnified selfishness. It is curious that the word 'society' does not exist as an idea in Chinese thought" (p. 169). Perhaps it is Kim (2002) herself who resolved this apparent contradiction when she stated that all individuals in all cultures are always simultaneously interdependent and independent, depending on their situation and circumstance. In his theory of cultural values, Schwartz (1994a) described the degrees to which individuals are "embedded" in a group as opposed to becoming a "part of the social fabric" (p. 94). One's ability to master one's universe, which includes the welfare of others, including the weakest in society, determines the quality of one's life. Mastery is tied to individual values of achievement, often seen in business motivations and goals.

Business Motivations and Goals of the Chinese Micro-Business

The business motivations and goals described by the Chinese micro-business owner-managers showed them motivated by change, grounded in familial business structures upon which they set specific, and in general, quite optimistic economic goals. According to Tang and Parish (2000) what drives the current Chinese urban economy is the influx of information from international, macro-economic forces and socialist egalitarian views of the government through its media. In keeping with Kim's (2002) terms, the former "individualist" views are harvested largely from outside of the country and add to the independent self-construal of the population, while the latter interdependent views are produced inside the nation and added to the self-construal of interdependence in the population. Chinese businesses stay motivated through their relational networks.

This study revealed that even in "market-driven southern China" as seen in the city of Shenzhen, family firms are highly personalized, adaptable, and are ruled by, or are in the likeness of a central authority. The Confucian family, of course, is and remains the basic social and business unit. Loyalty to the family is the basis of all trust relationships, and all acknowledgement of one's reputation is in relationship to one's family loyalty. This family structure is extended through networks of kin and reciprocal relationships of *guanxixue.*

This grounding in familial business structures can be seen from the self-reported values of conformity and through interview experiences of the micro-business owner managers in this study, although their experiences varied in the degree to which they categorized their learning as organizational or personal. For example, one of the interviewees manufactured and sold products in contract with regional, national, and multinational companies. She downplayed the idea of actually "innovating' products even though her product designs were quite unparalleled. Her business strength was in the flexible adaptation of a specific prototype, an evolutionary, trend-defining process. Another focused on his personal goals of merging his business with another company in order to increase access to market opportunities. These kinds of organizational competencies were central to information and knowledge sharing along the multiple sets of business networks among the interviewees.

The business goals among the micro-business owner-managers related to their high priorities assigned to achievement and self-direction values comprised of practical, economic success. Four were within reach of sufficient earnings and on their way to becoming "middle-class." Their earnings, they informed me, were "comfortable" to their specific business situations, and their expectations were in keeping with the returns they expected from their success. They spoke in terms of prevailing standards of middle-class acquisitiveness: technology, cars, and homes.

The general optimism I found among the micro-business owner-managers, based on their higher cultural scores for the values of mastery and egalitarianism, at first seemed to be generated from the widespread effect of market transformation in society.

Liberal markets had a strong appeal to all the owner-managers who were interviewed, an appeal championed by the socialist government for nearly 2 decades. Zhang (2001) stressed that this appeal may be softening, based less on structural economic changes and more on historical experiences, internalized within the country such as the "push" for displaced workers to start small *getihu* businesses that could support families and a widespread movement of workers to various regions for purposes of inexpensive labor. Tang and Parish (2000) described the motivation and goals of the veritable micro-business explosion of the mid-1990s, an "erosion from the bottom" (p. 82) as the bureaucratic state-run companies started to collapse in the late1980s.

Despite the international ideal of a "morally neutral market," businesses in Chinese society remain embedded in their business institutions through networks, organizational structures, and memberships (Chinese Culture Connection, 1987). These structures are often tested for their reliability and meeting the shared goals interests of the network. Castells (2000) called this "network logic" a process so entrenched in Chinese business relationships that "market logic" is often a secondary consideration. Legal contracts are merely "guidelines" that inform an overall deeper relationship.

Macro-Economic Forces in Chinese Market Socialism

The current macro-economic forces in China have been affected by foreign direct investment, mostly from overseas Chinese investors and other large international economic institutions such as the IMF and World Bank for nearly 3 decades. The infusion of market forces corresponds with the rise of state-sanctioned market socialism.

Currently, the micro-businesses start-ups, those in high-tech incubators, increasingly require regulated and impartial responses to contingencies that occur when they enter business negotiations in local and foreign markets. Interviewees spoke about the relief of not always having to do business through traditional Chinese style banqueting, rather based on the merit of managements and deliverables of the firm. The growing expectation of market "neutrality" puts the highly personalized business networks such as those in Asia in a position that requires great adaptability of their entrenched structures in order to harness market opportunities and avoid market pitfalls.

Historically, China's family-owned businesses have been distrustful of the state. Trust is placed in consanguinity and regional, conditional business network affiliates. However, since the last few decades of the 20th century, the role of the state in China provided political support and financial assistance to help Chinese business networks to grow into competing, globally profitable entities. Castells (2000) used the term "the developmental state," to describe China's current communist regime:

A state is developmental when it establishes as its principle of legitimacy its ability to promote and sustain development, understanding by development the combination of steady high rates of economic growth and structural change in the economic system, both domestically and in its relationship to the international economy. When such a societal project involves a fundamental transformation of the social order, I refer to it as a revolutionary state, based on revolutionary legitimacy, regardless of the degree of internalization of such legitimacy by its subjects, for example the Communist party state. When the societal project carried forward by the state respects the broader parameters of social order -1 consider it to be a developmental state, (p. 198)

Castells' (2000) argument, that the "historical expression" of China's developmental turn by the communist state, is a growing Chinese national identity, culture, and re-emergence in the world as a powerful nation, based on these developmental economic. In this study, the term "developmental" best describes the truth of the situation for micro-business owner-managers as shared goals between them and the state.

A key component of this developmentalism is the ways in which the family-based networks endure market socialism. In his opinion, the family network-based structures of China and other Asian countries resemble the most dominant organizational feature of what he called the "new information society" based on the concept of "network logic" (p. 17). Network logic has the consistency and flexibility to suggest that more local businesses will try to walk the fine line of broadening market participation within the state's guidelines, while retaining familial controls. Some micro-businesses would remain outside of these government institutions because of the historical contradictions that are imposed from the center. For those family business networks that operate within the existing institutional guidelines, there are ways to exploit the grey areas left by the state by enhancing their local networks, for example through banking centers, to increase "loose" affiliations with others in order to remain flexible, and to diversify.

International Development Ethics Complemented by Confucian Business Ethics

International development ethics and Confucian ethics would at first seem to collide. Sen (1999), who won the Nobel Prize for his work on the nature of economic well-being, wrote about the complexity of the ancient collective cultures colliding with modern Western liberalist economies. Economic liberalism, according to Sen (1999), requires unlimited accumulation of wealth and growth. Market socialism, so far, has required incremental accumulations and unlimited growth. In both cases, the consequences of unlimited growth may breach social contracts.

The micro-business owner-managers in the study described a newfound or strengthened sense of individualism from starting their own companies. Several described this freedom as tied to a greater societal motivation. One owner-manager, for example, stated that he and his partners felt like their company was "nearly democratic" in its structure, except for the fact that the oldest and most experienced partner in the firm was like the "godfather." Part of this new freedom allowed the owner-managers to take responsibility for giving back to society in unique and creative ways.

On the one hand, international development ethics contains economic variables that relate to broad-based intellectual and organizational freedoms, protections, and rights. On the other hand, Confucian business is a hybrid of familial customs and ideals provided by traditional culture, but recently modified, in China, by socialist revolutionary ideals. International development ethics seemed peripheral to the everyday lives of the micro-businesses owner-managers in the study, whereas Confucian business ethics are embedded in the culture. Therefore, the more the owner-managers were engaged with larger markets and selling to larger companies, the more their Confucian ethics seemed to recede.

There were only a small number of discourses among the interviewees on the need to socialize the nation for the purpose of mutual economic aid. These conversations came up in the context of something that may be lost if attention is not paid to the greater social welfare of the country, or when an ancient ethic had been lost and needed to be regained.

In the context of an urgent search, international development ethics and Confucian business ethics were complementary.

Summary Implications of the Survey and Interview Discussions

Schwartz's (2003,2004) survey and evolving analytical framework, while validated for mainland China (2003), is still a western model and usually interpreted based on western understanding of the individual, identity, cultural views, and their meanings. This western interpretive practice is relevant to this study since the instrument will be oriented towards the original meanings of the values based on Schwartz's definitions and interpretations. The relevance of gathering interview data from the study sample provided the survey data with interpretations of the contexts and meanings of owner-manager lives through a cross-cultural, or even perhaps a bi-cultural lens, whenever possible.

Micro-business owner-managers placed priority on security and conformity values that can be interpreted as their personal need to maintain harmonious social relations among group members. Harmonious relationships depend on the strategies they use to avoid social conflicts and defiance of group norms. These security-conformity values give the owner-managers a long-term view of the actual circumstances of then-business situations because, as has been described, the forces of the international macro economy and institutionalization of market socialism in the country remain in a "developmental" dynamic. The flexibility seen in these businesses is a deeply ingrained cultural feature of Chinese small businesses (Huang, 2004; Tang & Parish, 2000). It will most likely remain an important feature in the socialist market economy. The reason for this is the way in which Chinese businesses adapt and diversify as they become successful in their extended networks. There is, perhaps, a chance that some of this business flexibility may be hampered by some government regimes trying to control the private markets, or from an influx of bureaucrats and academics into the private market bringing different "institutional" structures. It is difficult to predict how well these controls would work in the actual circumstance.

Cultural priorities of Chinese teachers and college students placed highest importance on meeting and mastering skills. This could be the ancient influence of Confucian academies that required a broad competency in five primary subjects. The comparison of Chinese teachers and students to micro-business owner-mangers showed that universal socialist education in China aims students towards achieving the highest levels. Individuals are expected to attain success, not so much for personal fulfilment, but in order to attain the nation's goals, a moral phenomenon. Education provides the Chinese citizen with the social standards of success.

The educational project of Communism is carried forward in the new socialist market economy that pushes students to be the best in sciences, technology, and information. Micro-business owner-managers in this study who had higher education levels had moved into the private sector because of the rewards both in monetary and work satisfaction. The issues of social status and work seem to recede in importance as these owner-managers became successful according to the new cultural standards.

The combined quantitative and qualitative data in this study showed that Chinese urban micro-business owner-managers, while preserving their deeply rooted traditions, behave in revolutionary ways and see themselves as moving their society forward toward a new re-emergence of power based on their economy. To a Western outsider, some assert, China may appear to want to become a new America, but this study suggests that micro-business owner-managers are not thinking or feeling that way. The interviews substantiate that this study's participants are deeply engaged in theoretical and practical reforms of themselves and their businesses, ultimately for their nation.

The interviewed micro-business owner-managers described their overall values and the ways in which they handled them daily. In some instances, they moved forward and tried new business models, and at other times they proceeded slowly and backtracked in order to assess progress before moving forward once again. The market-based economy, for them, appears to be simultaneously family-based and private, socialist and capitalist, representing, as they see it, China's best prospects for the future.

CHAPTER SIX

SUMMARY, CONCLUSIONS, and RECOMMENDATIONS

Chinese Micro-Business Owner-Manager's Value Alignment and Adaptations to International Development Ethics

Summary

This study was based on the premise that urban micro-businesses, often viewed as the economic engines for growth in both developed and developing nations, are associated with concurrent changes in social values and provide fertile ground for studying change in global economics. This study examined the individual and cultural value priorities of two types of urban micro-business owner-managers in China: 108 ordinary store-front owners and 89 government-sponsored high-tech "incubator" owners who receive subsidized rent for 3 years during their start-ups. This revealed some of the subtle individual values related, in part, to China's emerging socialist market economy.

In 2004, 197 micro-business owner-managers from Shenzhen, China, completed the Mandarin Chinese version of the Schwartz (2003) Values Survey and subsequently 10 owner-managers were interviewed.

The values rated as most important were security, conformity, achievement, self-direction, followed by benevolence, and then, universalism, power, hedonism, tradition, and stimulation. These ratings are slightly different from Chinese teacher and student individual value priorities, This indicates that there may be sectors of the Chinese society contesting individual value priorities. Within the sample, I was able to quantify and describe the values and motivational goals of two types of micro-businesses that had types of micro-businesses that had emerged from the pilot. These were ordinary and incubator micro-businesses. These groups presented some unique characteristics for study including their social status, general locations and contexts. Ordinary micro-business owner-managers in neighborhood storefronts valued privacy and choosing one's own goals more than the incubator micro-business owner-managers whose businesses were housed in high technology buildings and who tended to value stimulation more and security less than did those in ordinary micro-businesses.

Compared to their counterparts in incubator micro-businesses, the ordinary micro-business owner-managers preferred choosing their own goals and privacy, expressing the view that larger companies did not give them the freedom they needed, possibly including freedom to innovate. On the other hand, participants in incubators seemed to place relatively higher emphasis on stimulation, which incubator locations may, in fact, provide due to the environment of information sharing and international trade opportunities.

The findings suggest that both types of Chinese urban micro-business owner-managers were concerned with balancing social order in terms of conformity with self-direction, but that greater education and more experience in business may motivate them toward these more self-oriented goals. As these owner-managers become more self-directed, the degree of consensus in their values may diminish both among themselves and relative to government values. Although the Chinese government is currently supporting market reform, it is unclear concerning the ways in which it will deal with changes in self-enhancement oriented individuals in the society.

For example, it is uncertain if the government will still support micro-businesses as they become more hedonistic, a domain of self-enhancement values.

Six qualitative interviews asked specific questions about the micro-business owner-manager's business behaviors, influences, attitudes, and ethical outlook. Most interviewees described the importance of intellectual freedom and choosing their own business goals. These value priorities and thematic discussions reflect the complex social and economic orientations among micro-business owner-managers in China and what they may imply about attitudes and behaviors in the nation's emerging middle class.

Conclusions

The SVS values survey of the Chinese urban micro-business owner-managers examined in this study provided a small slice of Chinese business society in what some argue is a post- reform era. Due to their sheer numbers, owner-managers of micro-businesses in China will likely begin to influence the general culture through their emergence into the ranks of the growing Chinese middle-class.

In the interview cases, micro-business owner-managers retained many of the norms of traditional Chinese family organizational structures, but those in these cases tended to be willing to extend these family networks in new directions (Schwartz & Bardi, 2004). This could be seen in very concrete ways—for example, in the ways they instituted hiring employees from outside their own families and how they used international laws to protect their rights in national and international markets.

Among the 6 interviewees, the incubator owner-managers were largely part of the officially accepted technocrats who were moving from state-owned companies and university departments to found private, high-tech incubator start-ups. The ordinary owner-managers resembled the Western model of "self-made" individuals and were largely disaffected either by intellectually dead-end careers or by economic lures to migrate.

Yet, the ideals of all the owner-managers appeared to be slightly more interdependent and culturally bound than one would expect in the West. Most of the interviewees discussed their achievements in terms of meeting their economic goals in the context of new market socialist goals, accomplishments that appeared to be motivated by their own sense of self-direction, but are seen in the values of the nation as a whole.

The issues, however, proved complex. The micro-businesses offered a consensus on overlapping security/conformity dimensions and achievement/self-direction dimensions. The socialist state, often the intersection of the first, more conservative dimensions, may have been the impetus for the pulls and pressures, tensions and turbulences in the other more open dimensions. The democratizing processes of international development ethics is one of the powerful pulls, but will also instill other, including opposite, Confucian tendencies. For example, there may be more of a plurality of beliefs fostered under democratic-styles of economic reforms. In turn, the familiar cultural hierarchies may be adapting to these reforms.

Whether economic development is planned by micro-business owner-managers themselves or by the state, it turns out that Sen's (1999) idea of well-being is quite adaptable to individual goals and motivations. Indeed, the consequences of China's current incarnation of the reform era has been a period of breakneck speed experiments, mid-course corrections, and adaptations, all that makes economic life for the micro-businesses in these reforms crave some security (Schumacher, 1975).

Based on these combined data sets, the values study of Chinese urban micro-business owner-managers provided perspectives on international development ethics in the new socialist market economy, and in terms of what the people want.

Recommendations

Because of this summary and conclusions, the following recommendations are made. If the SVS is the sole instrument used in a cross-cultural study, some form of exit interview should augment it to assess the impact of such surveys on micro-business owner-managers. There is strong evidence from this study's pilot exit interviews (Appendix 11) that micro-business owner-managers, though somewhat difficult to attract as participants in the study, were highly likely to find benefits in completing the SVS survey. In many instances, the exercise made them feel as if their thoughts on the state of the world mattered. The survey also provided a break from the owner-managers' daily routines and inspired them to think in fresh ways.

In addition, qualitative interview research on urban Chinese micro-businesses should be conducted on a much larger scale, with far more participants, in order to obtain a more precise measure of their values. This kind of research should allow ways for any number of illiterate and semi-literate Chinese micro-business owner-managers (although rare) to participate.

Implications for ordinary micro-businesses.

The question of how ordinary storefront owner-managers needs further study regarding the ways in which they affect local values, and what occurs when these businesses face competition from foreign market competition. The use of values surveys, especially the SVS, which focuses on personal and cultural guiding
principles, is a rarity in the Chinese business community. Thus, I recommend an assessment of the business values in China that can contribute to the understanding of what Chinese micro-businesses need to do to prosper and grow even more. To retrieve this information, I suggest that the demographic page of the SVS be modified to include several questions specific to ordinary micro-business finances, hiring practices, and looking ahead, include questions on their awareness of sustainable environmental issues.

Implications for incubator micro-businesses.

Studies should also examine business associations that provide loans and management to promote incubator micro-business development. The adniinistrators of high technology incubators could invite entrepreneurs from other parts of the world to incubate businesses in China. In that way, there would be more of a cross-fertilization of ideas and marketing practices.

Recommendations for additional and future research.

This study focused on the core values of China's micro-business owner-managers to understand how these values are representative of a growing segment of the Chinese business population; and the content of these values.

Apply other statistical methods to the research.

Now that this study has profiled the background and content of values among two types of urban Chinese micro-business owner-managers, additional research is needed to develop deeper insights into the effectiveness of micro-businesses in creating jobs. For example, it would be helpful to have multi-dimensional spatial analysis (SSA) of the individual and cultural values, which could then be used to understand long-term relationships in the sample.

Extend the scope of research

In addition, a study could be completed comparing teachers and students to micro-businesses controlled for demographics. These values could then be compared to the pan-cultural studies that are underway in various cross-cultural academic communities.

On the incubator side, of the 25 complexes in Shenzhen, the managers of only 14 agreed to let the survey be circulated to their tenants. More efforts to encourage participation will increase the research focus on that group's specific values.

Combine data collection instruments.

Illiteracy and unfamiliarity with formal written surveys may have been barriers to participation in this study. Kulich (2004) is testing a Chinese analogy supplement to the SVS in order to engage participants in the identification of their
values through a culturally consistent approach to talking about values (through analogy and parables). The combination of the Schwartz (2003) SVS and Kulich (2004) could improve the overall quality of the data collection.

Future research on micro-business owner-manager values.

Future research on urban Chinese micro-business owner-managers might be extended to other provinces of China beyond Shenzhen in order to gain a more representative sample of this socioeconomic sub-group. The sample could also be considerably larger than what was possible in this study with a lone researcher.

In addition, in the future, private associations might be surveyed to find out what unemployment alleviation groups are operated by local business groups. This kind of research would address the growing need to understand the social issues that accompany economic growth and coupled with wealth distribution in the nation. The data compiled in such studies might be used, for example, to track the allocation of private sector resources to the public sector in the form of philanthropy. The rising "third sector" in China offers quite a unique opportunity for scholarship.

Limits of the Study

In certain cases, participants may have provided socially desirable responses in order to accommodate perceptions of the researcher's expectations. This is also a common problem for researchers using survey methodology as described by Yang (1995) in her experiences with fieldwork in China. Less educated participants may also have felt intimidated by the language or structure of the surveys.

Another limit may have been the cross-cultural nature of the survey and interviews, which were conducted using Western methods and procedures. I approached this endeavor with the words of Lin Yutang (1935/1998) firmly in mind:

Indeed, the business of trying to understand a foreign nation with a foreign culture, especially one so different from one's own as China's, is usually not the for mortal man. For this work there is need for broad, brotherly feeling, for the feeling of the common bond of humanity and the cheer of good fellowship. One must feel with the pulse of the heart as well as see with the eyes of the mind.

There must be, too, a certain detachment, not from the country under examination, for that is always so, but from oneself and one's subconscious notions, and from the deeply embedded notions of one's childhood, and the equally tyrannous ideas of one's adult days, from those big words with capital letters like Democracy, Prosperity, Capital, and Success, and Religion and Dividends, (p.7)

Strengths of the study

This study had several strengths. Anecdotal reports showed that the study participants received the study in a positive light. Participants seemed to feel that it was timely to discuss personal values and the survey stimulated a lot of discussion, contributing to participants asking for copies of the survey to give to their friends and acquaintances. The SVS provided a well-validated survey instrument that permitted discussion of values in an international context, as well as permitting comparison of values within segments of one society.

The sample size of 197 micro-business owners was also appropriate to the purpose of the study and permitted a respectable investigation of values in two segments of Chinese society, comparing people working in ordinary and incubator micro-businesses, that has not had scrutiny in the research literature.

From A Cross-Cultural to Bidimensional Analysis

The exposure to multiple cultural encounters provided alternate ways for me as a researcher to cross the cultural chasms in China. The essential chasm standing between individualistic and collectivist societies such as a researcher from the U.S.A. in China, is the independent and interdependent self. The principles that "meet in the middle" of cross-cultural analysis can be used to identify when the researcher is acting bidimensionally.

Cultural cross-over.

Kim (2002) illustrated a West-East continuum of conceptions of the self, which I used for much of my self-reflection. Kim (2002) outlined several bidimensional principles in cross-cultural communication theory, the most important of which is to recognize that all individuals are simultaneously independent and interdependent (Appendix J). Therefore, as I continue to move between the West-East cultural systems it can lead to a systematic desensitization or a kind of "marginality." This desensitization is not a negative. For example, as a bicultural researcher, I was "desensitized" or took for granted many of the behaviors of the 6 interviewees and their "work" situations that I found myself in. My readers were often shocked, puzzled, or curious at what they considered the "rudeness" of someone scheduling an interview and not giving undivided attention. To me, these encounters were natural to China and the many informal "etiquettes of situations" I found myself in for the 4 years I lived there. It was clear that my "locus of control" could be defined as "other directed" - that is to say, the feelings of those helping with the study, the interpreters, and the interviewees, were my greatest concern.

Cultural tone.

It was important to me as a researcher to set the tone for each aspect of the study. I placed equal weight on confidentiality and efficiency goals for the survey as opposed to the interviews, where I placed more weight on specific contexts and situations as they emerged. There has been an attempt in this study to "mix" methods while both the quantitative survey and qualitative interview sections retain their research integrity.

The interview biases.

The interview section of the study results had bias principally because the interviewees volunteered, which sets a certain amount of bias from the outset. This self-selection allowed, perhaps, some amount of skew toward the more literate, and in some cases, the very curious among the sample participants. Due to the cross-cultural nature of the study, several methodological alternatives were incorporated in order to describe the rich contextual differences and the minute and subtle relationships of personality, attitudes, and behaviors of interviewees.

The bi-dimensionality of cross-cultural research

As a researcher, I brought bias to the study in terms of my socioeconomic research assumptions in terms of my role as an American scholar in China.

My overall research approach in the interviews stemmed from my personal view that cross-cultural researchers must be aware of and analyze for interview bias. In other words, I was aware that my being a female American scholar created a certain kind of power relationship with my interviewees. This was particularly true with respect to doing research in a developing country, and using a filter of translated conversation texts.

While I accept these biases, I found that through my bicultural personal life as an American woman married to a Chinese American, living with his elderly parents, having raised bicultural children, and having lived and worked in China, my acquired knowledge of the Chinese culture moved my scholarly position from a cross-cultural to a bicultural research. That is, rather than dealing with an alien culture, I was dealing with China, a culture that was already part of myself.

REFERENCES

Appelbaum, R. P. (2005). Fighting sweatshops: Problems of enforcing global labor standards. In R. P. Appelbaum & W. I Robinson (Eds.), *Critical globalization studies* (pp. 369-378). New York: Routledge.

Appelbaum R. P., & Robinson, W. I. (Eds.), (2005). *Introduction: Toward a critical globalization studies-Continued debates, new directions, neglected topics.* In R. P. Appelbaum & W. I Robinson (Eds.), *Critical globalization studies* (pp. xi-xxxiii). New York: Routledge.

Amin, S. (1995). Approver's testimony, judicial discourse: The case of Chauri Chaura. In S. Amin & M. Van der Linden (Eds.), *Peripheral labour: Studies in the history of partial proletarianization* (pp. 166-202). Cambridge, England: Cambridge University Press.

Apter, D., & Saich, T. (1994). *Revolutionary discourse in Mao's republic.* Cambridge, MA: Harvard University Press.

Arrighi, G. (1994). *The long 20th century: Money, power, and the origins of our times.* New York: Verso.

Arrighi, G. (1995, April 6). *The rise of East Asia and the withering away of the interstate system.* Paper presented at the session on Global Praxis and the Future of the World-System at the 90th Annual Meeting of the American Sociological Association, Washington, DC.

Arrighi, G., Hamashita, T., & Seiden, M. (1997, December 6). *The rise of East Asia in world historical perspective.* Paper presented to the Planning Workshop held at the Fernand Braudel Center, State University of New York, Binghamton.

Asian Development Bank. (2000). *Managing urban change: Strategic options for municipal governance and finance in the People's Republic of China.* Available at: http://

www.adb.org/document/Reports/Consultant/TA2924_ PRCFinalReport.pdf.

Baines, S., & Wheelock, J. (1998). Working for each other: Gender, the household, and micro-business survival and growth. *International Small Business Journal,* 27(1), 1635.

Baker, J. A. (1998, March 11). *Diverging cultural values in contemporary China.* Paper presented at the Institute for Public Policy, Rice University, Houston, TX.

Bao, S., Chang, G. H, Sachs, J. D., & Woo, W. T. (2002). Geographical factors and China's regional development under market reforms, 1978-1998, *China Economic Review, 13(1),* 89-111.

Biggart, N. (1997). Explaining Asian economic organization: Toward a Weberian institutional perspective. In M. Orrù, N. W. Biggart, & G. G. Hamilton (Eds.), *The economic organization of East Asian capitalism,* (pp. 3-32). Thousand Oaks, CA: Sage.

Bond, M. H. (Ed.). (1996). *The handbook of Chinese psychology.* Hong Kong: Oxford.

Bond, M. H, & Hofstede, G. (1988). The Confucius connection: From cultural roots to economic growth. *Organizational Dynamics, 16(4),* 4-21.

Bond, M. H., & Yang, K. (1982). Ethnic affirmation versus cross-cultural accommodation. *Journal of Cross-Cultural Psychology, 13,*169-185.

Bourdieu, P. (1977/2002). *Outline of a theory of practice* (R. Nice, Trans.). Cambridge, England: Cambridge University Press.

Bourdieu, P. (1997) *Pascalian meditations.* Palo Alto, CA: Stanford University Press.

Bourdieu, P., & Waquant, L. (1992). *An invitation to reflexive sociology.* Chicago: University of Chicago Press.

Brahm, L. J. (1998). *Zhong nan hai - The essential China political handbook for every real China hand.* Hong Kong: Naga Publications.

Braudel, F. (1979). *Civilization and capitalism 15th to 18th century* (Volume 1, S. Reynolds, Trans.) New York: HarperCollins.

Cardoso, F. H, & Faletto, E. (1978). *Dependencia y dessarollo en América Latina* [Dependency and development in Latin America]. Mexico City: Twenty-first Century Editors.

Castells, M. (2000). *The information age: Economy, society, and culture* (Vol. 1): *The rise of the network society* (2nd ed.). Malden, MA: Blackwell.

Chattergee, P. (1986). *Nationalist thought and the colonial world: A derivative discourse?* Minneapolis, MN: University of Minnesota Press.

Cheek, T. (1994). From priests to professionals: Intellectuals and the state under the CCP. In J.N. Wasserstrom and E. J. Perry (Eds.), *Popular protest and political culture in modern China* (2nd ed.). Boulder, CO: Westview Press.

Chinese Culture Connection (CCC). (1987). Chinese values and the search for culture-free dimensions of culture. *Journal of Cross-Cultural Psychology, 18,* 143-164.

Chodorkoff, D. (2003). Redefining development. *International Journal of Inclusive Democracy,* 3(1). Available at http://www.social-ecology.org/article.php7story=20031125143847456/

Chua, B. L., Ho, K., & Le, Z., (2003). *Global entrepreneur monitor: Hong Kong and Shenzhen.* Hong Kong: Trade Industry Department and SME Development Fund.

Chu, M., Castellop, C, Churchill, C, & Nourse, T. (2001). *Preliminary analysis of an institutional crisis in microfinance.* Buenos Aires, Argentina: Corposol/ Finansol.

Cleary, J. C. (1991). *Worldly wisdom: Confucian teachings of the Ming dynasty* (J. C. Cleary, Trans.). Boston: Shambhala.

Coombs, C. (1964). *A theory of data.* New York: Wiley.

Cronbach, L. J. (1963). A liberalization of reliability theory. *British Journal of Statistical Psychology, 16,* 137-163.

DeBary, W. T. (1962). *Sources of Chinese tradition,* (Vol. 1). New York: Columbia University Press.

Deng, X. (1978). Third plenary session of the 11th central committee. Available at: http://www.china-sd.net/80th/photos/032.htm. Deng, X. (1996). Deng Xiaoping wenxuan (Selected works of Deng Xiaoping), Vol. III, 1982-1992. Beijing, China: People's Publishing House.

Dewey, J. (1921/1973). *John Dewey: Lectures in China, 1919-192HR.* Clopton & T.-C. Ou, Eds. & Trans.). Honolulu, HI: University of Hawaii Press.

Easterly, W. (2002). *The illusive quest for growth: An economist's adventures and misadventures in the tropics* (4th ed.). Cambridge, MA: MIT Press.

Eastman, L. E. (1988). *Family, fields, and ancestors: Constancy and change in China's social and economic history, 1550-1949.* New York: Oxford University Press.

Egri, C, & Ralston, D. (2004). Generation cohorts and personal values: A comparison of China and the United States. *Organization Science, 15(2),* 210-220.

Egri, C. P., Ralston, D., Stewart, S., Terpstra, R. H., & Yu, K. C. (1999). Doing business in the 21st century with the new generation of Chinese manager: A study of generational shifts in work values in China. *Journal of International Business Studies, 30,*415-428.

Escobar, A. (1995). *Encountering development: The making and unmaking of the third world.* Princeton, NJ: Princeton University Press.

Featherstone, M. (1990). Global culture: An introduction. *Theory, Culture and Society,* 7(2-3), 59-66.

Fei, X. (1947/1992). *From the soil: The foundations of Chinese society* (G. G. Hamilton & W. Zheng, Trans.). Berkeley: University of California Press.

Fligstein, N. (2001). *The architecture of markets: An economic sociology of 21st century capitalist societies.* Princeton, NJ: Princeton University Press.

Fontana, A., & Frey, J. H. (2000). The interview: From structured questions to negotiated text. In Denzin, N. K. & Lincoln, Y. S., (Eds.). *Handbook of Qualitative Research* (2nd Ed.), (pp. 645-672),Thousand Oaks: Sage.

Frank, A. G. (1995a). *The Asian-based world economy, 1400-1800: A horizontally integrative macro-history.* Amsterdam: University of Amsterdam.

Frank, A. G. (1995b). The expansion of the south: Development, democracy and the market. *Society & Nature,* (3)1,7-23.

Frank, A. G. (2002). *ReOrient: Global economy in the Asian age.* Berkeley: University of California Press.

Fu, P. P. (2002). *Exploring the effect of cultural values on the relationship between social beliefs and managerial influence strategies in 12 cultures.* Hong Kong: Chinese University of Hong Kong.

Fukuyama, F. (1999). *The great disruption: Human nature and the reconstitution of social order.* New York: The Free Press.

Gallagher, M. (2002). Reform and openness: Why China's economic reforms have delayed democracy. *World Politics, 54(3),* 338-372.

Gao, G., Kim, H. S., Lin, S.-L., & Ting-Toomey, S. (1991). Culture, face maintenance, and styles of handling interpersonal conflict: A study in five cultures. *International Journal of Conflict Management, 2,* 275-296.

Geertz, C. (1983). *Local knowledge: Further essays in interpretive anthropology.* Princeton, NJ: Basic Books.

Geertz, C. (1990). *Peddlers and princes: Social development and economic change in two Indonesian towns.* Chicago: University of Chicago Press.

Gennep, A. van. (1909/1960). *The rites of passage.* London: Routledge.

Gergen, K. J. (1991). *Toward transformation in social knowledge* (2nd ed.). London: Sage.

Government Accounting Office. (2005, June 17). U.S.-China Trade: Commerce faces practical and legal challenges in applying countervailing duties, Available at http://www.gao.gov/new.items/d05474.

Gramsci, A. (1988). *An Antonio Gramsci reader: Selected writings, 1916-1935* (D. Forgacs, Ed.). New York: Schocken.

Greenbank, P. (2001). Objective setting in the micro-business. *International Journal of Entrepreneurial Behaviour and Research,* 7(3), 108-127. Gu, Z. (1957/2001, August 13-19). *Political liberalism in contemporary China* (C. Wang, Trans.) Available at www.cWna21century.org/.

Gudeman, S., & Rivera, A. (1990). *Conversations in Colombia.* Cambridge, England: Cambridge University Press.

Hamilton, G. G., & Biggart, N. W. (1990). Explaining Asian business success: Theory No. 4. In M. Orru, N. W. Biggart, and G. G. Hamilton (Eds.), *The Economic Organization of east Asian Capitalism* (pp. 97 -110). Thousand Oaks, CA: Sage.

Hamilton, G. G. (1997). Organization and market processes in Taiwan's capitalist economy. In M. Orrù, N. W. Biggart, &

G. G. Hamilton (Eds.), *On the limits of firm-based theory* (pp. 33-54). Thousand Oaks, CA: Sage.

Harrell, S. (Ed.). (1996). *Cultural encounters on China's ethnic frontiers.* Hong Kong: Hong Kong University Press.

Harvey, B. (1999, May). Gentle merchants: A contemporary view of Confucian business ethics. *Journal of Business Ethics,* 2(1), pp. 85-92.

Hinton, W. (1966). *Fanshen: A documentary of revolution in a Chinese village.* New York: Random House.

Hinton, W. (1972). *Turning point in China: An essay on the cultural revolution.* New York: Monthly Review Press.

Hinton, W. (1990). *The great reversal: The privatization of China, 1978-1989.* New York: Monthly Review Press.

Hofstede, G. (1983). The cultural relativity of organizational practices and theories. *Journal of International Business Studies, 14(2),* 75-89.

Hofstede, G. (1997). *Cultures and organizations: Software of the mind.* New York: McGraw-Hill.

Hofstede, G. (2001). *Cultures consequences: Comparing values, behaviors, institutions, and organizations across nations* (2nd ed.). Thousand Oaks, CA: Sage.

Hoong, Y. L. (2001). *New China rising: A social economic assessment of WTO entry.* Singapore: Hoong's China Economic Series.

Hu, F. (1961/1978). *Practice is the sole criteria for testing truth.* Nanjing, China: Nanjing University Philosophy Department Press.

Huang, J. (2004). *The dynamics of China's rejuvenation.* London: Palgrave Macmillan. Mich, I. (1974/2003). Development as planned poverty. In M. Rahnema and V. Bawtree (Eds.), *The post-development reader* (pp. 94-101). London: Zed Books.

International Development Association (IDA) (2005). China and the International Development Association. Available at: http://genevamission/tom.fmprc.gov.cn/eng/4363.html.

International Development Ethics Association (IDEA) (2002). *What is development ethics?* Available at: http://www. developmetethics.org.

International Finance Corporation (IFC) in China, (2005). Available at: http//www.web.worldbank.org/WBSITE/ EXTERNAL/COUNTPJES/EASTASIAPACIFICEXT/CHIN AEXTN/0,contentMDK:20600349~menuPK:14.

Jiang, X., & Neville, R. C. (2002). *The examined life—Chinese perspectives: Essays on Chinese ethical traditions.* Binghamton, NY: Global Publications.

Kerlinger, F. (1979). *Behavioral research: A conceptual approach.* Orlando, FL: Holt, Rinehart, & Winston.

Kerlinger, F. (1986). *Foundations of behavioral research* (3rd ed.). New York: Harcourt Brace Jovanovich.

Kim, M.-S. (2002). *Non-western perspectives on human communication: Implications for theory and practice.* Thousand Oaks, CA: Sage.

Kitayama, S., & Markus, H. R. (1991). Culture and self: Implications for cognitive emotion and motivation. *Psychological Review, 98,*224—252.

Kitayama, S. (2004). Shinobu Kitayama research interests. Available at Error! Hyperlink reference not valid interests.

Koch, R. (1998). *The 80/20principle: The secret of achieving more with less.* New York: Bantam.

Kohn, M. L. (2001). Job complexity and adult personality. In D. B. Grusky (Ed.), *Social stratification: Class, race, and gender in sociological perspective* (2nd ed. pp. 532541). New York: Basic Books.

Kulich, S. (2004, August 10). *Impacts of development and globalization: Longitudinal shifts in Chinese values?* Shanghai International Studies University. Paper presented at 6th Conference on International Association of Cross-cultural Psychologists, Xian, China.

Leavitt, T. (1973). The globalization of markets in managing in a borderless world. In C. Bartlett, S. Ghoshal, & J. Birkinshaw (Eds.), *Texts, cases, and readings in cross-border management* (pp. 180-190). Cambridge: McGraw-Hill International Editions.

Leys, C. (1996). *The rise and fall of development theory.* Bloomington, IN: Indiana University Press.

Licht, A. N., Goldschmidt, C, & Schwartz, S.H. (2001, December 2). *Culture, law, and finance: Cultural dimensions of corporate governance laws.* Department of Psychology, Hebrew University in Jerusalem. Paper draft for European Association for Law and Economics annual meeting.

Lincoln, J., Gerlach, M. & Takahashi, P. (1992). Keiretsu networks in the Japanese economy: A dyad analysis of intercorporate ties. *American Sociological Review 57*, pp. 561-585.

Littrell, R. (2003). Culture, geography, and business theory. In *Business ethics in East Asia.* Auckland, NZ: Auckland University of Technology.

Marcus, G. (1998). *Ethnography through thick and thin.* Princeton, NJ: Princeton University Press.

Martinez-Vazquez, J., & Bahl, R. (2004). Fiscal federalism and economic reform in China. In T. Srinivasan (Ed.), *Fiscal federalism in a global economy* (pp. 34-50). Palo Alto, CA: Stanford University Press.

Merchant, J. (1998, May, 14). *Cross-cultural values and employee orientations: A proposed model for maximizing human potential.* Tenth World Productivity Congress,

World Confederation of Productivity Science, School of Engineering, Universidad del Mar, Spain.

Newell, M. E. (1999). *From dependency to independence: Economic revolution in colonial New England.* Ithaca, NY: Cornell University Press.

Noorderhaven, N. G., & Tidjani, B. (2001). Culture, governance and economic performance: An explorative study with a special focus on Africa. *International Journal of Cross-Cultural Management, 1,* 31-52.

Nurkse, R. (1952). Some international aspects of the problem of economic development. *American Economic Review, 62,* 571-583.

Nurkse, R. (1959). *Patterns of trade and development.* Stockholm: Almquist, Wiksell.

Obadina, T. (2000). *The myth of neocolonialism. African economic analysis.* Available at http://www.abfis.com/analysis.neo-colonialism.

Ohmae, K. (1996). *The end of the nation state: The rise of regional economies.* New York: Simon & Schuster.

Olson, M. (2000). *Power and prosperity: Outgrowing communist and capitalist dictatorships.* New York: Basic Books.

Orru, M., Biggart, N. W., & Hamilton, G.G. (1997). Organizational Isomorphism in East Asia. In M. Orrù, N. W. Biggart, & G. G. Hamilton (Eds.), *The economic organization of East Asian capitalism* (pp. 151-187). Thousand Oaks, CA: Sage.

Ozkrimli, U. (2000). *Theories of nationalism: A critical introduction.* New York: St. Martin's Press.

Pareto, V. (1897/1906). *Optimization.* Principia Cybernetica. Available at: http://pespmcl.vub.ac.be/ASC/PARETO_OPTIM.

Park, A. F., & Kaja, S. (2001). Test of Financial Intermediation and Banking Reform in China. *Journal of Comparative Economics, 29(A):* pp. 608-644.

Park, A. F., & Zhang, J. W. (2005). What is China's true unemployment rate? *China Economic Review 16(2).* pp. 149-170.

Peng, W.T. (1995) *The origins of Chinese kongsi.* Sengalor Darul Ehsan, Malaysia: Pelanduk Publications.

Peters, P. E. (2000). *Development encounters: Sites of participation and knowledge.* Cambridge, MA: Harvard University Press.

People's Daily, March 5,2001. *Facts and figures: China's progress in 9th 5-year plan period.* Available at: http://www. english.peoplesdaily.com.cn.

Polanyi, K., (1944). *The great transformation.* New York: Rinehart & Company.

Polanyi, K., (1968). *Primitive, archaic and modern economies: Essays of Karl Polanyi.* Boston, MA: Beacon Press.

Postrel, V. (2000). Populist Industrial Policy, Available at http:// www.reason.com/

Prahalad, C. K. (2005). *Wealth at the bottom of the pyramid: Eradicating poverty through profits-Enabling dignity and choice through markets.* Upper Saddle River, NJ: Wharton School Publishing.

Prebisch, R. (1950/1962) The economic development of Latin America and its principal problems. Reprinted in *Economic Bulletin for Latin America,* 7(1). p. 1-22.

Prebisch, R. (1956). Commercial policy in underdeveloped countries. *The American Economic Review, 9(1),* pp. 251-273.

Prebisch, R. (1981). Transformación y dessaroyo: The Latin American periphery in the global system of capitalism, *Economic Review for Latin America Review, 8(1). pp. 122.*

Pym, A. (2001). The return to ethics, *The Translator, (2),* Special issue, 14-24.

Qi. Y. (1999). *The implementation of China's science and technology policy.* Westport, CT: Quorum Books.

Rahnema, M., & Bawtree, V. (2003). *The post development reader.* (M. Rahmena and V. Bawtree, Eds.). London: Zed Books.

Ravallian, M., & Anand, S. (1993). Human development in poor countries: On the role of private and public incomes. *Journal of Economic Perspectives, 7,* 89-103.

Ravallian, M., & Chen, S. (2001, August) *Measuring pro-poor growth.* New York: Development Research Group, World Bank.

Rescher, Nicholas (2001). Paradoxes: Their roots, range, and resolution. Chicago, IL, Open Court.

Robertson, R. (1992). *Globalization: Social theory and global culture.* Aberdeen University Press.

Robinson, W. I. (2004) *A theory of global capitalism: Production, class, and state in a transnational world.* Baltimore, MD: Johns Hopkins University Press.

Rokeach, M. (1960) *The open and closed mind.* New York: Basic Books

Rokeach, M. (1973). *The nature of human values.* New York: Free Press.

Rokeach, M., (1979) *Understanding human values.* New York: Free Press.

Ros, J., (1994). Financial Markets and Capital Flows in Mexico. In J.A. Ocampo and R. Steiner (Eds.), *Foreign Capital in Latin America,* Washington, D.C.: Inter-American Development Bank,

Ros, J., (2000). *Development theory and the economics of growth.* Ann Arbor, MI: University of Michigan Press.

Rostow, W. W. (1964/1991). *Stages of economic growth* (3rd ed.). Cambridge, England: Cambridge University Press.

Sachs, J. (1997). *Development economics.* New York: Blackwell Publishers.

Sachs, J. (2005). *The end of poverty: Economic possibilities for our time.* New York: Penguin Press.

Sahlins, M. (1995). *How natives think: About Captain Cook, for example.* Chicago: University of Chicago Press.

Said, E. W. (1983/2002). *Orientalism: Reflections on exile and other essays* (3rd ed.). Cambridge: Harvard University Press.

Schumacher, E. F. (1975). *Small is beautiful: Economics as if people mattered.* New York: Harper & Row.

Schumpeter, J. A. (1911/1934). *The theory of economic development.* Cambridge, MA: Harvard University Press.

Schwartz, S. H., & Bilsky, W. (1987). Toward a universal psychological structure of human values. *Journal of Personality and Social Psychology, 53,*550-562.

Schwartz, S. H., & Bilsky, W. (1990). Toward a theory of the universal content and structure of values: Extensions and cross-cultural replications. *Journal of Personality and Social Psychology, 58,* 878-891.

Schwartz, S. H. (1992). Universals in the content and structure of values: Theory and empirical tests in 20 countries. In M. Zanna (Ed.), *Advances in experimental social psychology* (Vol. 25, pp. 1-65). New York: Academic Press.

Schwartz, S. H. (1993, March 22). *Toward explanations of national differences in value priorities.* Paper presented at the XXIV Congress of the Interamerican Society of Psychology, Santiago de Chile.

Schwartz, S. H. (1994a). Are there universal aspects in the content and structure of values? *Journal of Social Issues, 50,* 19-45.

Schwartz, S. H. (1994b). Beyond individualism-collectivism: New cultural dimensions of values. In U. Kim, H. C. Triandis, C. Kagitcibasi, S-C. Choi, & G. Yoon (Eds.), *Individualism and collectivism: Theory, method and applications* (pp. 85-119). London: Sage.

Schwartz, S. H., & Sagiv, L. (1995). Identifying culture-specifics in the content and structure of values. *Journal of Cross-Cultural Psychology 26,* 92-116.

Schwartz, S. H. (1996). Applying a theory of integrated value systems: Value priorities and behavior. In C. Seligman, J. M. Olson, & B. M. P. Zanna (Eds.), *The psychology of values: The Ontario symposium.* (Vol. 8, pp. 1-24). Hillsdale, NJ: Lawrence Erlbaum.

Schwartz, S. H, & Bardi, A., (1997). Influences of adaptation to communist rule on value priorities in Eastern Europe. *Political Psychology, 18,* 385-410.

Schwartz, S. H. (1999). Cultural value differences: Some implications for work. *Applied Psychology: An International Journal, 48,* 23-47.

Schwartz, S. H. (2000). Value consensus and importance: A cross-national study. *Journal of Cross-Cultural Psychology, 31(4),* 465-497.

Schwartz, S. H. (2001a, August). Value hierarchies across cultures: Taking a similarities perspective. *Journal of Cross-Cultural Psychology, 32(2),* 268-290.

Schwartz, S. H. (2001b, September). Extending the cross-cultural validity of the theory of basic human values with a different measurement. *Journal of cross-cultural psychology, 32(5):* 519-542.

Schwartz, S. H. (2003). *Schwartz values survey, Chinese version.* Available at: http://www.crossculturalcentre(a). yahoo.com.

Schwartz, S. H., & Bardi, A. (2004). Moral dialogue across cultures: An empirical perspective. In E. W. Lehman (Ed.),

Autonomy and order: A communitarian anthology (pp. 1-25). Lanham, MD: Rowman & Littlefield.

Schwartz, S. H. (2004, August). *Keynote address.* Conference of the International Association of Cross-Cultural Psychologists, Xian, China.

Scollon, R., & Scollon, S. B. K. (1981). *Narrative, literacy and face in interethnic communication.* Norwood, NJ: Ablex.

Scollon, R., & Scollon, S. B. K. (1995/2001). *Intercultural communication* (2nd ed.). Malden, MA: Blackwell Publishers.

Sen, A. (1987). *On ethics and economics.* Berkeley, CA: Basil Blackwell.

Sen, A. (1992). *Inequality reexamined.* Cambridge, MA: Harvard University Press.

Sen, A. (1999). *Development as freedom.* New York: Anchor Books.

Sen, A. (2004). *Commodities and capabilities.* New Delhi: Oxford University Press. Senge, P. M. (1990). *The fifth discipline: The art & practice of the learning organization.* New York: Currency Doubleday.

Sheff, D. (2002). *China dawn: The story of a technology and business revolution.* New York: HarperCollins.

Singer, H. W. (1950). The distribution of gains between investing and borrowing countries. *American Economic Review, 40 ft),* 210-222.

Singer, H. W. (1975). The distribution of gains revisited. In A. Cairncross and M. Puri (Eds.), *The strategy of international development* (pp. 231-245). London: Macmillan.

Solinger, D. J. (1999). *Contesting citizenship in urban China: Peasants, migrants, the state, and the logic of the market.* Berkeley: University of California Press.

Somé, M. P. (1999). *The healing wisdom of Africa: Finding life purpose through nature, ritual, and community.* New York: Jeremy P. Tarcher/Putnam.

Spivak, G. (1988). Can the Subaltern speak? In *Marxism and the Interpretation of Culture* (C. Nelson and L. Grossberg, Eds.). Urbana: Univ. of Illinois Press, pp. 271313.

Stiglitz, J. E. (2002). *Globalization and its discontents.* New York: W.W. Norton.

Sun, Y. (1961/1984). *On issues of financial and economic system within economy of the ownership of the whole people (Guanyu quanmin souyouzhi jingji neibu de caijing tizhi wenti).* Taiyun: Shanxi People's Publishing House.

Surin, K. (1998). Dependency Theory's Reanimation in the Era of Financial Capital, *Cultural Logic, 1(2),* 93 —127.

Tajfel, H. (1982). *Social identity and intergroup relations,* Cambridge, England: Cambridge University Press.

Tajfel, H., & Turner, J. C. (1986). The social identity theory of intergroup behavior. In S. Worchel and L. W. Austin (Eds.), *Psychology of intergroup relations* (pp. 234-263). Chicago: Nelson-Hall.

Tang, W., & Parish, W. L. (2000). *Chinese urban life under reform: The changing social contract.* New York: Cambridge University Press.

The Globalist: Meet the new China: China's top brands. September 28, 2005. *Facts of the Week.* Available at: http://www.chinatodav.com/org/cpc/html.

Thurow, L. (2003). *Fortune favors the bold: What we must do to build a new and lasting global prosperity.* New York: HarperBusiness.

Ting-Toomey, S. (1999). *Communicating across cultures,* New York: Guilford Press. Todaro, M. (1997). *Economic development* (6th ed.). New York: Addison-Wesley.

Trescott, P. B. (2002). H. D. Fong and the Study of Chinese Economic Development. *History of Political Economy 34(A)*, 789-809.

Triandis, H. C. (1993). Collectivism and individualism as cultural syndromes. *Cross-Cultural Research,* 27(3/4): 155 - 226.

Trompenaars, F., & Hampden-Turner, C. H. (1998). *Riding the waves of culture: Understanding diversity in global business* (2nd ed.). New York: McGraw Hill.

Tsai, K. S. (2002). *Back-alley banking: Private entrepreneurs in China.* Ithaca, NY: Cornell University Press.

Turner, J. C. (1982). *Towards a cognitive redefinition of the social group.* In H. Tajfel (Ed.), *Social identity and intergroup relations* (pp. 73-94). Cambridge, England: Cambridge University Press.

Turner, V. (1974/1995). *The ritual process: Structure and anti-structure.* Hawthorne, NY: Aldine de Gruyter.

UNCTAD Trade and development report (2002, April 29). Developing countries in world trade, (pp. 198). Available at: http://www.kuscholarworks.ku.edu

Van Manen, M. (August, 1997a). From meaning to method, *Qualitative Research,* 7(3), 345- 369.

Van Manen, M. (1997b). *Hermeneutic phenomenological reflection: Researching lived experience* (2nd Ed.). London: The Althouse Press.

Waley-Cohen, J. (1999). *The sextants of Beijing: Global currents in Chinese history.* New York: W.W. Norton & Company.

Wallerstein, I. (1996). *Eurocentrism and its avatars: The dilemmas of social science.* Keynote address at ISA East Asian Regional Colloquium, The Future of Sociology in East Asia. Seoul, Korea

Wallerstein, I. (2000, September 20). *Cultures in conflict? Who are we? Who are the others?* Y. K. Pao Distinguished Chair Lecture, Center for Cultural Studies, Hong Kong University of Science and Technology.

Wallerstein, I. (2004) *Alternatives: The United States confronts the world.* Boulder, CO: Paradigm.

Wallerstein, I. (2005) *World-systems analysis: An introduction.* Durham: Duke University Press

Walras, L. (1874/1954). *Elements of pure economics: Or the theory of social wealth.* Homewood, IL: Richard Irwin.

Wan, L. (1986, August 15). Democratic and scientific decision making is an important issue of political system reform. People's Daily (pp. 1).

Wang, M. (1998, March 11). Diverging cultural values in contemporary China. James A. Baker Institute for Public Policy, Rice University, Houston, TX. Available at http://www.ruf.rice.edu/~tnchina/commentarv/wang0398

Wang, Z. (1999) *Women in the Chinese enlightenment: Oral and textual histories.* Berkeley, CA: University of California Press.

Weber, M. (1922/1993). *The sociology of religion.* Boston, MA: Beacon Press.

Wei-Ming, T. (1980). The moral universal from the perspectives of East Asian thought. *Philosophy East and West, 31(3).* 259-277.

Whitley, R. (1994). *Business systems in East Asia: Firms, markets, and societies.* Thousand Oaks, CA: Sage.

World Bank Group. (2001). *China: Country assistance strategy.* Washington, DC.

Yang, M. (1995). *Gifts favours and banquets: The art of social relationships in China.* Ithaca, NY: Cornell University Press.

Yu, J. (2002). Virtue: Confucius and Aristotle. In X. Jiang (Ed.), *The examined life— Chinese perspectives: Essays on Chinese ethical traditions* (pp. 1-31). Binghamton, NY: Global Publications.

Yutang, L. (1935/1998). *My country and my people.* Shanghai: Foreign Language Teaching and Research Press.

Zhang, L. (2001). *Strangers in the city: Reconfigurations of space, power, and social networked within China's floating population.* Palo Alto, CA: Stanford University Press.

Zhang, Z., & Yao, S. (2001). Regional inequalities in contemporary China measured by GDP and consumption. *Economic Issues Part 2, 6(2).* Chongqing, China: Chongqing University.

Zheng, L. (2003, April 9). *Entry into the emerging private sector: An institutional analysis of entrepreneurship in urban China.* Paper presented at the Department of Sociology. Palo Alto: Stanford University.

APPENDIX A
SCHWARTZ VALUES SURVEY (SVS 2003)
CHINESE VERSION

人生价值观问卷调查

在这份问卷中，您要问您自己：“在我的生命中，什么样的价值对我而言是重要的，

什么样的价值不太重要?” 以下有两份价值观念表。这些价值观念来自不同的文化，

每一条价值观念后面的括号中是其解释，可以帮助您理解它的含义。

您的任务是标出每一种价值观作为您的<u>人生准则</u>有多重要。标准如下：

0 一 意味著该观念根本就不重要，与您的人生准则毫无关系。

3 一 意味著该观念重要。

6 一 意味著该观念非常重要。

数字越高(0, 1, 2, 3, 4, 5, 6)，该价值观作为您的人生指引就越重要。

特殊标准

另外，用

-1 表明与您的人生准则相反的任何观念。

7 表明您人生准则中极其重要的价值观念，一般而言，

大多数人最多会有两个这样的价值观念。

请把分数 (-1, 0, 1, 2, 3, 4, 5, 6, 7) 填写在每个价值观前的空格内，

以表明这个价值观对您个人的重要程度。请尽量利用所有的数字以区分各个价值观的

差别。当然，您需要重复使用这些数字。

请把分数 (-1, 0, 1, 2, 3, 4, 5, 6, 7) 填写在每个价值观前的空格内,

以表明这个价值观对您个人的重要程度。请尽量利用所有的数字以区分各个价值观的

差别。 当然, 您需要重复使用这些数字。

<u>作为我的人生准则</u>, 这个价值观是 :

与我的价值观相反	不重要			重要			非常重要	极重要
-1	*0*	*1*	*2*	*3*	*4*	*5*	*6*	*7*

I.　　在您开始之前, 阅读表(一)中的价值观,

　　　选择对您而言最重要的一条并标出其重要程度。

II.　　选择与您价值观念最相反一条, 标上-1。如果没有这样的价值观,

　　　选择不太重要的价值观, 按它的重要性, 标上0或1。

III.　　标出其它价值观的重要性。

价值观表(一)

1 _______ 平等 (大家机会均等)

2 _______ 心情安详 (内心平静)

3 _______ 社会权力(控制及支配他人的权力)

4 _______ 愉快(满足欲望)

5 _______ 自由(行动及思想的自由)

6 _______ 精神生活(生活中强调精神而非物质性的事物)

7 ______ 归属感(感受到别人对自己的关心)

8 ______ 社会秩序 (社会的安定)

9 ______ 刺激的生活 (一些刺激生活经历)

10 ______ 人生意义 (人生目标)

11 ______ 礼貌 (有礼节, 良好的举止)

12 ______ 富有 (拥有金钱和物质)

作为我的人生准则, 这个价值观是 :

与我的价值观相反	不重要			重要			非常重要	极重要
-1	0	1	2	3	4	5	6	7

13 _______ 国家安全 (保护国家免受敌人侵袭)

14 _______ 自尊 (对自我价值的尊重)

15 _______ 礼尚往来 (不欠人情债)

16. _______ 创造力 (独创性, 想象力)

17 _______ 世界和平 (没有战争和冲突)

18 _______ 尊重传统文化 (保留流传已久的习俗)

19 _______ 成熟的爱 (情绪和心理均完善发展的爱)

20 _______ 自律 (自我约束, 抗拒诱惑)

21 _______ 私隐权 (拥有属于私人空间的权力)

22 _______ 家庭安全 (保护自己亲属的安全)

23 _______ 社会的认可 (得到别人的尊重和承认)

24 _______ 融入大自然

25 _______ 多采多姿的人生 (充满挑战, 新奇与变化)

26 _______ 智慧 (对人生成熟的理解)

27 _______ 权力 (有发号施令的权力或地位)

28 _______ 真正的友谊 (亲密无间, 能支持您的朋友)

29 _______ 美好的世界 (感受大自然和艺术的美)

30 _______ 社会公义 (纠正社会上不公平现象，扶助弱小)

价值观表(二)

在这一部分中，请您标出下列价值观念对您而言作为人生准则的重要性。这些价值观念以行为方式诠释，以协助您判断它们对您是重要或是不重要。同样，尽量用所有数字来区别这些价值观，以彰显重要性的不同。

I.　　在您开始之前, 阅读表(二)中的价值观，

选择对您而言最重要的一条并标出其重要程度。

II.　　选择与您价值观念最相反一条, 或者, 如果没有这样的价值观，

选择最不重要的价值观, 按它的重要性, 标上-1, 0或1。

III.　　标出其它价值观的重要性。

作为我的人生准则, 这个价值观是 :

与我的价值观相反	*不重要*			*重要*			*非常重要*	*极重要*
-1	*0*	*1*	*2*	*3*	*4*	*5*	*6*	*7*

31 _______ 独立 (依靠自我, 自给自足)

32 _______ 中庸 (避免极端的感情行为)

33 _______ 忠诚 (对朋友, 集体忠心耿耿)

34 _______ 有抱负 (有理想，有志向，敬业)

35 _______ 胸怀宽广(能包容不同的思想及信仰)

36 _______ 谦虚 (虚心不自满，内敛)

37 _______ 冒险精神 (不怕危险，勇于挑战的精神)

38 _______ 环境保护 (保护大自然)

39 _______ 影响力 (对人和事物能起作用的力量)

40 _______ 敬老 (尊重父母和长辈)

41 _______ 选择自己的目标 (选择个人志向)

作为我的人生准则, 这个价值观是：

与我的价值观相反	*不重要*		*重要*			*非常重要*		*极重要*
-1	*0*	*1*	*2*	*3*	*4*	*5*	*6*	*7*

42 _______ 健康 (生理和精神上的健全)

43 _______ 能干 (有才能, 高效率)

44 _______ 接受命运的安排 (顺从人生境遇, 随遇而安)

45 _______ 诚实 (真实, 诚恳)

46 _______ 保持自我公众形象(在大众面前保持自己美好的一面)

47 _______ 服从 (不负使命，尽忠职守)

48 _______ 聪明 (有逻辑思维)

49 _______ 乐意助人 (热心公益)

50 _______ 享受人生 (享受食物, 性, 闲暇和各种精神生活等)

51 _______ 虔诚 (忠于宗教信仰和信念)

52 _______ 有责任感 (可信赖,依靠)

53 _______ 好奇心 (对万物感兴趣, 喜欢探索)

54 _______ 宽宏大量 (懂得宽恕他人)

55 _______ 成功 (达到目标)

56 _______ 清洁 (干净, 整齐)

57 _______ 我行我素 (做自己喜欢的事情)

58 _______ 遵守社会规范 (维护面子)

个人资料

性别（请圈出）： a. 男　　　b.　　　女　　　　　　　年龄：＿＿＿＿＿＿＿岁

在您成长的过程中（从出生到十五岁），谁在您家里住了至少两年？请于以下不同的分类中

写下该分类人物在您家住了至少两年的人数。如果没有，请写零。

＿＿＿＿＿父母　　　　　　　　　　　　　＿＿＿＿＿其他亲戚

＿＿＿＿＿兄弟姐妹　　　　　　　　　　　＿＿＿＿＿没有亲属关系的人

下列人各受过多少年的教育（从小学一年级计算起）？（如果不确定可以估计）

＿＿＿＿＿您本人　　　　＿＿＿＿＿您的父亲　＿＿＿＿＿您的母亲

婚姻状况（请圈出）：

a. 单身　　　　　　　　　c.　　同居　　　　　　　e.　　离婚

b. 已婚　　　　　　　　　d.　　丧偶

请从下表找出您现在的职业或您最后一次被雇佣的职业并填写相应号码：＿＿＿＿＿＿＿

1. 教师 — 幼儿园到小学二年级。　　　　9.　　其他蓝领

2. 教师 —小学三年级到初中二年级　　　10.　　农场主或农场工人

3. 教师 —初中三年级到高中三年级　　　11.　　中学生

4. 学校校长　　　　　　　　　　　　　12.　　大学生：社会科学和教育

5. 其他专业人员　　　　　　　　　　　13.　　大学生：人文，文科和法律

6. 经理或企业家　　　　　　　　　　　14.　　大学生：自然科学和医学

7. 白领或推销人员　　　　　　　　　　15.　　家庭主妇

8. 技术工人　　　　　　　　　　　　　16.　　其他：请注明＿＿＿＿＿＿＿

THE FOLLOWING QUESTIONS WILL NOT BE ASKED IN THIS SURVEY:

A question Prof. Schwartz would like included in the SVS is below; a concern is that in some regions including this question might affect willingness to complete and return the questionnaire. If you feel it is appropriate to include the question, please do so; if not, it may be omitted. It should be inserted in the demographic data collection at the end of the Chinese versions of the SVS follows:

With regard to religion, with which religious group do you identify? (circle)
[List major religious groups, "Other " and "None"]
1. Xxxxxxxxxx 4. Xxxxxxxxxxxxxxx
2. Xxxxxxxxxx 5. Other______________________________
3. Xxxxxxxxxx 6. None

您信仰宗教的程度，如果有的话 （请圈出）

    无   非常虔诚

    0   1   2   3   4   5   6   7

您属于以下哪一个民族？（请圈出）

  1. 汉族中国人   2.   非汉族中国人

  3. 其他，请注明______________

  4. 您成长的环境（请圈出）

  1. 大城市（500,000+）   2. 小城市   3. 郊区   4. 农场

居住地：______________省 ________________________市/县/镇

APPENDIX B

SCHWARTZ VALUES SURVEY (SVS 2003)
ENGLISH VERSION

In this questionnaire you are to ask yourself: "What values are important to ME as guiding principles in MY life, and what values are less important to me?" There are two lists of values on the following pages. These values come from different cultures. In the parentheses following each value is an explanation that may help you to understand its meaning.

Your task is to rate how important each value is for you <u>as a guiding principle in your life</u>. Use the rating scale below:

0—means the value is not at all important, it is not relevant as a guiding principle for you.
3—means the value is important.
6—means the value is very important.

The higher the number (0, 1, 2, 3, 4, 5, 6), the more important the value is as a guiding principle in YOUR life.

-1 is for rating any values opposed to the principles that guide you.
 7 is for rating a value of supreme importance as a guiding principle in your life; *ordinarily*
         there are no more than two such values.

In the space before each value, write the number (-1,0,1,2,3,4,5,6,7) that indicates the importance of that value for you, personally. Try to distinguish as much as possible between the values by using all the numbers. You will, of course, need to use numbers more than once.

AS A GUIDING PRINCIPLE IN MY LIFE, this value is:

opposed to my values	not important			important			very important	of supreme importance
-1	0	1	2	3	4	5	6	7

Before you begin, read the values in List I, choose the one that is most important to you and rate its importance. Next, choose the value that is most opposed to your values and rate it -1. If there is no such value, choose the value least important to you and rate it 0 or 1, according to its importance. Then rate the rest of the values in List I.

VALUES LIST I

1 _____EQUALITY (equal opportunity for all)

2 _____INNER HARMONY (at peace with myself)

3 _____SOCIAL POWER (control over others, dominance)

4 _____PLEASURE (gratification of desires)

5 _____FREEDOM (freedom of action and thought)

6 _____A SPIRITUAL LIFE (emphasis on spiritual not material matters)

7 _____SENSE OF BELONGING (feeling that others care about me)

8 _____SOCIAL ORDER (stability of society)

9 _____AN EXCITING LIFE (stimulating experiences)

10 _____MEANING IN LIFE (a purpose in life)

AS A GUIDING PRINCIPLE IN MY LIFE, this value is:

opposed to my values -1	not important 0	1	2	important 3	4	5	very important 6	of supreme importance 7

11____POLITENESS (courtesy, good manners)

12____WEALTH (material possessions, money)

13____ NATIONAL SECURITY (protection of my nation from enemies)

14____ SELF RESPECT (belief in one's own worth)

15____RECIPROCATION OF FAVORS (avoidance of indebtedness)

16____CREATIVITY (uniqueness, imagination)

17____A WORLD AT PEACE (free of war and conflict)

18____RESPECT FOR TRADITION (preservation of time-honored customs)

19____MATURE LOVE (deep emotional & spiritual intimacy)

20____SELF-DISCIPLINE (self-restraint, resistance to temptation)

21____PRIVACY (the right to have a private sphere)

22____FAMILY SECURITY (safety for loved ones)

23____SOCIAL RECOGNITION (respect, approval by others)

24____UNITY WITH NATURE (fitting into nature)

25____A VARIED LIFE (filled with challenge, novelty and change)

26____WISDOM (a mature understanding of life)

27____AUTHORITY (the right to lead or command)

28____TRUE FRIENDSHIP (close, supportive friends)

29____A WORLD OF BEAUTY (beauty of nature and the arts)

30____SOCIAL JUSTICE (correcting injustice, care for the weak)

•   •   •   •   •

VALUES LIST II

Now rate how important each of the following values is for you <u>as a guiding principle in YOUR life</u>. These values are phrased as ways of acting that may be more or less important for you. Once again, try to distinguish as much as possible between the values by using all the numbers.

Before you begin, read the values in List II, choose the one that is most important to you and rate its importance. Next, choose the value that is most opposed to your values, or--if there is no such value--choose the value least important to you, and rate it -1, 0, or 1, according to its importance. Then rate the rest of the values.

AS A GUIDING PRINCIPLE IN MY LIFE, this value is:

opposed to my values	not important			important			very important	of supreme importance
-1	0	1	2	3	4	5	6	7

31____ INDEPENDENT (self-reliant, self-sufficient)

32____ MODERATE (avoiding extremes of feeling & action)

33____LOYAL (faithful to my friends, group)

34____AMBITIOUS (hard-working, aspiring)

35____BROADMINDED (tolerant of different ideas and beliefs)

36____HUMBLE (modest, self-effacing)

37____DARING (seeking adventure, risk)

38____PROTECTING THE ENVIRONMENT (preserving nature)

39____INFLUENTIAL (having an impact on people and events)

40____HONORING OF PARENTS AND ELDERS (showing respect)

41____CHOOSING OWN GOALS (selecting own purposes)

42____HEALTHY (not being sick physically or mentally)

43____CAPABLE (competent, effective, efficient)

44____ACCEPTING MY PORTION IN LIFE (submitting to life's circumstances)

45____HONEST (genuine, sincere)

46____PRESERVING MY PUBLIC IMAGE (protecting my "face")

47____OBEDIENT (dutiful, meeting obligations)

48____INTELLIGENT (logical, thinking)

49____HELPFUL (working for the welfare of others)

50____ENJOYING LIFE (enjoying food, sex, leisure, etc.)

51____DEVOUT (holding to religious faith & belief)

52____RESPONSIBLE (dependable, reliable)

53____CURIOUS (interested in everything, exploring)

54____FORGIVING (willing to pardon others)

55____SUCCESSFUL (achieving goals)

56____CLEAN (neat, tidy)

57____SELF-INDULGENT (doing pleasant things)
58____ SAVING FACE (honor for family, self and others)

作为我的人生准则, 这个价值观是 :

与我的价值观相反	不重要			重要			非常重要	极重要
-1	*0*	*1*	*2*	*3*	*4*	*5*	*6*	*7*

13 _______ 国家安全 (保护国家免受敌人侵袭)

14 _______ 自尊 (对自我价值的尊重)

15 _______ 礼尚往来 (不欠人情债)

16._______ 创造力 (独创性, 想象力)

17 _______ 世界和平 (没有战争和冲突)

18 _______ 尊重传统文化 (保留流传已久的习俗)

19 _______ 成熟的爱 (情绪和心理均完善发展的爱)

20 _______ 自律 (自我约束, 抗拒诱惑)

21_______ 私隐权 (拥有属于私人空间的权力)

22 _______ 家庭安全 (保护自己亲属的安全)

23 _______ 社会的认可 (得到别人的尊重和承认)

24 _______ 融入大自然

25_______ 多采多姿的人生 (充满挑战, 新奇与变化)

26 _______ 智慧 (对人生成熟的理解)

27 _______ 权力(有发号施令的权力或地位)

BACKGROUND ITEMS

Your Sex (circle): a. Male   b. Female   Your age: ____Years

While you were growing up (birth to age 15), who were the people who lived in your home for at least two years? Write the number of people in each category. Write zero if no one in category.

____Parents   ____Other Relatives
____Sisters & Brothers   ____Persons who are not relatives

How many years of education has each person completed since 1st grade)? (estimate if not certain)

____Yourself   ____Your Father   ____Your Mother

Your marital status (circle):

a. Single   c. Cohabiting   e. Divorced
b. Married   d. Widowed

Describe your current occupation or your occupation when last employed (Choose from below and then write in your answer) __________
    1. Teacher grades k-2   9. Other blue collar
    2. Teacher grades 3-8   10. Farm owner or farm worker
    3. Teacher grades 9-12   11. Secondary school student
    4. School principal   12. University student: social sciences & education
    5. Other professional   13. University student: humanities, arts, & law
    6. Manager or business owner   14. University student: natural sciences & medicine
    7. Clerical or sales worker   15. Homemaker
    8. Skilled worker   16. Other _________________

How religious are you, if at all? (circle)
    Not at   Very
    all   religious
     0   1   2   3   4   5   6   7

Of which of the following groups are you a member? (circle)

    1. Han   2. Other _____________
    3. If other, what group _____________

In what kind of a place did you grow up? (circle):
  1. large city (500,000+)   2. small city   3. rural area   4. farm

Fill in your birthplace province _____________city _____________county________

How many years have you been owner/manager of your current business? _____________

APPENDIX C
INTERVIEW PROTOCOLS

Qualitative Interview Protocol for Doctoral Dissertation for Chinese Urban Micro Business Owner Managers

By

Elisabeth P. Montgomery

In partial fulfilment of
Fielding Graduate University

Content Validity and Findings

After completing my proposed interview questions, I solicited the advice of six businesspeople for content validity. Each participant had to first complete the 58 questions on the Chinese version of the Schwartz Values Survey (2003) or SVS. Later, they were given the 9 proposed interview questions and were asked specifically to critique these proposed questions using a simple agreement and comment form.

These businesspeople were selected based on a snowballing technique beginning with a Law Professor at Shenzhen University. The participants included a diverse range of professions and equal number gender among the group. Overall, the nine proposed questions developed for the face-to-face interviews with micro-businesses retain a simple structure to optimize open discussions. The important comments from businesspeople were about the content. Some asked for more probing and specific questions.

For example, comments from Doris about the meaning of the term "risk" for Chinese businesses required further investigation. She suggested I was likely to get a range of comments that would have nothing to do with the concept of "daring" as the word is understood in the West. Her contribution to the dilemma of cross-cultural meaning of the word "risk," was to suggest that I stay open to the possibility of using other terms that came up in the interview. For example, if an interview participant spoke a lot about loyalty, then I would use that value as a basis for discussion.

On the other hand, Frank thought the interview questions were all unproblematic. Yet, he concluded that I could be "overwhelmed" by the diversity of views in the micro-business milieu, and the cross-translation, which needs to be translated and interpreted. Figure I shows the full summary characteristics and general comments provided by the participants.

Name	Gender	Title	Responsibilities	Overall Agreement on Interview Quetions	Advice
Dories	F	Marketing Director, DBL-a Hong Kong based Mutual Fund Bak	Mututal funds, bank investments	Agrees with questions 1-8; says question 9 is not important	Marketing: Focus on a few single values to pursue in the Interview
Frank	M	General Manager, TV Broadcasting	Consolidation of broadcast media and culture	Agrees with all questions 1-9, says participants may not reveal their true feelings.	Media: Try to discover the kinds of thinking that these people have and make it relevant - no one cares much about them. Prove how important they are to society.
Feng	F	Partner, Manufacturing Firm-SZ	Shipping and coordination of 40 factories selling goods overseas	Finds all the questions reasonable	Business: Most important values to discover are about the hardship of entrepreneurial activities.

Nasha	F	Vice-Deputy, Bank of China, and SOE; Shen-Zhen branch	Provides policy and control of SOE mergers and acquisitions	Says questions 1-8 are good, suggests questions 9 is not necessary unless the participant talks about roles.	Government: Take the role of these owner-managers seriously to see if you can find who will be successful. Their idea of success may not be the same as the cultural norm.
Mark	M	Law Dept. Chair, Professor at ShenZhen University	Chair of Regional University law school; Editor in Chief of Entrepreneur magazine.	Agrees overall to the structure of the interview questions.	Legal: Ask about the relationships between the owner-managers and their employees
Liu	F	District Deput Director of Micro-business, Small Business, and Medium Business; Nan-shan	Responsible for high-tech industry incubation and facilitation	Overall, agrees to the questions and feels more information will be revealed in the actual interviews process.	Civic Culture: Wants me to learn more about the micro-business in order to better serve their needs and development.

Figure 1 Participants in the interview protocol development.

Summary of Protocol Participants' Characteristics and Individual Advice

The protocol participants helped to develop questions for Chinese microbusinesses in face-to-face interviews. These questions, while best understood by directly interviewing the target population of micro-businesses also benefited from the objective review of informed professionals.

The protocol began by proposing questions for rating and advice from business people prior to face-to-face interviews with the Chinese microbusinesses. The volunteer businesspeople understood that micro-business entrepreneurs take enormous risks to create companies and jobs in a socialist society entering an increasingly global environment. The protocol assessed the content of those questions in order to addresses the *pre-interview perceptions* of the micro-business communities from outsiders with social, economic, and political viewpoints. The questions were as follows:

Confidentiality: All information gathered from this interview will remain confidential and anonymous. Your answers will be tape-recorded for transcription purposes only. No statement you make or quotes from this interview will be used without your consent.

Demographic Data Administrative Data

Company Produces: _______________ Time Start: _________Stop:__________

Interviewee title: _________________________________ Code: _____________

Number of Years in business________________ Tape#: __________________

Number of Employees ______________ Followup ____________________

Interview Questions

1) In your opinion, what are three strongest resources of the micro-business?

2) In your opinion, what are three weakest resources of the micro-business?

3) What values do you hold as most important to operating your microbusiness?

4) How do you define risk?

5) In what ways, if at all, do you feel the effects of the international market economy in your micro-business?

6) Have you ever taken a survey like the SVS before?

7) How does it make you *feel or think* to take a survey about your values?

8) In your opinion, in what ways is a values survey relevant or useful to you?

9) In your opinion, how important are the roles listed below in your microbusiness development? Rate your *attitude* toward the roles list below from 1 - 5, 5 is very positive.

Role	1 Very negative	2 Negative	3 Neutral	4 Positive	5 Very positive
Partners					
Employees					
Customers					
Banks					
Family Members					
Loan Guarantee Corporation					
Foreign Investors					
Venture Capitalists					

Local Business Associates					
Universities					
Attitude - is defined as a propensity for a particular view or sentiment and is assessed through a rating from very negative (1) to very positive (2).					

To enter a Chinese micro-business and have a conversation about the owner-managers values required relationship building, openness to dialogs, and adroit questioning to determine if their experience of international development is a new phenomenon or a general pattern of historical development. It also required seizing opportunities to further descriptions.

The interview research protocol, in the current Chinese micro-business environment, required me to use intense, gad-fly-like and iterative questions. I evoked the ambiguity of a double hermeneutic stance explained by Nicholas Rescher (2001) as:

Any theoretical scheme in natural or social sciences is in a certain sense a life, once the concepts have mastered the practical activity of generating specific descriptions. That then is already a double hermeneutic (p. 87).

Mindful of my broader dissertation research, what follows provided the context and content for face-to face interviews that fulfilled the descriptive detail of my broader inquiry and investigation. I asked six participants to review the proposed questions for content validity. I provide some of the results of their advice. I conducted all six interviews with English-speaking Chinese nationals, in China, between April and July 2004.

Other advice from the protocol participant Mr. Feng suggested that all comments in the interview conversation should be taken with a grain of scepticism because he insists that people may not tell the truth in this research situation.

According to him, micro-business owners will not place much importance on their values nor will they find the information useful. Therefore, they may just be curious to be interviewed by a foreigner.

Nasha, because of her head position in one of China's largest SOE, understands the necessity for the micro-business sector to prosper and thrive. Despite recent attempts at reforms, the Bank of China has very few capabilities or intentions to fund micro-businesses.

More to the point of the interviews, Mark said he would approach the owner-manager with questions on attitudes, roles and relationships with his/her employees. He felt this line of questioning would reveal a lot about the structure of the company and that its values would largely derive from that structure.

Ms. Liu works specifically with micro-businesses and wants to see internal capabilities rise in the entire sector. Her spoken English was the most limited among the participants, but she reads English perfectly and understood the issues on a day-to-day level as Deputy of the small business sector in this large district of Shenzhen.

In response to the protocol advice sought I made the following changes in the ten interviews conducted after this assessment:

- I changed the term "risk" in question #8 to keep that value open to the conversation possibilities as they naturally evolved in the interview.

- I eliminated the Likert scales of question #9 and used it only when the conversation stalled, or I felt I could tease out more descriptions by providing a range of topics for a shy participant.

In conclusion, this protocol assists in the research practice to provide me with more in-depth details about situated micro-businesses in Shenzhen, China. Based on the advice of six protocol participants, there will be three main interview questions, 4-6 and the remaining questions for owner-managers will be used to prompt if the situation warrants. More importantly, the intimate, face-to face interviews juxtapose the practice of static survey tallying that took place beforehand. One key component is to provide descriptive details of the interview. This protocol advice solicitation process engaged the opinions of a range of people in the diverse professions and provides me an optimal interview format and a sharper focus on the interview questions.

APPENDIX D
PILOT STUDY RESULTS

International Development Values
in Chinese Micro-Businesses

A Pilot Results Using the Schwartz Values Surveys
and Exit Interviews

Conducted in Three Provinces of China, April 2004

By Elisabeth Montgomery

The Pilot
Chinese Micro-Businesses in Three Provinces

Background

This pilot study was conducted in three Chinese provinces in April 2004 to examine the data collection instrument and the procedures and methods surrounding the collection data. Changes were made to strengthen the survey gathering procedures and to ensure full participation.

The pilot and lessons learned at various locations revealed that the overall procedures and methods were appropriate for the larger undertaking of the full dissertation research. What follows is an account of the pilot methods, results, analysis, considerations, and recommendations.

In tandem with respondent selection, it was important to establish relationships with local development groups and organizations in order to conduct the research, especially in a cross-cultural venue. Due to the comparative language barrier (at least two Chinese dialects), using local translator/ researchers weigh heavily in this proposal. Research activities entailed ways to gain access, authority, and document translations. *Pilot Sample Description*

This pilot research used a multi-site, qualitative, research approach based on surveys, exit interviews, observations, and analysis of 17 small businesses in five cities in Mainland China. The term "small business owner-managers" defines businesses owned and operated by a manager and that have between three and as many as seven employees. The survey took place during a ten-day period between April 16th and 26th 2004. Specifically, each business was selected from information provided by a local business loan development office and based on geographic accessibility. This database showed a universe of approximately 28,000 micro-loans throughout the Province of Guangdong, including Shenzhen City and out-laying factory districts of Longgang and Nanshan. Surveys were also completed in two other Provinces: Heiliongjiang, Hebei and Shanghai. These latter names were people who had obtained loans in Guangdong Province but who subsequently returned to their hometowns to do business.

During the pilot, 20 randomly identified participants were selected based on quota sample variable of location. The survey locations were 5 urban cities, each with 5 million citizens or more (Shenzhen, Wuhan, Harbin, Shanghai) or large districts (Longgan, Nanshan) with approximately 2 million in population. For instance, Shenzhen City boasts huge economic growth over the past 5 years, which attracts people from all over China. However, the differences among these cities and districts prove vast. Shenzhen is a thriving new metropolis with a bourgeoning high-tech industry, Hebei is a heavily industrialized province in a transition from manufacturing to newer economic industries, Heiliongjiang, in the far northeast of the country is China's industrial "rust belt" with exceedingly high unemployment. Shanghai is a city of international economic status and charm.

Each participant was given *two* survey forms to complete: one to complete with the researcher and interpreter present and one to complete on their own within a ten-day timeframe. Of the 20 who filled out the survey, 17 responded to all 58 questions. Only the 17 surveys were used in the Pilot Results. Various reasons for non-response are analyzed in Pilot Results.

Pilot Results

Of the 20 participants, 17 provided complete responses to all the 58 questions in the survey and 10 participated in a brief exit interview. Participants came from the provinces of Guangdong (11) 65%, Hebei (4) 23%, Heiliongjiang (1) 6%, and Shanghai (1) 6%. Of the 17 participants, all completed the retest surveys for a total of 34 surveys to be coded, analyzed, and compared.

Background demographics.

The background data collected on the participants includes the following: Participants were 11 males (64%) and 6 females (35%). They ranged in age from 27 to 54 years and a median age of 33, a mode of 32 and an average age of 36 years old. A full 95% are married. They had a range of education from 7th grade to post graduate school, a median of 14, a mode of 15 and an average education of 13 years. Among these participants, 20% grew up in large Chinese cities, 33% in the small cities, 26% in suburbs, and 20% on a farm. Primarily, they grew up in households with two parents, an average of 2.5 siblings and one other relative living in the household.

The participant's fathers had an education range of 3.5 years to 12 years education level, a median of 9.5 years, a mode of 10th grade, and a 9th grade average. Their mothers' education ranged from 0 to 16 years, a median of 6th grade, a mode of 6th grade, and an average of 7th grade.

All 17 participants considered themselves to be a part of the Han Chinese ethnic group and 70% characterized themselves as being non-religious.

Of interest, the self-identifying descriptions of the business owner by occupation categories, shows the diversity of the pilot sample along with the percentage of employees. The small business owner-managers' report a total of 55 years in business, and 108 employees. The self-selected business profile includes eleven entrepreneurs of various types (65%), three manufacturers (18%), two health and beauty services (12%), and two corner-store owners (12%).

Revised assumptions.

Two fundamental changes took place regarding my initial research assumptions and terminology. First, through discussions with Chinese officials, academics, and executives, I discovered my use of the US-based international development term "micro-business" means something quite distinct in China. The micro-business definitions and terms and conditions fluctuate worldwide. The international development community typically defines a micro-business as a business with five or fewer employees requiring initial capitalization $50 and $100 USD and up to $5000 USD.

Some definitions also characterize a micro-business as having maximum annual revenues of $2500 USD. By contrast, in Shenzhen, P.R. China, the micro-business is defined by CGC and other development groups as a business with five or fewer employees requiring initial loans of a minimum of 100,000 RMB or ($12,500 USD) to a maximum of 10,000,000 RMB ($1,250,000 USD).

The indigenous definition of micro-business in this Chinese context, forced me to adjust in my purpose in order to more clearly fit the Chinese reality. In other words, the sources for data collection in the micro-business community may include owner-managers who are more prosperous and more educated than at first anticipated.

Table 1		
Small Business by Number of Employees and Years in Business		
Type of Business	**Numbers of Employees**	**Years in Business**
Manufacturer	1	3
Manufacturer (Stove tops)	1	1.5
Beauty Shop (Hair)	6	6
Film developer	2	12
Corner Store (sundries)	3	5
Drugs store	3	2
Tailor	2	10
Photographer	1	10
Bicycle Repair	5	8
Corner Store (Grocer)	4	3.5
Marketer	1	2.5
Medical device	1	2
Housekeeping services	6	8
Eye glass	4	5
Audio-visual Duplication	6	8
Bookstore	3	17
Facial and Beauty	6	5
Totals	55	108.5

The pilot test scores below for 17 participant samples include the following ranking of value priorities:

Table 2

Chinese-SVS Pilot Test/Retest on Micro-Business Owner-Manager Ranking of Individual and Cultural Values.

Test-Rated of Values Based on Composite Scores		Retest-Rated Values Based on Composite Scores	
Individual Values	Cultural Values	Individual Values	Cultural Values
Universalism	Embeddedness	Universalism	Embeddedness
Security	Egalitarianism	Security	Egalitarianism
Benevolence	Affective Autonomy	Benevolence	Affective Autonomy
Self-Direction	Mastery	Self-Direction	Mastery
Achievement	Hierarchy	Achievement	Hierarchy
Confirmity	Intellectual Autonomy	Conformity	Harmony
Power	Harmony	Power	Intellectual Autonomy
Tradition		Tradition	
Hedonism		Hedonism	
Stimulation		Stimulation	

Pilot Reliability.

The pilot test-retest correlations indicate that the SVS is a very reliable survey to use with the target sample of Chinese small business owner managers (See Table 3) based on an overall reliability mean of *0.85.*

Each SVS survey took an average participant 35 minutes to complete. The exit interviews took an average of 10 minutes to complete. Therefore, the entire process took roughly 1 hour of the owner-manager's time. This time constraint needs to be taken into consideration for a survey sample goal of 200.

Two sets of 17 completed test-retest surveys (See Table 3); along with 10-survey exit interviews affirmed the reliability of the SVS with this target population of small businesses. The exit interview responses elicited unprecedented conversations about individual and cultural values.

See: Appendix I –Schwartz Values Survey Scoring Sheet for SVS Data: Table 3.

Pilot scorability.

The SVS rating provides for researchers to use longer lists of values and add to the instrument without affecting the overall core results. It also neutralizes "negative" values, so people do not feel like they are advocating certain values over others. Schwartz stated that "rating may be phenomenologically closer than ranking to the way in which values enter into situations of behavioral choice, even though people are typically aware only loosely of the possible contradictions between relevant values when making most behavioral choices." (Schwartz, 1994a, P. 26)

Once the pilot survey data was gathered and data-entry completed, the analysis followed the SVS scoring sheet, method of scoring the individual values, then compiling them into Individual and Cultural Value Dimensions.

The data analysis in this pilot centers on the percentages of agreement between the survey test and re-test for reliability. Notes on what participants said about the survey were also written down for this evaluation. In the future, running more complex computerized social science systems software using SPSS -10 or 11 are imperative. Further data analysis strategies must include entering the survey scores into an SPSS database to prepare correlations.

SVS.

The correlations made from the pilot include only the test-retest results. On the one hand, the results research suggests using an SPSS software program to correlate the data is essential to the questions asked. The SVS is designed for extensive quantitative survey data and sorts, tabulates, and handled a wide range of univariate and multivariate analysis. SPSS software programs offered a range of graphics procedures and can link directly to the database materials and making significant correlations.

Exit Interviews.

Three brief questions were asked of 10 participants regarding their reaction to taking the SVS survey. Although the questions have yet to be validated, the compiled narrative indicated patterns and themes for further analysis.

Pilot utility.

Primarily, I first considered the small business owner manager's time because they tend to have little time to do much else but work. When anything goes wrong, or unexpected tasks arise, the owner managers must respond.

Secondly, the interpreters played a significant role in conducting the surveys and translation of the exit interview materials and content.

Pilot cost.

The cost of the pilot in US dollars included airfare to China ($680), lodging ($150), translator fees ($150), respondent stipends ($65), and local transportation ($240). Total costs slightly exceeded $1000 USD.

Pilot language translation and validation.

Interpreters were hired to set up the surveys and exit interviews, and to provide translation services in 12 out of the 17 locations. In 5 other instances, only the interpreters distributed and collected surveys and wrote the participant exit responses.

During the pilot period, hired translators made data gathering observations and suggestions about obtaining results from two Provinces outside of Guangdong. The two translators signed agreements of confidentiality. They also took the SVS survey themselves and discussed the terms and procedures. Therefore, interpreters assisted with 12 of the 17 final surveys and solely administered five of them in the outer provinces of Hebei and Heiliangjiang.

For the purposes of this pilot, the derived interpretations and meanings come from too small of a sample and do not provide an entirely accurate measurement of values of this sample population. Full population samples will correct this discrepancy. The sample of 17 in this pilot assessed a small degree of variation in the pilot test- retest but reliability was maintained.

Exit research questions.

In any research, the researcher, as purely as possible, begins with a deep-seated curiosity and care for the people targeted in the research process. This pilot study attempts to keep the exit questions very specific and yet open for conversation. The three questions engaged participants and informed me about the survey reliability.

The three exit interview questions asked were:

1) Have you ever taken this kind of survey or a similar kind of values survey?

2) Overall, how did taking this survey make you feel? Or what kinds of things did it make you think about while you were taking it or afterwards?

3) In what ways is this kind of survey useful to you, or not?

The ensuing conversations among the 10 exit interview participants also provided insights into the delicate nature of researching values among the Chinese small business owner manager population. The "researcher as variable" although hard to determine or prove, came up as an issue in more than one instance.

If Chinese small business owner-managers provide primary roles in job development and job creation, their values, attitudes, and behaviors structure their relationships around their individual guiding principles and their dominant cultural values. In this study, the individual micro-business values may tend to collide with the dominant cultural values as represented by the loan programs. These two groups, while disparate in power, operate and obtain similar objectives: economic development (measured by personal financial success), and community development (measured by job creation and business growth).

Pilot summary.

In summary, the issues that arose during this pilot research included (a) interpreters' understanding of their role in conducting the survey; (b) participants not entirely understanding the directions given by interpreters for completing the survey; (c) interpreter perception and perspectives of answers to exit interviews; (d) how to use and analyze the qualitative data collected from the exit interviews; and (e) how to manage the data according to Schwartz and the cross-cultural community using this instrument. A discussion of these issues and my response follows:

On the first day of surveying I found the largest hurdle for me as a cross-cultural researcher was to make the interpreter understand how to explain, conduct, and collect the surveys without giving too much direction to the participant. For example, when they collected the surveys, they made sure all 58 answers were completed. However, on two or three occasions the participants did not choose to complete all the questions. The interpreters gave them a chance to finish the test survey, but the participants did not want to do it at that point. One interpreter tried to convince a participant to complete the survey, but I intervened to say it did not matter - this was part of conducting surveys.

The uncompleted surveys were not used in the sample results, although according to Schwartz there is a way to do use the data. Action Plan: Train the interpreters thoroughly by modelling through role-playing situations where they might find themselves wondering how to respond. Clearly state and model non-coercive behaviors that underlie the research expectations on participants.

Each participant was given directions about the use of the Lickert-style rating scale, and how to use the numbers "-1, or values opposed to your principles" and "+7, or values of supreme importance to you." In one instance, the interpreter suggested the participant must change their scores to indicate a -1 or a 7 at least once on the survey if they do not do so, or to change several evens to 6's. However, in the actual wording on the survey instrument, it was only suggested that participants mark opposing values (-I's) and choose only 1 or 2 supreme values (7's). After explaining the survey again to the interpreters I found they let the other participants alone on this issue. Action Plan: Have the interpreters take the survey and give them a sense of exactly what is being asked of the survey participant.

Interpreter perceptions on the content of exit interviews vary. I know this because I had two interpreters on several occasions and I listened to the subsequent disagreements they had about what important details came out of the exit interviews. We worked out a way where the interpreter who gave the three questions and wrote them down would have the final say, once they reviewed the answers directly with the participant. Action Plan: Defer to the interpreter handling each case even if the nuances seem not to be caught.

After collecting the qualitative surveys and the exit interviews I wondered how to use the interview data in the final dissertation. At that point I was informed that the three exit interview questions needed to have some form of validity in order to use them. Collecting and entering the SVS data linked me to dialogs with many international students and professors who were also using instrument as a cross-cultural methodology on values.

The survey goal of 200 participants creates a data log of 11,000 basic entries. Calculations for Individual and Cultural Dimensions include another 956 programmable entries. The data entry proved laborious and detailed with a 5% margin of error. <u>Solution</u>: Set up an online template and hire data entry clerk to do the work.

Pilot conclusions.

The pilot was effective in several ways. First, in terms of administering and using the survey, the problems I thought I would have with participant misunderstandings turned out to be greater among the hired interpreters. Second, I understand several administrative pitfalls and ways to overcome them. For example, each participant was paid a token amount of money to complete the survey. Given the volume of surveys needed in the dissertation, I shall request a written signature for the stipend to track the money. Hiring and training considerations provide the greater sense of urgency. The pilot results also indicate a need for improved communication between the researcher and interpreters, and for improved data collection statistical analysis before going to full scale dissertation interviews. The overall effectiveness prompted the following considerations. The small business owner manager responses collected during the pilot confirm and codify the survey's reliability, scorability, utility, and cost.

The exit interviews also provide some contextual aspects of Chinese cultural representation and participation.

The commitment to conduct this research in China begins with the commitment to make the translation process viable. The pilot experience informs about the cross-cultural difficulties of this type of research. The difficulties produced some key ethical considerations and knowledge about effective ways to present the survey to research participants

In China, a person does not instantly "materialize" for the people. Foreigners can present a bit of a mirage effect in the community. Getting to know people occurs over time. This research process at some point may need to understand the cultural aspects of time and time management.

Maintain awareness of power relationships between the lenders and business owner managers.

According to Hofstede (1983), the Chinese people perceive degrees of separation between those in power and those not prove greater than in Western countries. For this pilot research, awareness of power relationships centered on how the research participants are identified and recruited for the survey and follow-up interviews. Develop sensitivity to the research survey processes and the "researcher as a variable" while interviewing anyone, anywhere in the Chinese culture.

Surveys, while common in some parts of China, are not that common to the owner manager business communities of China (Bao, Change et. al, 2002) This is not to say that they have not been surveyed in the past, it is simply to state that this target population may have different methods of explaining their values and decisions.

They may have more limited contacts with foreigners and some may sit in fear because they may or may not be literate. Some may have only an elementary education.

The translator needs to be on-hand to assist with interview questions and record answers.

Recommendations based on pilot study.

This pilot showed how long the average survey takes to complete, code and analyze. Therefore, the following recommendations apply

Conduct all surveys in a limited geographic area in order to provide the most efficient and effective study. Set up the tabulation templates and corresponding SPSS statistical analysis programs for the final dissertation project. Include the following background data about the participant in the background section of the survey. I will include the following questions:

1) How many years did you work in the industry before you started your own business? One year; two - four years, five to 8 years; More than 8 years?

2) How many times have you applied for small business loans from government agencies or banks? 1-2 loans; 2-5 loans; more than 5 loans?

3)   Hire 15 — 20 bi-lingual Chinese graduate students to conduct 10 or more surveys each. The full dissertation research allows for multi-sited research approach.

4)   Collect between 200 or more surveys for the dissertation research to be valid.

5)   Conduct twenty semi-structured interviews as randomly selected case studies in order to deepen questions and observations of Chinese small business owner managers discovered during the pilot.

6)   Prepare a budget for the research and adhere to administrative and ethical practices regarding academic research.

Pilot IRB approval.

Approval for the pilot was obtained in March 2004, prior to contacting any participants for the survey and exit interviews. Rigorous reporting standards were used to correct data bias in the pilot and to act with professionalism in administering the correct confidentiality forms, honoring commitments, and following-up on agreements. Awareness of coercion and favoritism must be addressed and prevented. One of the best ways to balance issues of coercion includes coaching and articulating these issues for the Chinese translators. The translator, in turn, must understand that for the study to be valid it must include un-coerced participants - that is the goal.

APPENDIX E

CODEBOOK

Rater-Check for Analysis

7/1/2005

MR Z.	Mr. ZOU, CEO OF COMPANY IN INCUBATOR LOCATION IN NANSHAN DISTRICT, SHENZHEN	EPM	G.S	K.C.	A.D.
SPEAKERS	**NARRATION**	CODER 1	CODER 2	CODER 3	FINAL CODE
ELIZABETH	Thank you for filling out the survey and for agreeing to meet with me for this interview. I want to restate that my research is about the values of Chinese urban micro-businesses. I will ask Mr. Zou several questions about what he sees and the strengths and weaknesses of his company. But I hope he feels free to talk about his own interests and topics related to this subject. This is an open exchange of ideas and information.	A1	A1, D1	B1, A1	D1
CHINESE	XXXXXXXXXXXXXXXXXXXXXX XXXXXXXXXXXXXXXXXXX				
INTERPRETER:	Mr. Zou says he is a fan of the open exchange of conversation. He says the strength of his micro-business is to survive in the society today.	B1			B1
CHINESE	XXXXXXXXXXXXXXXXXXXXXX XXXXXXXXXXXXXXXXXXX				
ELIZABETH:	When you say the society today, can you tell me a little more of what that means to you?				
CHINESE	Mr. Zou says for him it means the market society	A2, C1			
ELISABETH	The market society of China today. Is it hard or easy to survive?				
CHINESE	XXXXXXXXXXXXXXXXXXXXXX XXXXXXXXXXXXXXXXXXX				
INTERPRETER:	Historically, it is the most important thing -- that everyone wants to be successful.	B2, D1	D2,B1	B2, C1	D2,D3
ELIZABETH:	So this is from the Chinese history? Is personal achievement and success from his personal history?	A3			
CHINESE	XXXXXXXXXXXXXXXXXXXXXX				

SPEAKERS	NARRATION	CODE 1	CODE 2	CODE 3	FINAL CODE
INTERPRETER:	Yes – but to create his own business, he means it is the way of the market. The history of how the market works. If you know how to do this it is easier, if you have no experience with the market, it is difficult to survive.	A4		A2, C2	A1, D3
ELIZABETH:	In Mr. Zou's personal life, was there anyone he modeled his business after, or did anyone in his family start their own company?				
CHINESE	XXXXXXXXXXXXXXXXXXXXX XXXXXXXXXXXXXXXXXXX				
INTERPRETER:	No, it was his idea. Totally unique to his own idea.	A5		A3	B2
ELIZABETH:	So it was his idea. Are there any other strengths or strong points that Mr. Zou can think of as to starting a business?				
CHINESE	XXXXXXXXXXXXXXXXXXXXX XXXXXXXXXXXXXXXXXX				
INTERPRETER:	Also, one advantage is that Mr. Zou was a college professor but he always wanted to put his knowledge into full use. So he developed his ideas and applied to the incubator and was accepted in part because he had the university experience. Bu this was not market experience. He left his position to start something new.	A6,D2,E1,C2	A2	B3, A4	A2, B3,E1,E2,
ELIZABETH:	His college teaching was in what subject?				
CHINESE	XXXXXXXXXXXXXXXXXXXXX XXXXXXXXXXXXXXXXXXXXX				
INTERPRETER	Computers and electronics. The incubator only accepts hi-tech companies.	D3	F1		B4
ELIZABETH:	Then he wanted to create a product. What does he think is the difference between being a professor and being his own businessman?				
CHINESES	XXXXXXXXXXXXXXXXXXXXX		D3	A5	
INTERPRETER:	There is a difference between theory and practice. The professor looks at theory. But what the client wants and what the professor thinks is no the same.	A7,B3,C3			B5,C1

SPEAKERS	NARRATION	CODE 1	CODE 2	CODE 3	FINAL CODE
ELIZABETH:	What are the constraints? What keeps the business from growing?				
CHINESE	XXXXXXXXXXXXXXXXXXXXXXXX XXXXXXXXXXXXXXXXXXX				
INTERPRETER:	Our company is based on IT technology and the company focuses on developing more and more new products to meet the demands of the market. But the constraints are determined by the market - in the sense that there is a lot of pressure.	B4,E3,E2 ,D4	F3	D1	C2, B6
ELIZABETH:	How much pressure is coming from the market in terms of competition?				
CHINESE	XXXXXXXXXXXXXXXXXXXXXXXX XXXXXXXXXXXXXXXXXXX				
INTERPRETER:	Yes, there is always so much pressure with the competition – he's always looking at that.	A8, C4			B7, E3, C3
ELIZABETH:	Does that pressure make him change the way he does things? Does he change his strategy or the way he trains people? From that pressure from the market or outside competition?				
CHINESE	XXXXXXXXXXXXXXXXXXXXXXXX XXXXXXXXXXXXXXX				
INTERPRETER:	Sometimes he must make a change in the way things are done.	B5		D2, A6	E4
ELIZABETH:	What about his values? Do his values change – again, values are the beliefs that he holds -- and values are how he might think about things or how he has to act.		D4		
CHINESE	XXXXXXXXXXXXXXXXXXXXXXXX XXXXXXXXXXXXXXX				
ELIZABETH:	Are there any values from the outside China - or global values - that he thinks are important to bring into the company or keep away from the company? For instance, one value that is important internationally would be transparency – letting people see what is on your accounting records - that kind of thing. Are there any international values that he thinks are important?				

SPEAKERS	NARRATION	CODE 1	CODE 2	CODE 3	FINAL CODE
INTERPRETER:	It is invaluable to be influenced by the international values, In his mind also he thinks that the international values are helpful to think about and try to work into the company.	A10,B6. C5	C1	C3	A3, D4, E5
ELIZABETH:	What does he see as the most important Chinese values in growing a business?			B4	
INTERPRETER:	All of our employees and the boss Mr. Zuo are Chinese in their way of thinking which is the Chinese way -- the traditional Chinese way.			B5, D4	B8, D5, E6
ELIZABETH:	Is the traditional Chinese Confucian – how does he define traditional Chinese?		B3		
CHINESE	XXXXXXXXXXXXXXXXXXXXXX XXXXXXXXXXXXXXXXXX				
INTERPRETER:	Um, yes it is the Confucian Chinese values. He thinks in his company the relationship between employee and employees is the most important thing – that there is harmony among them.	A12, C7	B4, D5	B6,D5, A7	A4, B9, C4, D6
CHINESE	XXXXXXXXXXXXXXXXXXXXXX XXXXXXXXXXXXXXXXXX				
ELIZABETH:	So harmony is very important and that is a traditional Confucian value. Are there any other values?	A13,B8	B5		A5
INTERPRETER:	Yes, but it is harder to describe. Sometimes the relationship between a businessman and an employee or even a client is based on some emotion – how you feel about that person.	A14, E6	D6, B6	B7	
CHINESE	XXXXXXXXXXXXXXXXXXXXXX XXXXXXXXXXXXXXXXXX				
ELIZABETH:	I find Chinese people to be very emotional. Can you tell me more about that?				
INTERPRETER:	Yes, ganshing – it means emotional because it is a close connection and relationship. But this is also deeper than the personal relationship—it may be that the relationship is also extending beyond the personal and becomes an important obligation between two people.	D5	B7	B8, D6	D7

SPEAKERS	NARRATION	CODE 1	CODE 2	CODE 3	FINAL CODE
INTERPRETER	In this way a deeper connection is made and trust is formed, over some amount of time.	C8		B9, D7	D8
ELIZABETH:	I see, so Chinese people make connections not too quickly, but over time very deeply.				
ELISABETH	I also see that that is changing in Shenzhen and that makes people a little different, because -- what is his lao jia (hometown)? Hunnan? -- Chairman Mao's Hunnan? Yes. Many microbusinesses are thinking about their hometown -- the towns where they were born and have family still_ -- many want to help that hometown to prosper. But they come to Shenzhen and maybe they don't want to return to live in their hometown anymore.			B10,D8,A8	B10, D8, E7, E8
CHINESE	XXXXXXXXXXXXXXXXXXXXXX XXXXXXXXXXXXXXXX				B11, D9
INTERPRETER:	Yes, but Mr. Zou says Shenzhen doesn't influence him very much because he is more influenced by his hometown and he lived in the north of China for some time.	B9,A15, D6, E7	A3	A9	A6, E9
ELIZABETH:	I see, so he is influenced by other places in China. So, at this point, what challenges does he face for his company to grow?		A4		
CHINESE	XXXXXXXXXXXXXXXXXXXXXX XXXXXXXXXXXXXXXXXXX				
INTERPRETER	The company must develop -- like the development of the whole society. In a company, if it does not develop what it has it will lose. Because it faces a challenges from a steady line of competition.	A16,A8. B10,A17, C9	A5	A10	B12, C5
	XXXXXXXXXXXXXXXXXXXXXX XXXXXXXXXXXXXXXXXXX				
	He also says, that the employees want to work in the company which is developing steadily and rapidly. They want to contribute more if they see progress and prosperity in the company.		D7	D9	A7, B13, D11
CHINESE	XXXXXXXXXXXXXXXXXXXXXX XXXXXXXXXXXXXXXXXX				
INTERPRETER:	The most important thing to know is that as the microbusiness grows, so the entire society will grow.		A6, D8	D10	B14, D12

SPEAKERS	NARRATION	CODE 1	CODE 2	CODE 3	FINAL CODE
ELIZABETH:	The whole of society develops when the micro-business grows. XXXXXXXXXXXXXXXXXXXXXX XXXXXXXXXXXXXXXXXX How important is job creation in the micro-business? Is it a goal to create jobs? One of the jobs is profits, is or are there other goals?				
CHINESE	XXXXXXXXXXXXXXXXXXXXXX XXXXXXXXXXXXXXXXXXXX				
INTERPRETER	No. First goal is to keep the company developing steadily and rapidly – or you could say once there are substantial profits.	B11, E9	D9	D11	A8, B15, D13,E10
CHINESE	XXXXXXXXXXXXXXXXXXXXXX XXXXXXXXXXXXXXXXXXX				
INTERPRETER:	The goal is what Mr. Zou focuses on all the time – the goal of survival.				B16
ELIZABETH:	I see, so everything comes from that – from the goal of keeping the company steady. What are the most important values he wants to pass on when for training employees? Rather, what are his goals for training the employees?	A18			
CHINESE	XXXXXXXXXXXXXXXXXXXXXX XXXXXXXXXXXXXXXXXXX				
INTERPRETER	His goals are to develop the skills of the employees to solve the problems. Because in a small business flexibility and speed are the most important.	A19,E10, B12	D10	D11	B17, C6, D14, E11
ELISABETH	Is that his most important business goal – speed and delivery to the customer?				C7
INTERPRETER:	Yes.				
ELIZABETH:	Does he feel his micro-business structure is set up as a team or is he mainly the decision maker? Would he say it is a traditional company structure, a pyramid, or team oriented? How would he say the company is organized?		D11, D12	A12,D13	
CHINESE	XXXXXXXXXXXXXXXXXXXXXX XXXXXXXXXXXXXXXXXXX				
INTERPRETER	What is is what you call a pyramid.				
ELIZABETH	A pyramid? It is sort of like a top down structure, a triangle.				
INTERPRETER:	How so you describe a pyramid? Is it not like a triangle?				
ELIZABETH:	Yes, it is a triangle.				

SPEAKERS	NARRATION	CODE 1	CODE 2	CODE 3	FINAL CODE
CHINESE	XXXXXXXXXXXXXXXXXXXXXX XXXXXXXXXXXXXXXXXXX				
INTERPRETER	The company is not a pyramid -- it is a modern style structure with the awareness that sometimes it must bring some change according to the demand.	A20, E11	D13	D14	B18, C8
ELIZABETH	I see. It is a modern structure that has some flexibility for allowing changes. Is there anybody in China who influenced his ideas on how to organize the company?	B13, E12		A13	
INTERPRETER:	Friends helped him and influenced him.				A9, D16
ELIZABETH:	From college times? From when he was in university?				
CHINESE	XXXXXXXXXXXXXXXXXXXXXX XXXXXXXXXXXXXXXXXXX				
INTERPRETER	His friends in college and colleagues in former companies and also a lot of help from clients.	A21			A10, D17
CHINESE	XXXXXXXXXXXXXXXXXXXXXX XXXXXXXXXXXXXXXXXXX				
INTERPRETER:	There are many times when the clients can bring in new ideas and they are very good ones. They are often more efficient, or he has to make changes that makes the customers orders faster and better quality.	A22		A13, D14	A11, C9, D18
ELIZABETH:	How many years has the company been operating? Nine years? Hen hao (very good). So from the time Mr. Zou started until now, what does he think is the most important or significant change in his own thinking and feeling?			E1	
CHINESE	XXXXXXXXXXXXXXXXXXXXXX XXXXXXXXXXXXXXXXXXX				
INTERPRETER	Before he was a technician and now he is a technician with a sense of the market.	A23	E1		A12, D19, E12
CHINESE	XXXXXXXXXXXXXXXXXXXXXX XXXXXXXXXXXXXXXXXXX				
INTERPRETER:	He also understand better the values of the market.	E13	E2		C10, D20, E13
ELIZABETH:	What are the values of the market?				

SPEAKERS	NARRATION	CODE 1	CODE 2	CODE 3	FINAL CODE
CHINESE	XXXXXXXXXXXXXXXXXXXXXX XXXXXXXXXXXXXXXXXXXX				
INTERPRETER	The market can bring opportunity and sometimes disaster.	A24	E3,E4		A13, C11, D21, E14
CHINESE	XXXXXXXXXXXXXXXXXXXXXX XXXXXXXXXXXXXXXXXXXX				
INTERPRETER:	The opportunity is there if the company is able to see it and carefully work on it. If not, there is disaster that can happen too.	B11, C10			C12, E15
ELIZABETH:	How does he as a Chinese businessman define risk?				
CHINESE	XXXXXXXXXXXXXXXXXXXXXX XXXXXXXXXXXXXXXXXXXX				
ELISABETH	Risk must be cautious and follow nature – the natural flow of things – otherwise the rhythm of the relationships in the company will not be harmonious.	A25, D7, B15	D14, A7,B8	A16, B11	A14, B18, D22, E16
CHINESE	XXXXXXXXXXXXXXXXXXXXXX XXXXXXXXXXXXXXXXXXXX				
INTERPRETER:	Mr. Zou has many experiences where he has to feel the understanding of his company and its many parts.	C11			A15, E17
ELIZABETH:	Would Mr. Zou act more by his feeling or his thinking?				
CHINESE	XXXXXXXXXXXXXXXXXXXXXX XXXXXXXXXXXXXXXXXXXX				
INTERPRETER:	It is inevitable to go with the thinking. It is the most important step after feeling. First to feel and then to think about that and understand how to act but that is based very much on thinking about a problem.	A26,E14, D8,C12, C13	A8	A17	A16, E18
ELIZABETH:	What was the most difficult thing he had to work through as an owner-manager – what was his most difficult time?				
CHINESE	XXXXXXXXXXXXXXXXXXXXXX XXXXXXXXXXXXXXXXXXXX				

SPEAKERS	NARRATION	CODE 1	CODE 2	CODE 3	FINAL CODE
INTERPRETER	In two periods of time -- when he first started, he had no business, and now after 9 years of experiments, and 3 years in the incubator he has too much business to do. Both the early stage and the stage of the company growing to a very big level is demanding.	B16,D9		A18,E2	A17, C13, D23, E19
CHINESE	XXXXXXXXXXXXXXXXXXXXXX XXXXXXXXXXXXXXXXXXXX				
INTERPRETER:	Mr. Zou says he wonders how this demand is changing the company too.				C14, E20
ELIZABETH:	Does Mr. Zou ever fear success? Is there any time of personal fear?				
CHINESE	XXXXXXXXXXXXXXXXXXXXXX XXXXXXXXXXXXXXXXXXXX				
INTERPRETER	Some success you can foresee and some you can't, so sometimes when he is not ready for it -- he was scared because he didn't know how to accept it.	A27,E15		A19	A18, E21
CHINESE	XXXXXXXXXXXXXXXXXXXXXX XXXXXXXXXXXXXXXXXXXX				
INTERPRETER:	But in general he is not too fearful because he is a careful risk taker.	B17		A20	A19, B19
ELIZABETH:	Does he have to think very far ahead? If so, how many days, months, or years out does he plan?				
CHINESE	XXXXXXXXXXXXXXXXXXXXXX XXXXXXXXXXXXXXXXXXXX				
INTERPRETER	Mr. Zou says he must always think ahead, every day -- it is the reason he has survived for nine years	A28,E16, D12	E5	A21,D15	A20, C15, E22
CHINESE	XXXXXXXXXXXXXXXXXXXXXX XXXXXXXXXXXXXXXXXXX	18	A10		
INTERPRETER:	Mr Zuo is often planning the business for the long-term.	B			A21, C16, E23

SPEAKERS	NARRATION	CODE 1	CODE 2	CODE 3	FINAL CODE
ELIZABETH:	Does he believe long-term thinking is part of Chinese traditional values?				
CHINESE	XXXXXXXXXXXXXXXXXXXXXX XXXXXXXXXXXXXXXXXXXX				
INERPRETER	In Chinese tradition to have long-term thinking is more of a political thing and usually there is a difference in market. The market is short-term. This is speaking of an international type of market, but still the view of the company can be very short because it must respond to change.	A29,D13, D14	B9	B12, D16	A22, D24
CHINESE	XXXXXXXXXXXXXXXXXXXXXX XXXXXXXXXXXXXXXXXXXX				
INTERPRETER:	Mr. Zou seeks harmony and balance in this idea of long-term thinking. He is mainly planning long-term and not thinking too much about it. Then he is living in the short term and thinking about it a lot. This may be the way of the Chinese…in business we "look at our shoes."	D15,C13, D16	A11, B9, D15	B13, A22	A23, D25
ELIZABETH:	The last question relates to that – what values does he believe China as a nation should give to the rest of the world?				
CHINESE	XXXXXXXXXXXXXXXXXXXXXX XXXXXXXXXXXXXXXXXXXX				
INATERPRETER	Oh, Mr. Zou thinks there are so many values that China wants give to the world.				A24, D26
CHINESE	XXXXXXXXXXXXXXXXXXXXXX XXXXXXXXXXXXXXXXXXXX				
INTERPRETER:	There are many – to give an example to the outside world -- China is an agriculture society and a Confucian society, and it is an industrial or scientific culture. And everything is mixed together in this new opening up China to the world, so maybe one day in the future the idea of Confucian values – the ideas of harmony and benevolence and peacefulness, and good governors will move the rest of the world. The scientific part is a kind of work spirit that is from recent times.	A30,D17, E17 C14	B11	C4, B14	A25, B20, C17,D27

SPEAKERS	NARRATION	CODE 1	CODE 2	CODE 3	FINAL CODE
ELIZABETH:	Spirit of working in the Chinese culture – is very unique – but one that spirals– does he see most of China as beyond the agricultural society?		B12		
CHINESE	XXXXXXXXXXXXXXXXXXXXXXX XXXXXXXXXXXXXXXXXXXX				
INTERPRETER	China has moved beyond this time of agriculture, but it is a deep part of society today and it will always be that way. Science is the path that was chosen for the people to prosper and that is a reality. But there re many realities.	B19,D18, D19, D20,	B13	B15	B21
CHINESE	XXXXXXXXXXXXXXXXXXXXXXX XXXXXXXXXXXXXXXXXXXX				
INTERPRETER:	What do you hope to do with this information and research?				
ELIZABETH:	I hope to understand the Chinese microbusinesses because I believe they represent a hope in this society and that hope is for jobs and family prosperity, but also for the beginning of an international development ethics. By that I mean, a feeling of well-being for the greatest number of people.				
CHINESE	XXXXXXXXXXXXXXXXXXXXXXX XXXXXXXXXXXXXXXXXXXX				
ELISABETH	I thank you for this interview time and for your thoughtful remarks. They make me understand my research topic is quite deep even though micro-businesses may not seem like a powerful force for change.				
CHINESE	XXXXXXXXXXXXXXXXXXXXXXX XXXXXXXXXXXXXXXXXXXX				
INTERPRETER:	It is Mr. Zou's pleasure to hold your audience and attention.				
ELIZABETH:	Xiexie (thank you).				

APPENDIX F

FINAL CODEBOOK

For Interview Analysis and Interpretation

FROM ZUO TAPE					
CODES	BROWN	BLUE	RED	GREEN	Pink
	Types of Chinese urban micro-business owner-managers	Chinese Micro-business Owner-Manager Individual values	Chinese Micro-business Owner-Manager Cultural values	International development values	Business values and attitudes to business ethics
1	1/history of personal achievement;	1/economic necessity	1/the idea is to survive as a society	1/small business mirrors a society	everyone wants personal success
2	2/former IT college professor;	2/prosperity	2/historically, Chinese people want success	2/–create a product	2/teacher turned businessperson; administrator turned businessperson; engineer turned entrepreneur; professor turned marketer;
3	3/company based on IT;	3/personal achievement	3/There is a division between intellectual and practical pursuits	3/client wants and theory are not the same	3/ focus on IT professions; service sectors;
4	4/growing from a small to a large business changed the company values	4/create own business	4/There is a focus on market demands	4/focus on market demands	; 4/started small
5	5/pattern is to be open to international values;	5/my idea	5/companies must change their values	5/the company growth changes its values	5/openness is good
6	6/focus on employee/employer harrmony	6/put knowledge to full use	6/invaluable international influences	6/Chinese way of thinking	6/business is homogenous.

7	7/hometown is same as Chairman Mao	7/practice over theory	7/our way is a traditional one	7/employer/empl oyee relationships is first	7/value of harmony
8	8/the company mirrors society	8/always aware of pressure	8/harmony is traditional	8/develop or lose	8/business ties are sometimes emotional.
9	9/first goal is growth	9/personal values are	9/not influenced by the modern citiy life	9/skills to solve problems	9/influences from origins
10	10/speed and flexibility	10/outside influences are invaluable	10/small business must develop with the whole society.	10/modern and flexible organizations	10/challenges are steady
11	11/demand changes structure	11/traditional thinking and acting	11/.first goal is steady, rapid development	11/risk is following nature cautiously	11/steady and rapid growth
12	12/changes in thinking	12/relationships in the company	12/train employees to solve problems	12/always think ahead	12/trains in problem solving skills
13	13/cautious intuition	13/importance of harmony	13/business structure must adapt to demands	13/Long-term thinking in reference to the market are different	13/adapttructure to demands
14	14/inevitable thinking	14/relationship based on feelings	14/market is always a crisis	14/must give to the outside world	14/consults friends, colleagues, and clients
15	15/scred of acceptance	15/influenced by north China	15/risk balances with caution.		15/sense of market and humor
16	16/far thinking combines with survival	16/a company and society need to develop	16/difficult with too much and too little business.		16/bases actions on thinking

17	17/Confucian idea of the future	17/.employees want steady growth	17/fear of not knowing how to accept success.	17/too little and too much are difficult times
18		18/everything comes from steady growth	18/think ahead	18/some success you can't foresee
19		19/flexibility and speed	19/the future ideas of an old society are how to endure	19/the market and tradition don't always mix
20		20/company is modern.		20/agricultural, Confucian, and industrial socialist are China's gifts
21		21/influences from friends and colleagues		
22		22/helped by clients		
23		23/a technician with a sense of the market.		
24		24/market brings opportunity and disaster.		
25		25/risk requires caution		
26		26/thinks more than feels.		
27		27/we are not ready for some of our successes		
28		28/survival from thinking ahead.		
29		29/traditional Chinese values differ on the market.		
30		30/export Chinese culture		

APPENDIX G

LETTERS OF ACCESS AND PARTICIPATION

<u>Participant Information Sheet</u>

<u>Bank and Institution Letter</u>

<u>Professional Assistance Confidentiality Agreement</u>

<u>Chinese Translation of Letter</u>

<u>Participant Information Sheet</u>

Project Title: A Study of Cross-cultural Values in Chinese Micro-businesses

Invitation

What is the purpose of this study?

This cross-cultural study is a part of a dissertation document and connected to a multi-national, project to obtain research data comparing opinions, attitudes and beliefs about individual values and desirable leadership behaviour from business managers. This project deals with business managers in China, and, those defined as participating in micro-business loan programs. It is expected that the knowledge generated will be used in part to compare managerial qualities across many national cultures.

How is a person chosen to be asked to be part of the study?

Volunteers from organizations from which the micro-business management has agreed to allow participation in the study.

Can I join the study?

Joining the study is voluntary; you merely must request a survey.

What happens in the study?

A questionnaire describing business owner behaviours and I or your individual values is given to you to complete, along with a demographic data sheet.

What are the discomforts and risks?

There should be no physical discomforts; if you choose to participate you need to take the time to accurately complete the questionnaire, usually about a half-hour to one hour. There are no risks; your anonymity will be protected.

What are the benefits?

The benefits are that we will collect data and provide information on how to facilitate the mutual engagement of micro-business owners from China; the benefits to you are that you may be able to operate in a more efficient and effective manner in your business from reading the results of the study.

How is my privacy protected?

The questionnaires will be completed anonymously; no company affiliation or individual name data will be collected.

Costs of Participating

30 to 60 minutes of your time

Opportunity to consider invitation

Participation is completely voluntary; you may decide to participate or not at any time. After the survey is sent to the researcher, we cannot identify your questionnaire, so it cannot be returned.

Participant Concerns - Any concerns regarding the nature of this project should be notified in the first instance to the Researcher Elisabeth Montgomery at (001-510-601-6286) or fax (001-510-658-7289). Concerns regarding the conduct of the research should be notified to Dr. Marie Farrell, Fielding Graduate Institute 2112 Santa Barbara Street, Santa Barbara, California 93105. Telephone: (001) + (805) 687-1099.

Approved by the Fielding Graduate Institute Ethics Review Committee on:

Date: ____

Reference Number: _________________________________

Bank & Institution Letter

Bank/Institution

xxxxxxxx

xxx:xxxxx

Date _______________________

Dear XXXX:

I am writing to request official permission to gain access to bank clients that are participating in any of your programs designed specifically for micro-finance, or business loans between $50 and $500 USD. The purpose of my study is to understand the business and personal values of Chinese business owners at this level of business practice.

This study is part of my dissertation work at The Fielding Graduate Institute in Santa Barbara, California and part of a cross-cultural international database of on business values research. With your esteemed permission, I will survey business owners using an internationally developed questionnaire called the Schwartz Value Survey or SYS (see attached). The survey, translated in Chinese, has been tested several times in China, Singapore, Hong Kong, and on Chinese nationals in other foreign countries with business professionals and teachers.

Participants in this survey need to be randomly selected and anonymous. Therefore, the bank nominators will not be advised who was selected or participated and who was selected or chose not to participate. All selected nominees and their answered questionnaires will remain confidential. No names of participants will be asked, and no names will be given.

In order to maintain confidentiality and anonymity, each survey will be numbered according to location and interview sequence. Collected survey answers will be tabulated using the international research scoring and databank. This information will then be compared to business values in other countries using available information.

The final research document and aggregate conclusions of the values survey will be made available to the bank after the dissertation research is approved and reviewed.

Thank you in advance for your kind consideration of this important research request and any assistance you can provide. If you have any questions, please feel free to call me.

Sincerely,

Elisabeth P. Montgomery
USA (001-510-601-6286)
CHINA (755-2653-2106)
Email: info@TDRinc.com Email: elisbeth170@aol.com

Professional Assistance
Confidentiality Agreement

Study for doctoral coursework in Human Organizational Development "Cross-cultural values in micro-businesses in China"

Elisabeth Montgomery, HOD/HOS Doctoral Student

Fielding Graduate Institute
Contact: USA - 001-510-601-6286 Email: info@TDRinc.com
Contact: China- 755-2654-2106 Email: elisbeth170@aol.com

I, ____________ have agreed to assist Elisabeth Montgomery in her research study on cross-cultural values in Chinese micro-businesses in the role of interpreter. I have no direct or indirect relationship to the Bank or lending institution providing the names of participants. I understand and agree that all participants in this study have been assured that their responses will be confidential and anonymous. I understand the participation in the project is strictly voluntary. Participants can drop out of the survey for any reason and at any time. Part of my job ensures there will be no pressure on participants, of any kind, to take the survey. I will remain watchful in this aspect of my interpreter job.

I further agree that no materials will remain in my possession beyond the operation of this research project and I further agree that I will make no independent use of any of the research materials from this project.

Signature ____________________

Date ____________________

Printed Name (Pin yin) ____________________

Title ____________________

APPENDIX H

PROTECTION OF HUMAN SUBJECTS

Informed Consent Letter
The Fielding Graduate Institute, Santa Barbara, CA

Elisabeth Montgomery, HOD/HOS Doctoral Student
Contact: USA - 001-510-601-6286 Email: info@TDRinc.com
Contact: Shenzhen. P.R. China- 755-653.0422
Email: info@TDRINc.com

Study for doctoral coursework in Organizational Theory
"Cross-cultural values clarification
with micro-businesses in China:
Is the Schwartz Values Survey (SVS) a fit?"

Dear ___________________: You have been randomly
selected from a list of businesses in the Bank of China micro-
lending program to participate in a volunteer research study
conducted by Elisabeth Montgomery, a doctoral student in
the School of Human Organizational Development at Fielding
Graduate Institute, Santa Barbara, California, USA. The
purpose of the study is to understand cross-cultural values
in Chinese micro-businesses. The study asks you to fill out
a cross-cultural values survey. In addition, Elisabeth will
interview you briefly about the survey and ask you a few
questions about the survey. The benefits of this study include
a deeper understanding of the patterns of relationships
between local business values and attitudes and international
institutions. Any questions you may have please feel free to
ask Elisabeth at any time using the contact information above.

The study will be arranged at your convenience and last
approximately one and a half hours. The total time may not
exceed two hours. The results of this study will be used in a
Knowledge Assessment paper on Organizational Theory and
may be used as added support for conducting further research

on micro-businesses in China Participants in this study will be given the results in written format and Elisabeth will also call each participant to talk about the survey results.

The name on the survey and our interviews are strictly confidential and your real name will not be mentioned in any paper or publication. Two copies of this **Informed Consent Letter** are provided. Sign both and may keep one of for your records. You will also be given a **Professional Assistance Confidentiality** Agreement to understand the role of the hired interpreter. The Institutional review Board of Fielding Graduate Institute retains access to signed informed consent forms. **Contact:** Fielding Graduate Institute, 2112 Santa Barbara Street, Santa Barbara, California 93105 Telephone: (001) +(805) 687-1099.

The Fielding Graduate Institute, Santa Barbara, CA
Elisabeth Montgomery, HOD/HOS Doctoral Student

NAME OF PARTICIPANT (please print in Pinyin)

SIGNATURE OF PARTICIPANT

DATE

**FACULTY ADVISOR'S NAME, ADDRESS
& TELEPHONE NUMBER**

Dr. Marie Farrell
Fielding Graduate Institute
2112 Santa Barbara Street
Santa Barbara, California 93105
Telephone: (001) +(805) 687-1099

Yes, please send a summary of the study results to:

Name of Participant (please print in Pinyin): ______________

Street Address: ______________________________

City, State, Postal Code, ____________________

Country: People's Republic of China

Professional Assistance Confidentiality Agreement

**Study for doctoral coursework in Human
Organizational Development**
"Cross-cultural values in micro-businesses in China"

Elisabeth Montgomery, HOD/HOS Doctoral Student
Fielding Graduate Institute
Contact: USA-001-510-601-6286 Email: info@TDRInc.com
Contact: China- 755-2654-2106 Email: elisbeth170@aol.com

    I, ___________________ have agreed to assist Elisabeth
Montgomery in her research study on cross-cultural values in
Chinese micro-businesses in the role of interpreter. I have no
direct or indirect relationship to the Bank or lending institution
providing the names of participants. I understand and agree
that all participants in this study have been assured that their
responses will be confidential and anonymous. I understand
the participation in the project is strictly voluntary. Participants
can drop out of the survey for any reason and at any time. Part
of my job ensures there will be no pressure on participants,
of any kind, to take the survey. I will remain watchful in this
aspect of my interpreter job.

    I further agree that no materials will remain in my
possession beyond the operation of this research project and I

further agree that I will make no independent use of any of the research materials from this project.

Signature __________________________ Date _________________

Printed Name (Pin yin) _________________________________

Title ____

APPENDIX I

SCHWARTZ VALUE SURVEY SCORING SHEET FOR SVS DATA

Table 3

Test/Retest Reliability Scores for Individual and Cultural Values

Individual Level	TEST	RETEST	CORRELATIONS
Conformity	295	305	0.87
Tradition	227	215	0.84
Benevolence	370	401	0.71
Universalism	567	584	0.91
Self-direction	354	382	0.9
Stimulation	125	136	0.92
Hedonism	153	138	0.93
Achievement	318	354	0.83
Power	255	261	0.85
Security	401	402	0.73
Cultural Level			
Embeddedness	991	1005	0.81
Hierarchy	284	293	0.86
Mastery	307	333	0.91
Affective Autonomy	371	370	0.79
Intellectual Autonomy	279	287	0.88
Egalitarianism	433	465	0.83
Harmony	276	290	0.91

APPENDIX J

KIM'S THEORY OF BIDIMENSIONAL SELF-CONSTRUALS

Kim's Theory of Bidimensional Self-Construal (2002)

Independent	Marginality	Interdependent
WEST	Communicative adaptiveness of individuals as they move between cultures	EAST
Self-ways (Markus & Kitayama, 1997)		Self-construals (Kim, 2002)
Self is an independent; selves are separate wholes		Self is relational to groups; selves are family through blood-ties, membership, guanxi
Self is an achiever		Self is social
Mastery as a high cultural value		Harmony as a high cultural value
Independent		Interdependent
Individualism	Simultaneously Independent and Interdependent	Collectivism
Comfortable with Verbal	Systematic Desensitization	Comfortable with Silent
High Independence		High Interdependence
Cognitive dissonance/self-concept clarity		Cognitive connection/selves as context specific and situational based on relationships
Person stays the same in almost all situations; consistency is good; transituational		Person is seen as shifting variables of context, meaning and ethics is situational
Individual responsibility or dispositionalism		Whole context behavior or situationalism
Environment is obligated to them		Obligated to the environment
Believe attitudes can lead to actions; focused on attributes to behavior ; people have control over their and are responsible for their behaviors	Independent individuals place more weight on their attitudes and goals; Interdependent individuals place more weight on situations	Attend to situations in discussing reasons behind others' actions.
Attitude/behavior theories exclude external or ethereal causes		Situation/behavior is the most important
Conformity has a negative undertone in the west; unique has positive undertones; seen as yielding to the collective		Conformity has positive connotations of connectedness and harmony;
Ideal person is one who defines himself; noncompliance seen as an important milestone	Locus of control (Ward & Kennedy, 1992), LOC	Ideal person is one who is defined by others; foster empathetic connections with others
Feel they control and expect to control events; order and coherence achieved by seeking control and mastery over the world; direct coping mechanisms; can threaten harmony if deemed "necessary"; cultural context based on facts and theoretical interpretations	Control orientation come from culturally reinforced practices	Internal LOCs prefer harmony and attempt to adjust to social situations through strategies that focus on the changing self, rather than on changing the situation or other's opinion. Use indirect strategies e.g. reinterpreting; accepting and changing one's expectations;

Independent WEST	Marginality Communicative adaptiveness of individuals as they move between cultures	Interdependent EAST
		identifying with a powerful other.
Deception is always bad; truth is an absolute state; regardless of the circumstances; only deceive if issue is private or to protect	Independents are receptive to others by presenting themselves and their beliefs. Interdependents are receptive to others and they adjust their needs and demands by restraining their inner needs to serve others.	Deception is a useful situational strategy; look at strategies in the situation; lies or irrelevant information are relevant message responses;
Self-disclosure is important; confidence in self important; self-effacement in groups		Self-criticism is deep and frequent; modesty; promote fundamental connectedness
Promotion of goals is seen as a pursuit of gains and aspirations	Independents' self-enhancement is through methodological artifacts; Interdependents' self-enhancement is through security minded preventative measures	Prevention of goals refers to avoidance of losses and fulfillment of obligations
Silence is absence, discreet messages needed to communicate; silence are viewed as malfunctional; silencing women (male supremacy); silence as pathology; half empty.		Silence, rhythm and timing are needed to communicate as they are a complex part of nature; quietness is a way to control what goes on; the zero in math; skillful silence is maturity; half full.
Bi-polar values; black versus white; life versus death; yes versus no		Tact, wordless silence in indirectness is a form of communication, intuition are highly developed concepts
Appropriate rules for talking are learned behaviors; communicative competence; children talk more and appropriately	Independents and talking are important strategies. Interdependents use silence often as to mean being understood without putting one's meaning on the record	Appropriate rules for silence are learned behaviors; communicative competence; children talk less
		Refusal, resistance, and leaving strategies
Marginalization of minorities as they struggle to define and counter opposition of host country and language		Assimilation theory – identity is compete only after an individual joins the dominant group and acquires host communication competence
Alternation model – posits that an individual is able to gain competence in two or more cultures without losing her cultural identity or having to choose one culture over the other		Biculturalism (Ramirez, 1983) competencies of two cultures within one individual; cognitive and affective processes that allow this to come about are cultural frame of reference shifting
Host communication competence is a one-way street – a) maximum convergence of stranger to host b) minimum maintenance of primary culture	Independents view their Identity as choice; Interdependents view their identity as multifunctional within situations and contexts	Biculturalism views identity acquisition among different cultures and within groups as dynamic; a non-linear equation.

Source: Montgomery (2006)

www.ingramcontent.com/pod-product-compliance
Lightning Source LLC
Chambersburg PA
CBHW031051250726